PR   M

FOOD & BEVERAGE

MANAGEMENT

.

PROFITABLE
FOOD & BEVERAGE
MANAGEMENT

Richard Kotas, BCom, MPhil, ACIS, FHCIMA, FBHA
Emeritus Professor, Schiller International University
Visiting Professor, International Hotel Management Institute, Switzerland

Chandana Jayawardena, MSc, MCIM, FHCIMA
Visiting Professor, Ceylon Hotel School
General Manager, Forte Pegasus Hotel, Guyana

Hodder & Stoughton
A MEMBER OF THE HODDER HEADLINE GROUP

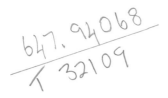

647.94068

T 32109

A catalogue record for this title is available from the British Library

ISBN 0 340 59512 4

First published 1994
Impression number 10   9   8   7   6   5   4   3   2   1
Year   1999   1998   1997   1996   1995   1994

Copyright © 1994 Richard Kotas and Chandana Jayawardena

Typeset by Wearset, Boldon, Tyne and Wear.
Printed in Great Britain for Hodder & Stoughton Educational, a division of Hodder Headline Plc, 338 Euston Road, London NW1 3BH by Bath Press, Avon

To Lucy and Shani

CONTENTS

CHAPTER 1

INTRODUCTION

The Hotel and Catering Industry

In most of Western Europe, and in many other parts of the world, the hotel and catering industry is one of the biggest there is. It comprises many thousands of establishments; indeed, according to the latest statistics in Great Britain we now have some 120,000 businesses within the commercial sector. This includes: hotels, holiday camps, restaurants, cafés, snack bars, public houses, clubs and catering contractors. And all this is in addition to what is described as the non-profit, or welfare, sector which essentially includes: industrial, school and college, and hospital catering.

Whilst it is quite common to speak of the hotel and catering industry, and hotel and catering services, it should be appreciated that the industry is an amalgam, a collection of multifarious food and beverage operations. Most of the catering establishments in the commercial sector are in many respects different from those in the non-profit or welfare sector. The meal experience – the food, its preparation, service and price, as well as the decor and atmosphere – in a four-star hotel is vastly different from the meal experience available in a works canteen. Indeed, even within the commercial sector, differences from one type of operation to another are quite substantial. Even in terms of the most obvious criteria, such as size of operation, number of employees, choice of foods and beverages offered, presentation and service, and, finally, price level, a 200-bedroomed four-star hotel is a very different thing from a Chinese restaurant. Perhaps the only thing they have in common is that they use similar raw materials and offer sustenance to people away from home.

One of the most important differences between the commercial and welfare sectors stems from their business orientation. Whilst hotels, motels, restaurants, country clubs and leisure centres are market-oriented, all the different types of catering operation within the welfare sector are cost-oriented. The orientation of a business has a most profound influence on all major aspects of its operations and is discussed in detail later in this chapter.

The present volume does not attempt to deal with all the different types of food and beverage operation. No single book can adequately cover all the special characteristics, operation, control and management of all the different establishments within both the commercial and welfare sectors. It is for this reason that the scope of this book is limited to, essentially, hotels, restaurants and similar food and beverage operations within the commercial sector.

Complexity of Food and Beverage Operations

Throughout this book, we tend to refer to hotels and restaurants only. We do so, however, in the full knowledge that in fact hotels and restaurants are very complex organisations and vary considerably from one establishment to another. In the sections which follow we look at some of the typical complexities and differences.

SIZE AND OWNERSHIP

Hotels and restaurants vary considerably in size and with regard to their ownership. Both in the UK and throughout Europe there is a high proportion of small, family-owned establishments – hotels with 10–20 rooms and restaurants and cafés with a seating capacity of 20–40. Many of these are small simply because they are older properties, built before World War II, where there were relatively few tourists and little business travel. Such small food and beverage operations are in many respects different from the more recently built establishments. In recent years we have witnessed the appearance of the so-called mega-hotel, with at least a thousand rooms.

Readers should note that size does not necessarily detract from quality or efficiency. Whilst the large establishment benefits from the economies of scale (whether you average 1,000 or 1,200 covers a week, you need one head chef, one restaurant manager, etc.), it is the small establishment that is well placed to provide a high standard of personal service. Indeed, guests frequenting some of the large hotels often feel that whilst the standard of food is very acceptable and food and beverage service competent and professional, they are simply 'guests', not personally known to the hotel staff. This not uncommonly high degree of impersonal service is an inevitable consequence of large size, and has to be compensated for by high gastronomic standards, friendly and competent service, and a high degree of comfort.

One of the important advantages enjoyed by the large unit is the ability to employ specialists. Thus a 400-bedroomed hotel will be able to employ a top-class executive chef, a highly experienced food and beverage manager, a fully qualified accountant and a marketing director. In addition to these top-level specialists, there are advantages available at a lower level. The kitchen brigade of a large hotel is divided into 8–12 parties, each specialising in a different part of the overall cuisine. This high degree of specialisation is a powerful factor in promoting high standards of gastronomy. In the case of privately owned restaurants – most of which tend to be comparatively small in size – neither the employment of specialists nor a high degree of specialisation in food production is normally possible.

Different patterns of ownership occur in the food and beverage industry. In the case of hotels, most of the larger units belong to hotel chains. It is invariably the smaller hotel that is an independent, privately owned business. Whilst some of the chains own hotels only, we do find those which belong to airlines or other organisations with a base outside the hotel industry proper.

With regard to restaurants, the independent, privately owned units are clearly in the majority, and the reason for this is the relative ease of entry into the restaurant industry. One requires considerably less capital to open a restaurant than to acquire a hotel. The minority of restaurants, which are not privately owned, belong to chains operating a variety of units, differing greatly in terms of size, extent of service provided, national cuisine, etc.

EXTENT OF SERVICE

The extent of food and beverage service provided by hotels and restaurants varies considerably. Whilst the large hotel will normally operate several restaurants (dining rooms), a coffee shop, a banqueting department, room service and a number of cocktail bars, the small 20-bedroomed 'private hotel' will typically offer a breakfast service and an evening meal.

The size of the hotel is not always a good indicator of the extent of food and beverage service. In some European countries, notably in Switzerland, there are numerous larger hotels with up to 120 rooms, which are known as 'garni hotels'. These offer accommodation only and do not operate food and beverage departments – though tea, coffee and snacks are always available.

The majority of motels are small and tend to concentrate on the provision of accommodation only – even where a motel has in excess of 50 rooms, and would be regarded as a medium-sized unit. Where a great deal of choice of food and beverage outlets is provided, there is a need for a great deal of planning, effective supervision and competent management.

The extent of food and beverage service, as a factor contributing to the complexity of the operation, is further aggravated by the existence of different styles (methods) of service, different menus and different pricing policies within each sales outlet. Some of these complications are considered below.

Menus: Profit Implications

Menus are traditionally thought of as table d'hôte and à la carte. A table d'hôte menu, often described as a 'set menu', offers a limited choice of items – typically not more than three main dishes. There is usually a fixed price which the customer pays irrespective of the menu items chosen. An important operational feature of table d'hôte menus is that the required food items are prepared before the actual arrival of the guests and in anticipation of their demand. Where identical or similar menu items are offered on the table d'hôte and à la carte menus, the table d'hôte portions tend to be smaller. The reason here is the lower price of the table d'hôte meal.

The à la carte menu offers considerably more choice and generally more generous portions. The food is cooked on receipt of the guest's order; and this makes the à la carte food preparation more labour-intensive and hence more costly. The average spending power (ASP) level of the à la carte menu is generally significantly higher than in the case of table d'hôte sales. From this it follows that the cash gross profit per cover is, as a rule, much higher in the case of à la carte customers – with obvious implications for the profitability of the sales outlet concerned.

Where there is a sizeable banqueting operation, banqueting menus are usually prepared in advance of the banqueting season. Many hotels prepare a series of menus – say four or five differently priced menus for each type of function: wedding receptions, business meetings, conferences, etc. All such menus attract different prices and result in different levels of cash gross profit per cover. Much care is therefore required when planning such menus to ensure that they result in satisfactory levels of gross profit.

Fixed price menus have tended to prove popular in recent years. Whilst this particular arrangement appears attractive to potential customers in that they know in advance what the meal will cost, it suffers from certain disadvantages. A fixed price is necessarily a compromise: an average price appropriate to an average customer. In terms of ASP levels, this average price will be rather more than some customers wish to spend, and rather less than others might be quite happy to spend. As far as the former is concerned, this arrangement is not conducive to generating repeat business. As for the latter, the fixed price results in inevitable underachievement in terms of ASP levels and resulting cash gross profits. A redeeming feature of fixed price menus is that they facilitate revenue control: the number of covers times the fixed price equals total food sales.

Nationality and Nature of Cuisine

During the last ten years or so we have seen the emergence of numerous new restaurants. Very many of these are restaurants which offer a specific national cuisine, rather than English or international fare. Chinese, French, Greek, Indian and Italian restaurants now constitute a substantial proportion of UK restaurant operations, and a similar situation prevails in other European countries.

In addition to the various national cuisines, we now see many food and beverage operations where the menu offerings are severely restricted and aimed at specific, hopefully not too narrow, market segments. The types of operation which come under this heading include fish restaurants, steak houses and vegetarian restaurants. In all these cases the nature of the cuisine and the entire food preparation process are different. The menu offerings are highly specific and specialised, lacking in diversity and breadth, but not ordinarily in terms of acceptable gastronomic standards.

We have witnessed a similar development in the case of larger hotels. Where a hotel operates a number of restaurants, then quite commonly, in addition to international cuisine, it is usual to offer hotel guests one or two restaurants serving the food of a specific foreign country. Quite a few hotels have recently opened Japanese restaurants, in addition to any French or Italian restaurant already in existence.

The choice of a particular national cuisine has important implications in terms of food and labour costs as well as gross profit margins. As an example, Egyptian, Lebanese and Italian restaurants tend to use quite inexpensive raw materials and generally operate at fairly low labour costs. This results in a high percentage of gross profit, even though the ASP levels are not high. French and German restaurants, on the other hand, tend to use costly raw materials and their cuisines require above-average skills. They have, in consequence, high ASP levels which sometimes reduce repeat business.

Finally, it should be remembered that where a hotel operates a number of restaurants offering distinctly separate cuisines, there is a strong element of rigidity and specificity in terms of the kitchen crew skills. Transfers of staff from one brigade to another are impractical in such circumstances, which makes the control of labour costs even more difficult.

Principal Characteristics

We have now mentioned the multiplicity of different types of food and beverage operation. As our principal aim here is to deal with the management of food and beverage operations of hotels and restaurants, it is appropriate that we should take a close look at their main characteristics.

COST STRUCTURE

One of the most important features of hotels and restaurants is their cost structure: they all operate at high levels of fixed costs and low variable costs. Let us look at hotels first. In the majority of hotels fixed costs account for some 75 per cent and variable costs 25 per cent of total cost. This ratio of fixed to variable costs will be found in the vast majority of hotels, irrespective of such factors as size, location or star rating.

We see a similar situation within the hotel food and beverage department. The main variable costs – those of food and beverages – tend to absorb some 25–30 per cent of departmental revenue. In addition to this there are other costs of a variable nature, such as part-time and casual labour. Even when this is added to food and beverage costs, the total variable cost of the hotel food and beverage department is not particularly high, averaging 35–40 per cent. From this it is clear that food and beverage departments tend to be rather low variable cost operations.

Low variable costs imply high profit margins, and in most hotels gross profit margins are relatively high – typically around 60–75 per cent. Variable cost levels and gross profit margins are very similar in restaurants, most of which maintain gross profits at 60–70 per cent.

DEMAND INSTABILITY

High profit margins, both in hotels and restaurants, have important implications for profitability, particularly in conditions of demand instability. Where there are appreciable changes in the sales volume there will, inevitably, be powerful changes in the amounts of profits earned by the establishment from one trading period to another.

CHANGES IN SALES MIX

Food and beverage sales consist of a large number of individual food and beverage items. The gross profit loading on some of these items is higher than on others. As an example, £100 of soups and appetisers will produce significantly more gross profit than £100 of main dishes. By the same token, £100 of business in the banqueting department will produce more gross profit than the same amount of food and beverage sales in the coffee shop. Changes in the composition of food and beverage sales (i.e. sales mix) have a strong impact on the total amount of gross profit earned by the establishment. This is illustrated in the example below.

EXAMPLE

A hotel operates, amongst others, an Italian restaurant, where the pricing policy is as follows. All starters are priced to produce 75 per cent gross profit; the main dishes are priced at 55 per cent; desserts produce 65 per cent of gross profit; and teas and coffees produce 80 per cent. Set out in Table 1.1 are sales volumes and the resulting gross profits for weeks 1 and 2.

Table 1.1 Sales volumes and gross profits

Sales mix	Gross profit	Week 1		Week 2	
		Sales	Cash GP	Sales	Cash GP
	%	£	£	£	£
Starters	75	1,000	750	400	300
Main dishes	55	3,400	1,870	4,600	2,530
Desserts	65	1,200	780	800	520
Teas, coffees	80	400	320	200	160
Total	–	6,000	3,720	6,000	3,510

During week 2 our total volume of sales was exactly as in week 1. Also we priced all food items in the same manner as in week 1. Yet, because of the change in the sales mix, our total cash gross profit in week 2 was £210 less than in week 1. There was also a significant decrease in the percentage gross profit: from 62.0 to 58.5 per cent.

PERISHABILITY OF FOOD

Food is perishable both as a raw material and in the form of prepared cooked dishes, and this results in several problems peculiar to catering operations. The quantities of food purchased are of great importance, particularly in the case of meat, fish and soft fruits, in that they must match the demand for the relevant menu items. Whilst, therefore, the so-called non-perishables are generally purchased on a monthly basis, the perishables will tend to be purchased several times a week.

Equally important is the matching of food preparation to the fluctuating demand (as measured in terms of the number of covers). All food operators have to predict the demand for the various menu items on a daily basis. Otherwise the actual production of food will either be excessive or fall short of demand. Any leftovers resulting from overproduction represent a loss and lead to inadequate profit margins. Unsatisfied demand results in customers having to accept a second choice; and this, clearly, is not the right way to secure repeat business. Many hotels and restaurants use a system of volume forecasting. This predicts, from one week to another, the number of customers and their choice of menu items. Volume forecasting is described in detail in Chapter 12.

SHORT CYCLE OF OPERATIONS

The 'cycle of operations' is the period of time taken from the purchase of raw materials to the sale of the finished product. In many industries the cycle of operations is long; quite frequently the complete cycle extends over several months. This is quite different in the case of food operations, where, typically, perishables delivered early in the morning are cooked and consumed a few hours later. Indeed, it is not unusual for the meals to be paid for and for the receipts to be banked before the end of the same day.

This speed requires a great deal of organising ability, appropriate systems and procedures, and a great deal of skill at all levels of the kitchen crew, food and beverage service personnel and the ancillary departments such as purchasing, stores and wash-up. The short cycle of operations provides numerous opportunities for mistakes and mishaps of all kinds. However well organised the food and beverage department, these will never be completely eliminated. We should therefore apply frequent checks on actual performance to ensure that shortcomings are reduced to a minimum.

MULTIPLICITY OF LOW-VALUE TRANSACTIONS

Another characteristic feature of food and beverage operations is the multiplicity of low-value transactions. What on the face of it is simply a meal consists in fact of many separate and distinctly different elements: the starter, the main course, the vegetables, the dessert, the coffee and, of course, the accompanying beverages. All these have to be planned, costed, priced and prepared/cooked separately; and this, as already suggested above, requires not only a wide range of culinary skills but also a great deal of clerical and control work.

HIGH DEGREE OF DEPARTMENTALISATION

Finally, we come to the last characteristic feature of food and beverage operations: the high degree of departmentalisation. This is particularly evident in larger hotels where, in addition to room service and banqueting, there may be several restaurants, each offering a different type of service and a different national cuisine. A high degree of departmentalisation necessitates first-rate management skills, effective supervision and a great deal of dedication on the part of the food and beverage manager.

Cost and Market Orientation

We noted at the beginning of this chapter some of the differences between the profit-oriented, commercial sector of the industry and the welfare sector. One of the main differences between the two sectors relates to their orientation. This may be of two kinds. Whilst hotels, restaurants and similar establishments are said to be market-oriented, the welfare sector is regarded as essentially cost-oriented.

There are four main factors which determine the orientation of a business:

1 Cost structure;
2 Demand for its product/service;
3 Capital intensity;
4 Nature of the product/service.

COST STRUCTURE AND PROFITABILITY

We have already noted that hotels and restaurants are high fixed cost operations. In general, the higher the percentage of fixed costs the greater the degree of market orientation, and the greater the dependence of the business on market demand.

Also, it should be noted that the higher the percentage of fixed costs the greater the effect on profits of any given change in the volume of sales. The message of high fixed costs is loud and clear. Hotel and restaurant profits are dependent on the volume of sales. In view of this, constant monitoring of the sales volume is required. As the volume of sales is a powerful determinant of profitability, the food and beverage manager should, essentially, concern him/herself with the revenue side of the business. Food quality standards, guest satisfaction, the percentage of repeat business, sales mix and the pricing of foods and beverages – all demand constant and unfailing attention. The high percentage of variable costs associated with cost-oriented operations enjoins a different philosophy and strategy. In trying to achieve the major objectives (as evidenced by the budget), the cost-oriented establishment will concentrate on the cost – not revenue – side of the operation. Cost control, cost analysis and cost management will be the catering manager's main preoccupations. It is, so to speak, the debit side of the profit and loss account that is of primary interest in such circumstances.

DEMAND FOR PRODUCT/SERVICE

The second major factor which determines business orientation is the nature of the demand for food and beverage facilities. This, essentially, relates to the stability of demand, and has been mentioned earlier in this chapter under the heading of Demand Instability. Some further comments are necessary.

Food and beverage operations experience peaks of intensive activity as well as relatively slack periods throughout the working day. In many establishments it is possible to observe a distinct weekly pattern of business. Finally, a large proportion of hotels and restaurants are, to some extent, seasonal and have a pronounced annual pattern of business. All such fluctuations in demand produce a condition of sales instability, which is aggravated by the fixed capacity of food and beverage outlets. When the restaurant is full, it is unable to take advantage of excess demand. When a business is slack, heavy fixed costs still have to be paid.

Sales instability and fixed capacity present a serious threat to the profitability of market-oriented food and beverage operations. This, combined with a high level of fixed costs, calls for a wholly different approach to profit management. As the debit side of the profit and loss account offers little scope for financial manoeuvre, solutions to problems can only be found on the revenue side of the business. Cost control and cost management will not provide all the answers, and the real solution is to develop a new approach to accounting and control – a concept of 'revenue accounting'. This recognises that costs have to be monitored, but at the same time concentrates on the credit side of the profit and loss account and all the things associated with the revenue side of the business. Within the revenue accounting approach, we concentrate on: total sales volume, sales mix, profit margins, pricing methods – including pricing devices such as cover charge, service charge and minimum charge – as well as techniques such as sales histories and volume forecasting.

Capital Intensity

Capital intensity may be measured by comparing the capital of a business with its sales volume or by calculating the amount of capital per employee. Capital-intensive businesses tend to have a high level of charges in the form of loan interest, depreciation and repairs, and maintenance, and these affect their cost structure. Fixed costs, as a result of such charges, tend to constitute a high percentage of total cost.

There is no evidence that hotel and catering establishments are particularly capital intensive. There are, however, exceptions: hotels and up-market restaurants do have a high level of capital employed in relation to their turnover. The higher the degree of capital intensity, the higher the level of fixed costs and the greater the dependence on consumer demand – and hence the stronger the element of market orientation.

Nature of the Product/Service

Earlier in the chapter we discussed the perishability of food and its consequences in terms of gross profit performance. Where product perishability is associated with demand instability, a market-oriented situation must of necessity exist, in that the business is at the mercy of the whims of the market. The greater the perishability of the product, the stronger the degree of market orientation.

From what we have already said about cost and market orientation, the reader will appreciate that differences between the two are substantial. The market-oriented food and beverage operation differs from the cost-oriented establishment in terms of its aims, capital intensity, cost structure, gross profit margins, stability of demand and, of course, the type of product, service and atmosphere. The term 'market orientation', although it may appear a simple, convenient label, carries with it a great deal of significance.

Organisation Charts

Earlier in this chapter we discussed the complexities of food and beverage operations. We mentioned the high degree of departmentalisation and the multiplicity of planning, production and control problems which are due to the wide selection of foods and beverages offered to hotel and restaurant guests.

In the section which now follows we show a number of organisation charts. These illustrate the organisation structures in different types and sizes of food and operation, and indicate the essential lines of responsibility and authority.

In Figure 1.1 we show the organisation chart of a 400-bedroomed four-star hotel. The hotel is divided into eight fully fledged separate departments and employs some 300 employees. Of all the departments – both revenue-producing and otherwise – the largest is the food and beverage department. Readers should note that in this type of hotel 45–50 per cent of all employees will work in the food and beverage department. Also it should be noted that although certain employees appear to 'belong' to the food and beverage department, they are in fact functionally responsible elsewhere.

The food and beverage controller used to be regarded as a member of the food and beverage department and report to the food and beverage manager/director. In recent years, however, a large number of hotels have moved the controller to the accounting/finance department. To be independent and impartial the controller needs to be responsible to someone other than the food and beverage manager/director. Similar

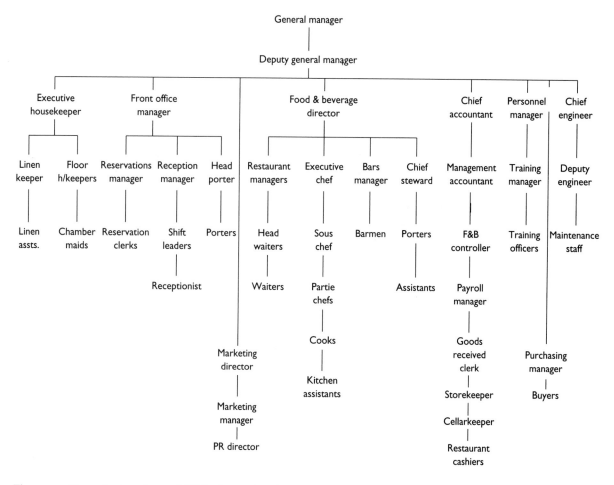

Figure 1.1 Organisation chart of 400-bedroom hotel

considerations apply in the case of employees such as storekeeper, cellarkeeper, goods received clerk and restaurant cashiers. Although they all appear to be members of the food and beverage department, in most hotels they are responsible to the chief accountant.

Also it should be noted that most of the specialist work that would in a smaller hotel be undertaken by an outside specialist/consultant will in a hotel of this size be done internally. This applies to marketing, repairs and maintenance, and personnel and training. From this point of view, the large hotel is a fully independent and self-sufficient entity.

Finally readers should note the rather different terminology associated with large hotels. We refer to the food and beverage director rather than food and beverage manager; executive chef rather than chef or head chef; executive housekeeper rather than housekeeper or head housekeeper, and marketing director rather than sales manager or marketing manager.

In Figure 1.2 we show the organisation chart of a three-star, 150-bedroomed hotel. It will be noticed that we have fewer departments here. Consequently some of the tasks performed internally in the large hotel will be done for this hotel by outside specialists and part-time employees. Activities such as marketing and periodic sales promotion campaigns would be planned and executed by outside specialists in conjunction with the general manager. Whilst some of the basic training would be undertaken by the appropriate department heads, outside specialist lecturers would be engaged for staff/management seminars. Any major engineering work, such as installation of a new air-conditioning system, would certainly be done by outside specialists rather than by the hotel maintenance staff. In our organisation chart we show a small department headed by a financial controller. Many medium-sized hotels do not, in fact, have a separate accounts/finance department, and rely on part-time employees who attend to tasks such as payment of suppliers' accounts and payroll.

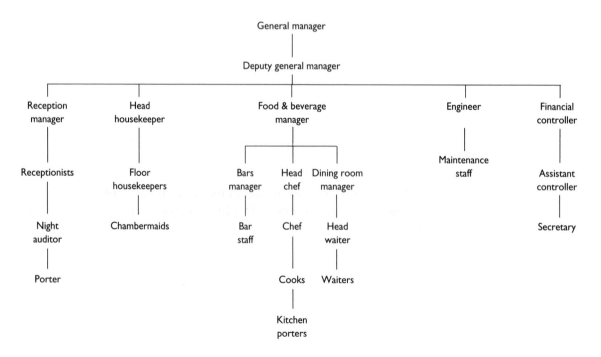

Figure 1.2 Organisation chart of 150-bedroom hotel

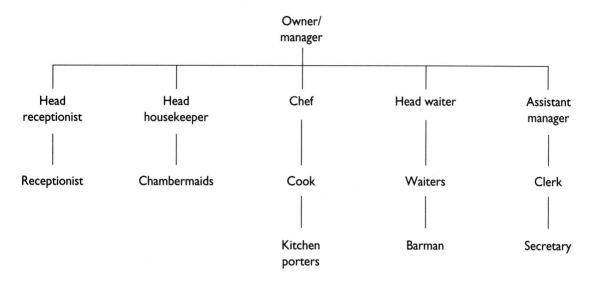

Figure 1.3 Organisation chart of 50-bedroom hotel

We now look at the organisation chart of a small, 50-bedroomed hotel. This is shown in Figure 1.3. Many hotels of this size are family businesses and are run by members of the family rather than paid managers. The organisation structure here is very simple, and the total number of full-time employees would probably not exceed fifteen. In most departments of the hotel we would see part-time employees. This offers the advantage of an easy adjustment of the labour force to the volume of sales and results in a relatively low cost of labour.

An important characteristic of many employees of a small hotel is their versatility. A given employee may start the working day by helping to cook the breakfast; then transfer from the kitchen to the food store to issue the required foods to the appropriate departments. From the food store he or she might transfer to the dining room to help lay the tables, and then from noon serve drinks in the cocktail bar. A similar routine would occur in the afternoon. This high degree of employee versatility associated with small hotels offers the advantage of low payroll costs and therefore contributes to the hotel's profitability.

KITCHEN OPERATIONS

Traditionally the work of the hotel kitchen has been based on the 'partie system'. This reflects a high degree of specialisation, where the work of the kitchen crew is divided into a number of separate sections, i.e.

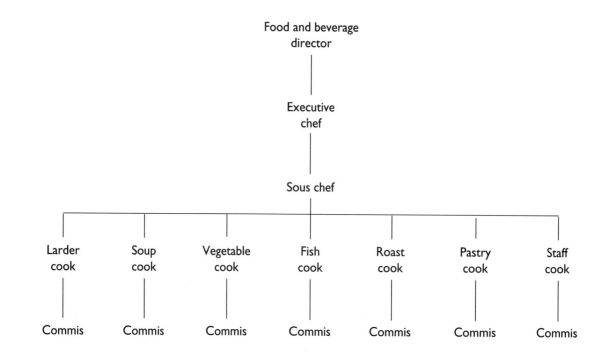

Figure 1.4 The kitchen brigade

parties. Each partie is in the charge of a 'chef de partie', who is regarded as a specialist in a particular aspect of food production.

In Figure 1.4 we show the traditional division of the kitchen brigade into seven parties, though in a large luxury hotel the number of parties could be in excess of ten. Each chef de partie – larder cook, soup cook, etc. – is assisted by a commis or two and sometimes by an apprentice.

Invariably one of the chefs de partie acts as a deputy to the sous chef. The traditional brigade system, though still very much in evidence in large hotels, has undergone a number of changes. In some smaller hotels some parties have been combined, and it is now not unusual for a chef de partie to act as a vegetable cook and a soup cook, or for the roast cook to have responsibility for grilling. Finally there has been a lot of change in the terminology of kitchen operations: French terms and titles have tended to disappear. *Chef garde manger* is now known as the larder cook; *chef potager* is referred to as the soup cook; *chef rôtisseur* is the roast cook. The *sous chef,* however, is still known as the sous chef.

FOOD AND BEVERAGE SERVICE

The organisation of food and beverage service personnel – sometimes referred to as the restaurant brigade – is also highly structured. All food and beverage service personnel are grouped into 'stations', each of which is in the charge of the station head waiter, who is assisted by a waiter and a commis waiter. The number of stations depends on the size of the hotel restaurant. Each station consists of a number of tables and probably serves about fifty covers during each (luncheon or dinner) service. In addition to the service of food, there are two or three wine waiters – frequently one wine waiter looks after two stations.

The structure of the restaurant brigade, as illustrated in Figure 1.5, has undergone similar changes to those mentioned in relation to the kitchen brigade. The use of French terminology has largely given way to more readily understood English terminology. Also the structure of the restaurant brigade is less rigid and more responsive to the needs and circumstances of each individual hotel.

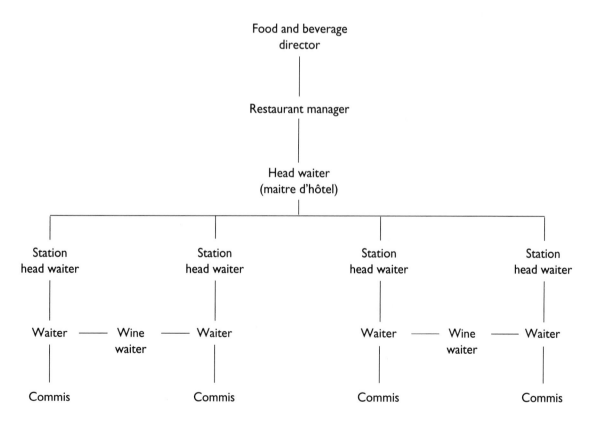

Figure 1.5 The restaurant brigade

Restaurants – unlike hotel food and beverage departments – are essentially simple as far as their organisation structure is concerned. In the vast majority of cases we see basically two departments: the kitchen and the dining room. Also, with few exceptions, the size of the restaurant is too small to justify the creation of specialist departments such as purchasing or accounts. In all probability, some 80–90 per cent of restaurants have an organisation structure such as shown in Figure 1.6.

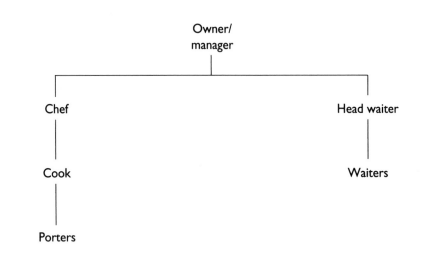

Figure 1.6 Organisation chart of a restaurant

In the six organisation charts shown above, we have illustrated structures and used terminology associated with British hotels. Some readers will be pleased to see further examples of organisation charts relevant to larger international hotels. These will be found in Chapters 8, 9 and 13.

QUESTIONS

1 Describe the following principal characteristics of food and beverage operations:

(a) high cost fixity
(b) demand instability
(c) sales mix instability
(d) perishability of food
(e) short cycle of operations
(f) multiplicity of low value transactions
(g) high degree of departmentalisation

2   Set out below is a list of a number of different types of food and beverage operation.

      (a)   hotel
      (b)   motel
      (c)   restaurant
      (d)   café
      (e)   country club
      (f)   industrial canteen
      (g)   flight catering
      (h)   airport catering
      (i)   outdoor catering

    Describe the essential characteristics of the above types of operation and decide which of them are cost-oriented and which market-oriented.

3   Discuss the composition of the hotel and catering industry, and divide all the major types of food and beverage operations into meaningful categories.

4   Explain what you understand by the orientation of a business. What are the main factors which determine the orientation of food and beverage operations?

5   Distinguish clearly between cost and market orientation. Give examples of cost oriented and market oriented industries.

6   Draw the organisation chart of a 300-bedroomed hotel, and indicate clearly the authority and responsibility of each of the following:

      (a)   food and beverage controller
      (b)   purchasing manager
      (c)   storekeeper
      (d)   restaurant cashier

7   Draw the organisation chart of the food and beverage department of a large, 500-bedroomed hotel. Assume that the hotel has four restaurants and a substantial banqueting department.

CHAPTER 2

OPERATIONAL AND ECONOMIC CHARACTERISTICS

In Chapter 1 we discussed the meaning and significance of market orientation, which was then – as a concept – presented as heavy dependence on market demand. Market orientation has yet another aspect – namely, the influence of the customer profile on practically all aspects of the food and beverage operation.

A market-oriented business, to be successful, must be sensitive and responsive to the needs, requirements and even whims of its customers. It is not surprising, therefore, that type of customer has an all-pervasive influence on practically every aspect of hotel and restaurant operations. In the section which now follows we present the customer profile as a powerful determinant of the major operating characteristics of hotels and restaurants and discuss its main economic implications.

Average Spending Power (ASP)

The concept of price in food and beverage operations is complex and essentially different from what is commonly understood by this term in other industries. In retailing, for example, each individual product has its own clearly defined price. The seller offers a range of products, and it is for the customer to respond. The customer has generally no freedom to purchase more or less of a given product and, in this way, decide how much he or she will spend.

The situation is wholly different in hotels and restaurants. As a general rule, the customer is offered a wide range of food and beverage items, each of which is priced separately, and is free to spend more or less on each meal. In a situation like this, the individual prices quoted for the starters, main dishes, vegetables, etc., are simply elements which contribute to the total amount paid for the meal. It is for this reason that most hotels and restaurants use the concept of the average spending power, which is the most relevant concept of price.

Whilst it is for the hotel or restaurant to establish the general price level, i.e. compose menus which will produce an ASP of, say, £10 or £20, the exact and final level of the ASP is a compromise – a joint decision by, so to speak, equal partners in the pricing process: the hotel or restaurant and the customer. Whatever the menu offerings and whatever the individual menu item prices, it is ultimately the customer's decision how many courses and which individual menu items he or she will have. In such circumstances, whether the ASP works out at £14.50 or £15.25 is very much dependent on the whims of the guests.

In controlling the ASP of the establishment – and hence its profitability – it is desirable to resort to a variety of measures which promote sufficiently high ASP levels. Menu engineering involves the examination of the performance of individual menu items as well as their prices. Where ASP levels are not satisfactory, the menu engineering routine will ensure that sufficient attention is paid to the price of each food item on the menu. Waiters' sales analysis is a particularly powerful weapon in ASP control in that it encourages the waiting staff to sell starters, desserts and beverages and, in this way, achieve the highest possible personal level of ASP. Finally, when ASP levels show a degree of under-achievement, consideration should be given to the imposition of a cover charge. This is not appropriate in all circumstances; where it is, however, it has a particularly strong impact on profitability: the whole of the cover charge is an addition to the net profit of the establishment.

Nature of Product

The nature of the product offered by hotels and restaurants is greatly influenced by the type of customer. Indeed in many cases, before a new establishment is open, a thorough feasibility study is undertaken with a view to determining the type of customer. What is then offered in terms of food, beverages, service and atmosphere is strictly based on the expected type of customer (i.e. customer profile).

The products we offer in hotels and restaurants consist of tangible and intangible elements. The tangible elements are the actual food and beverages, whilst the intangible elements consist of food and beverage service, decor and the atmosphere. The more affluent the guest, the higher generally his/her ASP and the greater the intangible element, and vice versa. This is illustrated in Figure 2.1.

Also it should be noted that the composition of the tangible element tends to change in response to the level of the ASP. At low ASP levels the

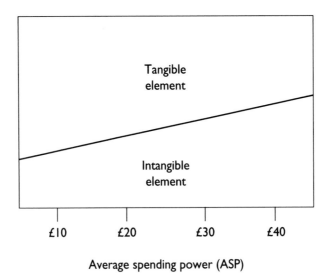

Average spending power (ASP)

Figure 2.1 Tangible and intangible elements of ASP

customer buys almost exclusively items of food. As the ASP rises, the customer's expenditure on beverages tends to become more prominent.

Gross Profit

The influence of the customer profile on the gross profit of an establishment is strong. As far as the percentage of gross profit is concerned, gross profits in hotels and restaurants tend to vary from 55 to 70 per cent. As a general rule, the more affluent the customer, the higher his/her ASP and the higher the percentage of gross profit. Cheaper popular restaurants and cafés tend to operate at 55–60 per cent gross profit, whilst more up-market establishments, charging in excess of £25 for food only, tend to earn gross profits of around 70 per cent.

From this it follows that £1 spent in a high ASP establishment will generate more for cash gross profit than £1 spent in a low ASP establishment. The table below will make this clear.

ASP	£10	£20	£30
Gross profit %	60	65	70
Gross profit £	£6	£13	£21

Every type of customer may be associated with a different level of ASP. This, in turn, has a strong impact on the cash gross profit per cover.

Where the ASP level and the resulting cash gross profit per cover are high, it is not surprising that 'the customer is always right' and that 'nothing is too much trouble' to please him/her.

Opening Hours

The opening hours of a food and beverage operation are an excellent example of the way in which the type of customer influences the major aspects of its work.

From observation we know that establishments with low ASP levels, say around £5 (and this includes so-called fast food operations, cafés and snack bars) tend to open early in the morning and remain open until fairly late at night. On the other hand, high ASP establishments tend to open for about three hours at lunchtime and five hours in the evening. There are two main reasons for this difference. The demand for snacks, teas and coffees, and light refreshments tends to persist throughout the day, whilst the demand for more expensive meals occurs around lunchtime and in the evening. As a sensitive and responsive business unit, the food and beverage operation tailors its offerings to match consumer demand. The opening hours are also influenced by the economics of each operation. Where the ASP is low, an establishment which opened for just a few hours twice a day would not achieve a sufficient volume of sales to break even, let alone make a profit.

Elasticity of Demand

Elasticity of demand measures the responsiveness of demand to changes in price. Where a small change in price results in a substantial change in the quantity demanded, demand is said to be elastic. Where a large change in price has little effect on the quantity demanded, demand is said to be inelastic.

From observation it seems that the higher the ASP level the less elastic the demand, and vice versa. It is fair to assume that the general position is as illustrated in Figure 2.2.

In the case of low ASP operations, demand tends to be very sensitive to changes in price. In such circumstances a relatively small increase in menu prices, say 10 per cent, may well lead to a substantial loss of business. Where ASP levels are high – say in excess of £30 – a similar

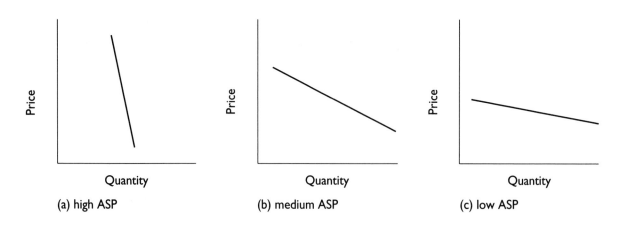

Figure 2.2 Elasticity of demand

increase in menu prices may not have any noticeable effect on the number of covers.

Similar considerations apply with regard to price reductions. Where the ASP is high, price reductions as a method of attracting customers are not likely to prove effective: the loss from lower prices is not likely to be compensated by the resulting addition to the total number of covers. High ASP establishments must, therefore, concentrate on high gastronomic standards and professional and friendly service as a method of securing the right results in terms of sales volumes and profits.

Profitability and Profit Stability

Profitability of hotel food and beverage operations is not only difficult to achieve, but also difficult to assess. One of the main factors which militate against profitability are the long opening hours. Frequently hotel dining rooms are open and staffed long after any guests are likely to materialise – simply because it is felt that hot meals should be available in case they are needed. In many countries it is usual for hotels to offer a 24-hour service in the coffee shop, even though it is obvious that few guests will use the facility after 12 p.m. Such long opening hours result in relatively low sales volumes per employee and make hotel food and beverage operations less profitable than restaurant food and beverage operations where – as noted earlier in this chapter – opening hours are adjusted to match demand.

Frequently the profitability of hotel food and beverage operations is hampered because it is not seen as a major goal of the total hotel operation. Where this view prevails, the thinking is that the main function of the food and beverage department is to offer a standard of service which will promote the sale of rooms: it is, after all, in the rooms department that most of the hotel's profit is made. It seems that, in the final analysis, the right attitude is: (a) to accept the crucial role of the food and beverage department in promoting room sales but, at the same time, (b) to recognise the food and beverage department as a major revenue-producing department of the hotel capable of making its own contribution to overall profitability. The food and beverage department should always be seen as, essentially, an independent entity with its own aims and a clearly defined profit target.

Earlier in this chapter we attributed to hotels and restaurant operations the characteristics of sensitivity and responsiveness. When, however, we look at their profitability, it is clear that they also have the characteristic of vulnerability. Both hotels and restaurants operate at high levels of fixed costs, have strictly limited seating capacity and face continual fluctuations in demand. All these three elements make their profitability vulnerable.

Example 1: hotel operations

From published statistics we know that food and beverage costs (which are fully variable) amount to some 35 per cent of sales; food beverage payroll tends to equal approximately 30 per cent of sales; and we assume here that of the 30 per cent, 25 per cent is fixed and 5 per cent is variable costs. Other departmental expenses (laundry and dry cleaning, china, glassware, silver and linen, contract cleaning, etc.) tend to be fixed rather than variable, and amount to some 10 per cent of food and beverage sales. Finally, let us assume that food and beverage sales amount to £7,000 per available room. In this example we assume that our hotel has 200 rooms.

From Table 2.1 we may see that a relatively small loss of sales revenue of 10 per cent results in a loss of departmental profit of 24 per cent. If we lose 20 per cent of our food and beverage sales, the loss of departmental profit will amount to 48 per cent. In a situation like this the rewards for hard work and high sales volumes are as substantial as the penalties for indifference and declining turnover.

We referred earlier in this chapter to the fact that the profitability of hotel food and beverage operations is difficult to assess. The problem of assessment arises because in the majority of cases the food and beverage

Table 2.1

	Usual F&B Sales	F&B Sales Less 10%	F&B Sales Less 20%
	£	£	£
F&B Sales	1,400,000	1,260,000	1,120,000
Variable costs (40%)	560,000	504,000	448,000
Dept fixed costs (35%)	490,000	490,000	490,000
Total	1,050,000	994,000	938,000
Dept profit	350,000	266,000	182,000
Loss of dept profit	—	24.0%	48.0%

operation is not charged with a proportion of certain fixed expenses (administration and general expenses, marketing, energy costs, property operation and maintenance, etc.). Whilst it undoubtedly benefits from such expenditure, the problems of apportionment are such that most hotel accountants are quite happy not to charge such indirect expenses against food and beverage sales. In consequence we calculate, from time to time, the departmental profit but not the food and beverage net profit.

In the case of restaurants such problems of assessing profitability do not exist. All fixed costs have to be recovered from the restaurant's sales and the true cost structure is clearly visible. We can also see clearly the impact of sales volume fluctuation on the net profit of the restaurant.

EXAMPLE 2: RESTAURANT OPERATIONS

Most restaurants are relatively small organisations. Currently the average restaurant has a turnover of just in excess of £0.5 million. Restaurant fixed costs tend to amount to approximately 40 per cent of sales revenue

Table 2.2

	Usual F&B Sales	F&B Sales Less 10%	F&B Sales Less 20%
	£	£	£
F&B Sales	500,000	450,000	400,000
Variable costs	200,000	180,000	160,000
Fixed costs	200,000	200,000	200,000
Total	400,000	380,000	360,000
Net profit	100,000	70,000	40,000
Loss of dept profit	—	30.0%	60.0%

(divided equally between labour costs and overheads). The total variable cost amounts to approximately 40 per cent of sales revenue. (Food and beverage costs account for some 35 per cent and part-time and casual labour some 5 per cent.) The net profit, in consequence, averages some 20 per cent of total turnover. In Table 2.2 we show the effect of changes in food and beverage sales on the net profit of a typical restaurant.

The vulnerability of restaurant profits is very clear from this table. Even a moderate loss of sales volume of 10 per cent will reduce the net profit by 30 per cent. A loss of turnover of 20 per cent will at least half the net profit of the average restaurant.

Questions

1   Describe the main factors which contribute to the complexity of hotel and restaurant food and beverage operations.

2   Explain the essential differences of table d'hôte and à la carte menus in terms of their respective contributions to profitability.

3   'A market-oriented business, to be successful, must be sensitive and responsive to the needs, requirements and even whims of its customers.' Discuss.

4   Discuss the average spending power as a concept of price in food and beverage operations.

5   Enumerate the various measures that may be resorted to in controlling the average spending power.

6   Explain what is meant by the 'tangible' and 'intangible' elements of ASP.

7   Why is it that, particularly in high ASP establishments, the 'customer is always right'?

8   Explain what you understand by 'elasticity of demand'. How does it influence the pricing policy of high ASP food and beverage operations?

9   The opening hours of restaurants vary quite considerably. Do they vary because of the sensitivity and responsiveness to consumer demand or due to economic considerations?

10 Frequently hotel dining rooms remain open long after any guests are likely to come. What are the reasons for this? What are the consequences?

11 Explain what is meant by the vulnerability of hotel and restaurant profitability. What are the main factors which contribute to vulnerability?

12 Your friends Fred and Mavis Jones have recently purchased a 100-bedroomed hotel. Until recently Mr Jones was director of a construction company; now, having inherited a small fortune, he has decided to branch out on his own.

Fred Jones has been in business for many years and is of the opinion that managing a hotel is not different from managing any other business. He has, however, approached you to ask if there is anything in particular he should know about the operation of the food and beverage department.

You are required, before meeting Fred Jones, to draft some explanatory notes on the following:

(a) the complexity of hotel food and beverage operations with regard to the extent of food and beverage service, types of menu and nature of the cuisine;
(b) the implications of the above for the profitability of the operation;
(c) the importance of repeat business and the maintenance of appropriate ASP levels;
(d) the overriding importance of the customer profile.

CHAPTER 3

MARKETING

Marketing is the management and social process of identifying, anticipating and satisfying the needs of present and potential customers whilst making long-term profits. The choice of marketing techniques may vary in the marketing of services from the marketing of products, but the basic principles and concepts of marketing are equally important and relevant in both.

Successful hospitality marketing regards the customer as the focal point of business.

Selling and Marketing

In the hospitality business, selling is often misunderstood as marketing. Personal selling, although important, is only one of many tactical areas of marketing and one of the five elements of promotion mix as shown in Figure 3.1.

Most 'front of house' hotel staff, especially the ones attached to the sales department, front office, banquet office, and food and beverage outlets, are involved in selling. Basically selling is a micro function which means offering existing products at an agreed price. Often sales people do not control (although they may influence) the production level or quality.

Marketing is a macro function, which, in addition to selling, is involved in many other tactical areas, such as:

1 Collecting, storing and analysing important information regarding markets, competition and future trends.
2 Segmenting the market and identifying specific needs of different customers.
3 Adjusting existing products and creating new products to suit the changing customer needs.
4 Deciding on price levels acceptable to the customers and to the company (ensuring value for money to the customers and ensuring long-term profitability for the company).

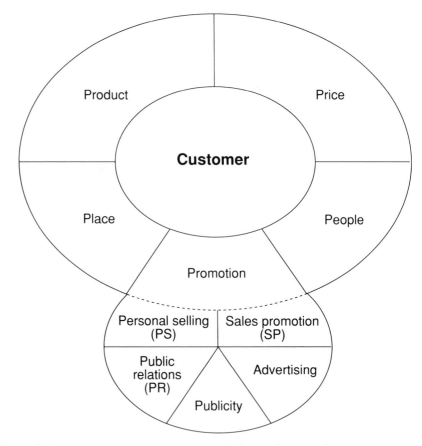

Figure 3.1 Promotion mix in the context of the marketing mix

5 Selecting suitable channels which can be used as 'pipelines', either to distribute the products to the customers or attract customers to the products/services. (In the case of the hotel and restaurant business, channels such as travel agents are often used for attracting potential customers, rather than actually distributing manufactured goods, as is done in most other industries.)

6 Communicating with the middlemen (agents and channel representatives), together with past, present and potential customers, by effectively using a suitable mix of advertising, direct mail, publicity, public relations and sales promotion to promote the products.

7 Recruiting, training and motivating staff who are directly or indirectly involved in selling and other marketing activities.

8 Planning short-term and long-term marketing with inputs from operations, finance, human resources and general management.

Hospitality Marketing

To be successful in the modern hospitality business, a market-oriented business philosophy is required. It is considered essential for hospitality companies to co-ordinate their marketing process. Most companies now spend around 2–5 per cent of total revenue on marketing.

To satisfy customer needs and enjoy a good 'bottom line' profit, hospitality companies need food and beverage managers, rooms division managers, personnel managers, financial controllers and general managers who are market-oriented and who appreciate the importance of marketing. Similarly, a good marketing manager in a hospitality business must understand the other important aspects of the company in order to achieve the desired long-term profits, as shown in Figure 3.2.

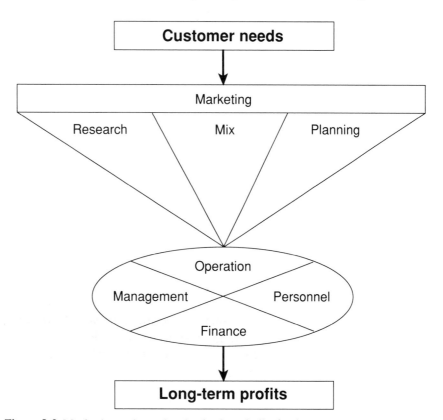

Figure 3.2 Marketing orientation in the hospitality business

In many ways, hospitality marketing seems different from the marketing of products owing to the following twelve unique characteristics of the hospitality industry:

1   Customers' presence during production and service. A hotel or a restaurant can be compared to a factory (for example the kitchen is similar to a production line) with show rooms (e.g. public lounges), sales outlets (e.g. restaurants), an after-sales service unit (e.g. maintenance services) and a customer complaint counter (e.g. guest relations desk) all rolled into one!

2   More personal contact between the service providers and customers.

3   Many hotel guests stay longer than just a day or two. Where a guest's meal experience is for some reason unsatisfactory, there is normally plenty of opportunity to demonstrate high food and beverage standards and extra attention to ensure guest satisfaction on subsequent occasions before the guest's departure. Such opportunities do not exist where physical/tangible products are sold.

4   A variety of products and services are combined and offered to the customers as a total and complex package. For example, a hotel customer who enjoys his/her meals, drinks, music, room service, restaurant service and mini-bar facilities may still be unhappy because of noise in his/her room. All elements of the total package have to be satisfactory.

5   Many elements of the total package are both intangible and unquantifiable. As an example, the smile of a waiter, the politeness of a restaurant hostess, the clarity of speech of a room service order taker, the showmanship of a cocktail barman and the playing of a lobby pianist are important but intangible and unquantifiable elements of a hotel product.

6   Most hospitality products cannot be examined in advance of consumption. The equivalent of a fit-on of a dress or a test-drive of a car prior to purchase is not possible.

7   In the hospitality industry, payment for products and services will generally be made after consumption.

8   As explained earlier, there is no actual distribution of products, although channels are used to attract customers.

9   Sales can be optimised through planned 'in-house' (internal) promotions and merchandising, as customers are to some extent a captive audience.

10 Heterogeneous services make quality control and standardisation difficult. As an example the smile of a waitress cannot be identical every day. Her personal life will have an impact on her smile, irrespective of the training and directions that she has received. Similarly a cream of chicken soup served from the same kitchen may taste different from one day to another depending on the chef on duty or the mood of the same cook. With the use of standard

recipes, communication and training one may achieve near perfection, but assuring the same standard day after day will be difficult.

11 High fixed costs, coupled with low variable costs, means generally high profit margins and a lot of scope for flexible pricing. (This is explained in considerable detail in Chapter 11.)

12 High degree of perishability. For example if a restaurant is ready to serve 100 customers for dinner and only 40 arrive, the restaurant will lose the man-hours, heating, flowers, lighting, etc., adequate to serve 60 customers. This obviously cannot be stored and reused and will affect profitability.

Market Research

Market research has not been given its right place by many hotels and restaurants. Market research is the systematic collecting, storing and analysing of data related to markets, competition, future trends and other factors influencing a business operation. It is done in order to improve the efficiency and effectiveness of the whole operation. Lack of formal research in food and beverage operations is frequently evident. Properly planned market research will help food and beverage managers to fine-tune their operations and to become more customer-oriented. Although there are numerous ways of collecting data, many hotels use only a few operational records. Most hotels analyse the information collected through guest comment cards, but unfortunately, owing to a very low response rate from most short-stay guests, the data collected are not truly representative.

For any industry there are six obvious steps which constitute the market research cycle. These are interlinked and should be an ongoing process. The fruitfulness of market research depends on the management and marketing decisions taken based on the research findings. The market research cycle is outlined in Figure 3.3.

Food and beverage operations market research can be broadly divided into three main categories:

External Desk Research

This means using information collected and stored by external organisations, such as:

- Governments and tourist boards: tourist arrival patterns, nationalities, tourist segments, tourist profiles, reports on periodical tourist surveys, special reports, etc.

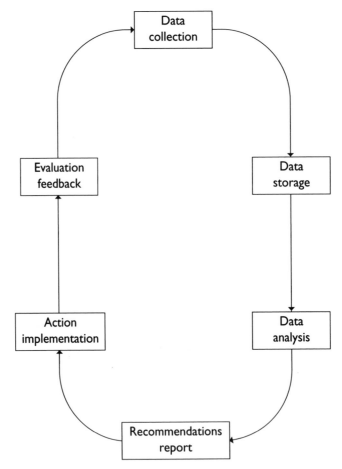

Figure 3.3 Market research cycle

- Associations (e.g. HCIMA) and publishers (of guide books and journals): lists of hotels and restaurants, information on competitors (type of food, number of covers, number of seats, average spending, food and beverage prices and segments), lists of suppliers, popularity surveys, trends in eating habits, etc.

- Educational establishments: research papers on current issues in hotel and restaurant industries, special research undertaken by faculty, postgraduate students and undergraduate students, etc.

Internal Desk Research

This means using information collected and stored by different departments of the hotel such as:

- Front office: customer profiles, nationalities, average stay, double occupancy, guest comments, booking patterns, etc.

- Sales: comments made by tour operators, travel agents, etc.

- Public relations: communication share (for example, calculating the space/air time given for advertisements and for publicity of a hotel in the local media as a percentage of total space given to all competitor hotels in the area), restaurant reviews of newspapers and journals.

- Food and beverages controls: average spending power, weekly restaurant patterns, dish popularity analysis, etc.

Field Research

This means carrying out surveys and collecting new data 'on the floor'. For example:

- Observations made in restaurants, bars, etc.

- Customer interviews by hostesses, guest relation officers and restaurant managers

- Blind tasting involving regular customers (e.g. new dishes, house wines and cocktails)

- Postal or telephone surveys

- Diner questionnaires – a sample taken from the coffee shop of a well-known hotel is shown in Figure 3.4 overleaf.

Market research is mainly carried out to collect more data in order to analyse the following four Cs as shown in Figure 3.5.

Community

- Whole population or total market

- Economic health in general terms

- Main segments – present, past and potential

- General trends, etc.

Customers

- Social and economic levels

- Ages, sex, etc. (profiles)

- Frequency of usage, average stay and product loyalty

- Consumer behaviour, etc.

The Nightingale Hotel

DODINTON · LONG SUTTON · SOMERSET TA19 0ER
TELEPHONE 0245 24556

Dear Guest

Did our hospitality shine through?

Our goal is to make you feel truly welcome and we will do our utmost to help you enjoy our facilities and services.

Please give a few moments of your time to complete this questionnaire. Your response will help greatly in our efforts to improve our services.

Thanking you for your assistance.

Yours sincerely

General Manager

Please tick ☑

	☺	☻	☹
Quality of service	☐	☐	☐
Value for money	☐	☐	☐
Employee attitude	☐	☐	☐
Employee appearance	☐	☐	☐
Speed of service	☐	☐	☐
Menu selection	☐	☐	☐
Quality of food	☐	☐	☐
Cleanliness	☐	☐	☐
Beverage selection	☐	☐	☐
Quality of entertainment	☐	☐	☐

Comments:

_____

_____

_____

_____

_____

We encourage our employees to exemplify our hospitality and we reward them when they do.

We invite you to nominate any of our staff who has impressed you with their hospitality:

Nominee _____

Department _____

Special comments _____

_____

_____

_____

_____

Name and address (please print):

_____

_____

_____

Tel:

Figure 3.4 A diner questionnaire from a coffee shop

36

Company (own)

- Strengths and weaknesses

- Position and image

- Products and services

- Advertising, etc.

Competitors

- Strengths and weaknesses

- Position and image

- Products and services

- Customers and channels, etc.

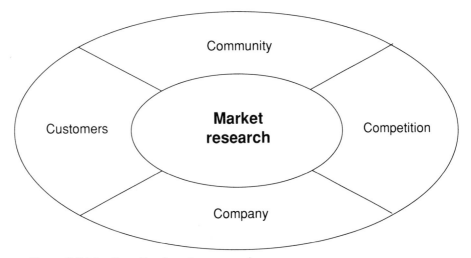

Figure 3.5 The four Cs of market research

Research findings often surprise hoteliers and restaurant owners. Some recent research in the UK indicates the following:

- Most popular for leisure eating out are steak houses, pubs, and Chinese and Indian restaurants. Only about 11 per cent of people go to hotel restaurants. (This may be very different in many overseas countries where eating out in hotel restaurants is quite common.)

- The main reasons for eating out, among less frequent consumers, are celebrating a special occasion or giving oneself or spouse a treat.

- The main reasons for eating out, among very frequent consumers, are to meet with friends and to make a change from eating at home.

- The most important attributes of eating establishments which customers frequent are:

    1   Cleanliness and hygiene;
    2   Well-cooked/good food;
    3   Efficient and pleasant service;
    4   Atmosphere;
    5   Acceptable price range.

- The factors influencing initial choice of an eating establishment are:

    1   Reasonable prices;
    2   Recommendations;
    3   Spacious and pleasant layout;
    4   Interesting or adventurous menu;
    5   Convenient to get to.

Hoteliers and restaurant owners with good business sense will use research findings to adjust/change the products and services, as well as promotions and prices, to ensure optimisation of the long-term profitability of their operations.

It is often observed that either research findings are not used in a systematic fashion or only ad hoc research is carried out, without proper planning. However, some hospitality organisations use research findings in a most systematic manner (for example tabulating guest comments with percentages and comparing monthly percentages to determine changing levels of customer satisfaction, improvements and trends). In the long run only such organisations will enjoy sustained success.

Market research helps organisations to be more customer-oriented in the whole operation. It helps in market segmentation and in fine-tuning of different products and services to suit the different needs of different market segments.

Market Segmentation

Market segmentation can be defined as the identification of a subset of consumers, so that a marketing mix can be devised specifically to satisfy its demand.

The market for the hotel product may be divided into several components or segments and this enables individual hotels to identify their actual and potential users according to various criteria. Segmentation then provides a basis for the marketing of hotel products, for paying close attention to the requirements of different users and monitoring the performance in the markets chosen by a hotel. Over the years the segment changes will prompt product and service changes in hotels. The British guest segment in London five-star hotels has decreased over the years. In the 1940s most London five-star hotels recorded over 70 per cent British guests, but by the 1960s this had dropped to 35 per cent. In the 1980s this fell to 20 per cent. Today, in most of these hotels American and continental (from other European Union (EU) countries) guests form a much larger and more important segment than British guests. In some London five-star hotels, fast-increasing numbers of Middle Eastern and Japanese guests have resulted in many product/service adjustments.

Marketing decision-making must be preceded by a clear identification of customers and their likely responses to different marketing actions. Hospitality marketers should ask the following questions in order to understand buyer behaviour and then to improve the business:

1 Who are the customers?
2 How do they buy?
3 Why do they buy?
4 What do they expect from buying?
5 What do they value when buying?

In market segmentation it is always worth considering the following questions:

1 Is segmentation relevant to the market situation?
2 Is the segmentation base appropriate to customer buying?
3 Is the segment sufficiently large to meet special efforts?
4 Is the segment reachable by media or serviceable by channels?
5 Is the segment really different from other segments?
6 Is the segment expected to grow?
7 Is the segment relatively resistant to substitution by competitors?

Customers seek benefits when they visit a restaurant. A clear understanding of the benefits sought by customers is a prerequisite for entering or developing hospitality business. Many markets are made up of customers oriented towards the following four core benefits:

1 Economy
2 Service
3 Quality
4 Status

Most customers will have a main orientation, with one or two other benefits sought, as shown on Figure 3.6.

Economic orientation	Service orientation
Quality orientation	Status orientation

Figure 3.6 Core Benefit Segments

A market can be segmented according to three main bases as shown on Figure 3.7.

What is bought?	Who buys?	Why?
• volume • price • outlets • geography • product characteristics	• geographic • demographic • socio-economic • behaviour patterns • consumption patterns	• benefits • attitudes • perceptions • preferences • other influences

Figure 3.7 Bases for market segmentation

Marketing Mix

The marketing mix has five closely linked variable elements – popularly known as the five Ps – controlled/adjusted by the management of any organisation.

These five – Product, Place, Promotion, Price and People – are in fact the critical elements which are used to influence demand according to market forces to improve the long-term profitability of organisations as shown in Figure 3.8.

In the context of food and beverage operations the marketing mix will include:

Product

- Quality of food and beverage products

- Quality of food and beverage service

- Restaurant and bar decor

- Furniture, fittings and equipment

- Menu design

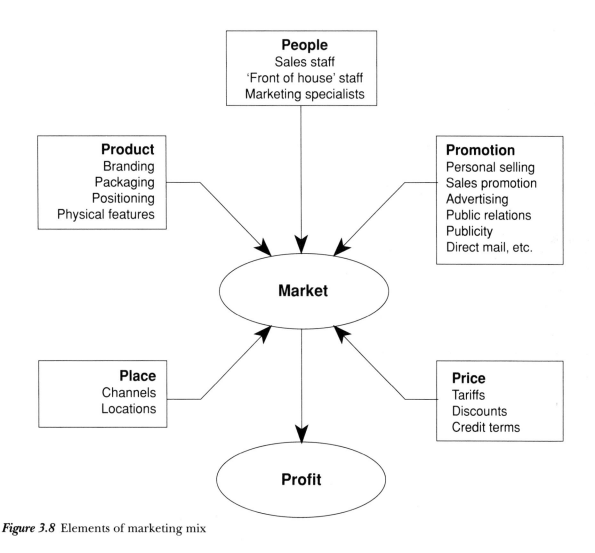

Figure 3.8 Elements of marketing mix

- Portion sizes
- Hours of operations
- Range of food and beverage outlets
- Brand names (e.g. reputed hotel chains)
- Well-known staff (e.g. chefs, managers)
- Entertainers, musicians
- Unique selling proposition (USPs), such as 'The only 24-hour gourmet restaurant in London'

Place

- Hotel locations

- Restaurant locations/easy accessibility

- Distribution (e.g. outside catering)

- Representatives/agents

Promotion

- External personal selling (e.g. banquet, sales staff)

- Internal personal selling (e.g. waiting staff)

- Food festivals

- Advertising (e.g. TV, radio, newspapers)

- Merchandising (e.g. lift posters, tent cards, food and beverage displays)

- Direct mail to regular diners

- Participation at exhibitions

- Sponsorship of public relation events

- Free sampling of items

- Cookery demonstrations

- Public relations (birthday cakes, anniversary cards, complimentary meals, Christmas hampers and cordial relationships) with regular customers, the media, opinion formers, food critics, local communities, etc.

Price

- Variable pricing of different menus

- Bar 'happy hours'

- Discounted rates for children

- Credit facilities

- Volume discounting (e.g. banquets and group bookings)

- Waiving of corkage

People

- Well-trained sales staff

- Sales-oriented 'Front of House' staff (e.g. restaurant managers and hostesses, bar staff, waiters)

- Other specialists (e.g. public relations staff, advertising agents)

Marketing Planning

Power in marketing is derived from gathering information through market research – information about us, our products, our customers and our competitors. The information gathered and analysed should be used effectively in the marketing planning process to make the business more customer-oriented and more profitable.

Hotel marketers should ask themselves questions such as:

1 What can we produce/create and sell?
2 What will our customers want to buy in the future?
3 What business are we in?
4 Is the market expanding or declining?
5 What can we do about it?
6 How much profit do we make per restaurant, per dish and per function?
7 Will our customers buy any other products from our hotel (for example in new restaurants, pastry shops, etc.)?

Hotel marketers should be very clear of the answers to such questions and be objective in their approach when engaged in marketing planning. The marketing plan should be devised in the context of and as a part of the corporate plan of an organisation. It should be practical and should be co-ordinated with other key plans such as the financial plan (budget) and operational plan. At the end of a marketing plan one will find a few action plans which will provide a 'To Do' list for a given period (usually a year) covering all the activities that need to be done to market the products successfully (such as a promotional plan with all costs). Figure 3.9 shows this concept.

The stages of a one-year planning process are:

1 **External macro environmental analysis**
   Opportunities and threats in the context of the Political, Economic, Social and Technical (PEST) environment – explained in Table 3.1.

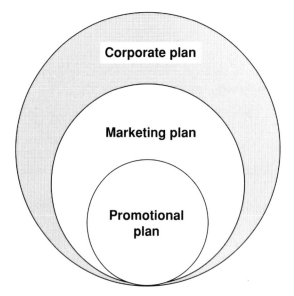

Figure 3.9 A plan within plans

2 **Marketing audit**
   An analysis of customers, suppliers, agents, etc., of an organisation as well as of the main competitors and the public, banks, unions, media, etc., and the anticipated opportunities and threats.

3 **Internal analysis**
   Identifying own strengths and weaknesses in the context of the operation, personnel, finance and marketing.

4 **'SWOT' analysis**
   Marrying of Strengths, Weaknesses, Opportunities and Threats

5 **Marketing objectives**
   An organisation can have one or many, such as survival, growth of restaurant revenue by 10 per cent, improving guest satisfaction from 78 per cent to 85 per cent, improving standards from two-star to three-star, or increasing food and beverage profits from 12 per cent to 16 per cent.

6 **Marketing strategies**
   In order to achieve the identified/determined marketing objectives. Basic strategic alternatives are shown in Figure 3.10.

Table 3.1 External macro environmental analysis: PEST factors

PEST Factors	Examples
Political	• Government legislation: fire regulations, health and safety acts, EU regulations. • Changes in the taxation structure of the United Kingdom regulations affecting business expense allowances. • Specific government taxes such as VAT (Value Added Tax).
Economic	• Rising costs: foods and beverages, labour, fuel rates and insurance. • Changes in expenditure patterns and people's disposable incomes. • Expansion and retraction of credit facilities. • Higher interest rates on borrowed capital.
Social	• Changes in population distribution: population drifting away from certain areas. • Changes in the socio-economic groupings of the area/ region. • Growth of ethnic minorities leading to a demand for more varied foods. • Changes in food fashion: popularity of takeaway foods, home delivery of fast foods, trends in healthy eating.
Technical	• Mechanisation of food production and food service equipment. • Computer technology: data processing in hotel and catering establishments. • Product development: textured vegetable protein, increased shelf-life of foods, meat and dairy produce alternatives.

	Existing products	New products
Existing markets	Market penetration	Product development
New markets	Market development	Diversification

Figure 3.10 Basic strategic alternatives

The following are examples of strategic alternatives for an Italian restaurant catering to business people:

(a) Market penetration — To get more business people to visit the restaurant to have Italian food (existing product and existing market)

(b) Market development — To attract tourists and 'after theatre' segments to visit the restaurant to have Italian food (existing product and new markets)

(c) Product development — To offer French and German food to existing 'business' segment (new products and existing market)

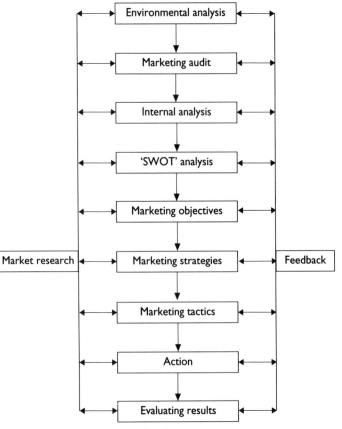

Figure 3.11 Marketing planning model (MPM)

<table>
<tr><td>(d) Diversification</td><td>To offer French and German food to tourists and 'after theatre' segments (new products and new markets)</td></tr>
</table>

7 **Marketing tactics**

Adjustments to the five Ps in the context of marketing strategies (e.g. change of positioning from an exclusive fine-dining restaurant chain to a medium-class restaurant chain ensuring better value for money, or vice versa).

8 **Action**

9 **Evaluating results**

10 **Feedback**

Each stage of the marketing planning process should be based on market research findings, and regular feedback should be channelled as shown in Figure 3.11.

The implementation of the concept of 'Marketing' can be summarised as shown in Figure 3.12. All marketing decisions should be based on inputs through market research – which is similar to the base of a toolbox. This toolbox contains everything the marketer needs. What keeps all the elements held together is marketing planning, which is similar to the handle of the toolbox. In a 'nutshell', the successful marketer bases decisions on the findings of market research and co-ordinates the various adjustments to the marketing mix with a good marketing plan, whilst being customer-oriented and profit-conscious.

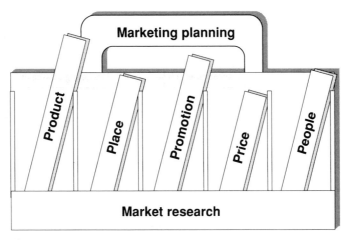

Figure 3.12 The marketing toolbox

QUESTIONS

1 'Marketing is a macro function which, in addition to selling, is involved in many other tactical areas.' Discuss this statement in the context of hospitality marketing, noting the ways in which it differs from the marketing of manufactured products.

2 Why is marketing orientation considered vital for success in the hospitality business?

3 List and explain the stages of the market research cycle and the main categories of market research in food and beverage operations.

4 'The market for the hotel product may be divided into several components or segments and this enables hotels to identify their actual and potential users.' Do you agree?

5 Write brief notes on the following:

   (a) Marketing orientation
   (b) Hospitality marketing
   (c) Promotional mix
   (d) Field research
   (e) The marketing toolbox

6 'The five Ps is a marketing concept concerning the closely linked variable elements of a mix.' Discuss this statement with examples of the five Ps in the context of food and beverage operations.

7 How will a change in one of the variable elements of the marketing mix affect other elements? Explain with examples from a hotel or restaurant.

8 What are PEST factors, and how do they influence hotel marketing?

9 Identify and explain the bases for market segmentation.

10 Explain the marketing planning process in detail.

CASE STUDY: THE QUEEN MARY HOTEL

The Queen Mary is a three-star hotel with 127 rooms, located near a golf course in a picturesque area just outside Edinburgh, Scotland. You are the newly appointed food and beverage manager of this poorly maintained hotel built in 1927. The available data are as follows:

1 Main market segments in comparison to the whole area.

Segment	Scotland %	Edinburgh %	Queen Mary %
North American	44	31	25
British	20	31	50
Continental (Mainly EC)	16	17	13
Middle Eastern	12	8	4
Others (Mainly Japanese)	8	13	8

2 237 beds.
3 Food and beverage operation.

Outlet	Seats	Covers per day	Average spend (£)
Grill room	40	24	42.37
Scot restaurant	40	31	17.58
Coffee shop	120	300	8.13
Bar lounge	50	—	
Room service	—	48	12.50
Banquet rooms	300	116	N/A
Outside catering	—	20	N/A
Total	550	539	—

4 Average occupancy (last year)   = 65 per cent
5 Food and beverage revenue   = 50 per cent of total
6 Food cost   = 37 per cent
7 Beverage cost   = 35 per cent
8 Male/female guest ratio   = 62:38
9 Double occupancy   = 59 per cent
10 Meals consumed by non-resident guests   = 167 a day
    (without banquets)
11 Food and beverage departmental profit   = 2 per cent
12 Hotel net profit   = 11 per cent

The family-owned Queen Mary Hotel is managed by Mrs Susy McQueen. Her husband is the current chairman. Mrs McQueen did not believe in advertising or sales promotion and often said that 'Good food needs no advertising.' The decor of all the restaurants and the menus were planned according to her taste. When, occasionally, a customer complained, the comments were ignored. The only plan for the whole organisation was the budget done by the accountant.

However, Mrs McQueen now wishes to be more marketing-oriented and has asked you to prepare a report covering the following for the food and beverage department of the hotel:

(a) Marketing orientation – proposed changes
(b) Plan for marketing research
(c) A proposed marketing plan

CHAPTER 4

ADVERTISING AND MERCHANDISING

Advertising is 'any paid form of non-personal presentation and promotion of ideas, goods or services by an identified sponsor'.

Advertising is universally regarded as one of the most important marketing weapons. Advertising, like other elements of the marketing programme, requires objectives. These can only be set when the hotel's position has been determined. At times it is observed that hotel advertisers are not clear about either the desired positioning of the hotel or the aimed market segments. The hotel advertiser must answer the following three questions as the first step in systematic advertising:

1   What are our advertising objectives?
2   How much should we spend on advertising?
3   To whom should we direct our advertising?

Timely analysis of the above will provide a better opportunity to the advertiser to increase the revenue of the hotel and ultimately optimise its long-term profits, which is the primary objective of any business organisation. Most hotel groups find that advertising is a cost-effective method of reaching a volume market.

Hoteliers should have a good understanding of the crucial role advertising plays in hotel marketing. A closer analysis of advertising effectiveness is important. This is not possible unless improved methods of advertising evaluation are implemented. Some hoteliers use in-house guest questionnaires to obtain a feedback from guests as to whether their visit resulted from seeing an advertisement. It is generally accepted that measuring the effectiveness of advertising is an extremely difficult task. Advertising effectiveness means different things to the groups responsible for different aspects of advertising. For some it is the popularity of the advertising campaign; for others it is the positive image built or the increased revenue.

It is interesting to study the contrasting views expressed by hoteliers, researchers and academics regarding the importance of advertising and how it works. The earliest attempts at explanation occurred in the 1920s. Today there is still disagreement about how advertising affects purchasing behaviour. A senior hotel marketer once said 'Certainly advertising can be a terrible waste of money. Few readers notice more than three or four advertisements in a newspaper or a periodical they are reading.' Little is known about how or why it works, yet billions are spent on advertising.

'People spend a lot of unnecessary money on paid advertising', another well-known hotel marketer said. Can we easily arrive at a conclusion that advertising is not required once your hotel becomes full and well established in the market? Is there a continuous need for advertising? Will a potential customer take a decision to patronise a hotel or restaurant purely because of an advertisement? These are questions well worth investigating. The purpose of advertising is defined by the Institute of Practitioners in Advertising (IPA) as: 'to influence a person's knowledge, attitude and behaviour in such a way as to meet the objectives of the advertiser'.

The stages of the advertising process are shown in Figure 4.1.

Advertising Objectives

Any advertiser will expect short-term or long-term benefits as a result of an advertisement. The objectives will vary from one organisation to another. The objectives will also vary depending on the environment at the time of advertising. Competition, consumer behaviour, revenue and profits will all influence the advertising objectives from time to time.

The following are some of the common objectives of advertising by hotels and restaurants:

1 Persuade customers to patronise the hotel or restaurant more often.
2 Create desire for a product/service in the minds of potential customers.
3 Emphasise benefits and advantages of the product/service.
4 Create an awareness of the product/service
5 Increase the market share.
6 Improve revenue.
7 Influence the attitude of the public towards the product/service.
8 Improve brand loyalty.
9 Confirm in the minds of customers that they have made the correct choice.
10 Enhance the desired image of the hotel or restaurant.

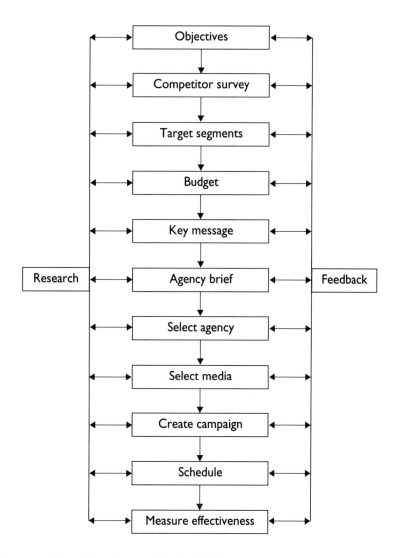

Figure 4.1 Advertising Strategy Model (ASM)

Communication Mix

An advertisement by itself may or may not stimulate a person to respond immediately by making a reservation to stay in a hotel or to visit a restaurant for a meal. It performs an intangible servicing in addition to any direct response it may evoke, by creating an image, making a memory impact, or paving the way for the future of some other sales tool you may utilise. A change in one of the elements of the communication mix such as public relations, sales calls, promotions and advertising has an effect on other elements. Each element, if properly managed, will help other elements of the mix to achieve goals and objectives. Paid advertising may be less cost-effective compared with face-to-face selling, telephone selling or sending personalised letters, but it is often felt to be an essential investment in the context of image-building, rather than a short-term expense.

To optimise results from advertising, hoteliers should be able to:

1   analyse the effectiveness of advertisements;
2   develop suitable advertising strategies; and
3   create novel ideas in communicating messages.

Being the first or being different, in marketing and positioning as well as in advertising, will give any hotel a distinct advantage over its competitors. According to one successful marketing consultant, 'Being the first to say that you are the first is a key point.' A main objective in advertising is to create a strong positioning for the product, ensuring that the customers will remember it. Advertising in tourism is similar to advertising for any other industry. It essentially follows the AIDA principle:

• Attract **attention**

• Create **interest**

• Foster **desire**

• Inspire **action**

Advertisements could be judged by their appeal to the main market segment of the hotel or hotel groups.

It is interesting to analyse the importance of advertising firstly in the context of the marketing mix and secondly as an element of the communication mix. Analysing the advertising mix of selected hotels, too, may provide useful information. In the 1930s most hotels were spending approximately 55 per cent of their advertising budgets on press and 45 per cent on other advertisements. By the end of the 1980s only 40 per cent was being spent on press, and only 30 per cent for other advertisements. Around 30 per cent of advertising budgets in most hotels now are reserved for television advertisements. By the end of the 1990s the advertising mix is expected to be different again. Have these changes of advertising mix influenced the revenue and profitability of hotels? Or were they changes that simply matched the trends in the industry?

Some of the leading advertisers among the major restaurants and hotel groups are listed below.

McDonald	Berni Inns
Kentucky Fried Chicken	Burger King
Pizza Hut	Inter-Continental
Wimpy	Holiday Inn
Harvester Steak Houses	Sheraton
Forte	Marriott

There should be a relationship between a hotel's market share and its communication share in the market. All competitor advertising material should be collected and quantitatively and qualitatively analysed on a daily, weekly, monthly and yearly basis. This will help the hotel, or its advertising agency, to determine the hotel's communication share. Lesser communication or advertising, when compared with the competitive hotels, may mean lesser chances of attracting clients. Availability of reader analysis of different newspapers or TV viewer analysis will be a tremendous advantage for a hotel in order to optimise results from advertising by directly aiming at the target segments.

Creativity in Advertising

Advertising can be defined as paid communication by an identified sponsor through a non-personal medium. It is also defined as paying for presentation of information and ideas in media outside the company. A leading British hotelier defined advertising as 'saying something interesting to clients whilst being the only one to say it or the one to say it better'. It should also be ensured that proof of a promise, or at least reasons to believe, should be given in an advertisement. Key points for positioning in advertising are:

1 Name (group or individual);
2 Location (e.g. London Hilton on Park Lane);
3 Unique selling proposition (e.g. the French touch – Le Meridian, London);
4 Size (small or large – both can be attractions);
5 Age (newest or oldest – both can be attractions).

One has to spend a considerably large sum of money to obtain the services of a good professional advertising agency. Some feel that a higher volume of average-quality advertisements will be better than a low volume of high-quality advertisements at the same cost. However, this depends largely on the class of the hotel and its desired image. Cheap and shoddy advertising reflects a cheap and shoddy product. Most clients believe that it is of vital importance for advertising to be consumer-oriented, simple and clean. Major problems in hotel advertising are product-oriented words – hotel jargon, creeping in instead of consumer-oriented words. This often confuses the potential consumer. A leading US advertising personality once stated that, in far too much advertising today, advertisers are talking to themselves, talking to each other and not primarily to the customer. They are talking in general, to the crowd, rather than saying something in particular to someone in particular. The shot-gun principle widely used in today's hotel advertising means one thing – a waste of money. Hotel advertising should be more memorable, more involving, more personal to the main market segments. It would be, if only it were less hotel-oriented and more customer-oriented.

To be successful in advertising, hotels and agencies should be willing to be original and must dare to be different. After identifying main market segments the crucial step in the advertising process is creativity in producing memorable pictures, words and slogans, expressing the essence of a product in a few words. Creative quality cannot be defined but it can be recognised and measured in terms of recall. In travel and tourism good examples of creative executions are:

- That will do nicely (American Express).

- We try harder (Avis).

- We speak your language (British Tourist Authority in USA Market).

- I love New York (New York State).

- Take me to the Hilton.

An analysis of some of the advertisements of international hotel groups indicate the following key messages:

Hilton – business
Intercontinental – service
Sheraton – style
Meridien – French touch
Hyatt – friendly attitude
Holiday Inn – belongingness

Advertising Budgets

The key to determining the advertising budget is to set clear, measurable goals. But how can this be done? Some hotels do not advertise and yet are successful in marketing their products and services. Some hotels advertise widely but still fail in marketing. Advertising expenditure does not guarantee a boost in sales unless it is used wisely and cost-effectively as an integrated component of the promotional mix with the marketing mix.

Advertising deserves a larger share of the sales promotion budget where:

1 Repeat business is insignificant;
2 Specific media allow cost-effective access to the target audience;
3 Market is too large;
4 Market is segmented on image;
5 Market is expanding too quickly;
6 The hotel is new;
7 Hotel products and services are changed.

Larger hotel groups usually need to develop a corporate image.

Different hotels and different hotel groups use different tools in determining the advertising budgets. The decision on how much to spend on advertising and other promotional activities is one of the more difficult budgeting problems that management is called upon to make.

Common advertising budgeting methods are:

1 Objective and task (allocating funds to advertisements to achieve the set objectives);
2 Percentage of sales (not practical in changing environments);
3 Profit excess (remaining profits utilised/what we can afford);
4 'Me too' approach (responding to competitors' actions).

In general, most fast food operations spend more than hotels on advertising. This is usually around 3 per cent of turnover. Comparison with the competition is a practical method. Ignoring what they spend would be like ignoring what the enemy spends on weapons during a war! When revenues fall short of budgets, some hoteliers are reluctant to reduce their maintenance budget, but do not mind cutting the advertising budget. Both cuts are similar, with serious long-term effects to the product and its image.

It is usual that a new challenger spends more than the established defenders who naturally have some advantages such as loyal customers.

Drawing up clear guidelines for advertising budgeting will be an impossible task as many external influences will have to be considered. The macro-economic environment, new competition, product changes, etc., have an important bearing on the advertising budget.

Advertising Research

It is generally accepted that good advertising strategies can be developed and improved only if the effectiveness of previous advertising can be determined. However, in most industries this is rarely practised.

Mature advertising is nothing more than common sense as revealed by research and experience. But, unfortunately, hardly any research has been done specifically on hotel advertising.

Advertising has played a vital role in increasing business and profits of most hotels and restaurants. In spite of high prices and increasing competition, some hotels continue to have a greater proportion of repeat clients. Most advertising works by encouraging an increase of the frequency of purchase of one brand against another.

Good advertising helps by confirming in the minds of the repeat clients that they have chosen the correct hotel again and again.

A gap is left when we do not evaluate advertising sensibly, a gap which is only too easily filled. 'The client likes it' or 'it won an award' replace 'it's selling the product'. The most important aspect is that advertising should work commercially. Good advertising helps hotels to build confidence in the minds of prospective customers. It is not enough to find out the reasons for past success or failure; we need to improve future decisions.

Hotel and restaurant managements must choose the advertising strategy best suited to their establishment according to a careful analysis of desk and field research data.

Merchandising

Merchandising in hotels and restaurants involves internal sales promotion or point of sale promotion of products and services. Merchandising aims at influencing the behaviour of customers already on the premises.

In a hotel/restaurant context, the merchandising objectives are as follows:

1   Increasing the average spend of an outlet;
2   Promoting specific seasonal dishes;
3   Encouraging customers to patronise more than one outlet (e.g. a drink at the hotel lobby bar before dinner at a restaurant, or patronising the hotel night club after dinner at a restaurant);
4   Ensuring another visit by the customer in due course;
5   Promoting food and beverage items with low material costs and high gross profit margins;
6   Promoting fast-moving food and beverage items;
7   Encouraging customers to visit a more expensive outlet (e.g. the grill room instead of the coffee shop);
8   Popularising a newly opened outlet;
9   Popularising an underused outlet;
10 Promoting a special event (e.g. Christmas lunch) or a food festival.

Some of the common types of merchandising in hotels/restaurants are as follows:

1   **Posters**
    In strategic positions within public areas (e.g. in lifts, entrance to restaurants, bars, lobbies, reception).

2   **Floor stands**
    Same as posters but on movable stands. Also used to advertise special events.

3   **Tent cards**
    On restaurant tables and bar counters to promote cocktails, house wines, food festivals, seasonal activities or entertainment programmes.

4   **Illuminated wall displays**
    Very common in fast food outlets, cocktail bars and discotheques.

5   **Blackboards**
    Common in bars, pubs and theme restaurants.

6   **Food and beverage displays**
    Usually at the entrance of restaurants and on buffet tables (in some restaurants live lobsters and fish too are used).

7   **Menus**
    Miniature and children's menus which the customers are expected to take away.

8   **Television screens**
    For night clubs and some restaurants.

9 **Menu clip-ons**
To highlight speciality items, day's special menus, etc.

10 **Announcements**
Mainly by entertainers in night clubs. Some resort hotels even use public address systems.

QUESTIONS

1 'Hoteliers should have a good understanding of the crucial role advertising plays in hotel marketing.' Discuss this statement with emphasis on the importance of advertising.

2 List and explain the common objectives of advertising with examples from hotels and restaurants.

3 What is communication mix? Explain with examples.

4 'To be successful in advertising, hotels and agencies should be willing to be original and must dare to be different.' Discuss this statement in the context of creativity in advertising.

5 Explain the circumstances in which larger budgets for advertising can be justified.

6 Describe the common advertising budgeting methods and the factors considered in deciding the size of the advertising budget.

7 Discuss the importance of advertising research.

8 Draw an advertising strategy model (ASM) and explain each stage briefly.

9 'Merchandising aims at influencing customer behaviour.' Discuss this statement, highlighting merchandising objectives.

10 Identify and briefly explain the common types of merchandising in hotels and restaurants.

CASE STUDY: LORD NELSON RESTAURANTS LTD

Ms Jane Miller is the general manager of Lord Nelson Restaurants Ltd, a small chain of four exclusive restaurants in London. Her main competitors, in her opinion, are fine-dining restaurants in four-star and five-star London hotels.

Ms Miller has personally handled advertising and merchandising of the four outlets for the last five years. She is now seeking applications for the newly created post of sales and promotion manager. The person appointed will be entrusted with responsibility for handling advertising and merchandising. She has interviewed many hotel school graduates and has shortlisted you for the final interview.

The kitchens operate under the direction of well-known chef, Mr Dieter Bachman. Lord Nelson Restaurants' aim is to offer a complete contrast in the type of dishes offered and supplement that by catering for special requests. Lightness is the keynote of most dishes, for Chef Bachman's conviction is that people should leave the table feeling satisfied, and not uncomfortably full. Classical French *haute cuisine* is the framework within which Chef Bachman has created his own unique style. Lord Nelson Restaurants have added a new dimension to that tradition, not only with their cuisine but with the style and flair with which it is served, and in the atmosphere of the surroundings. All four restaurants are situated in Mayfair, an area of London where fine restaurants are as plentiful as shoe shops in a high street. But even in the face of this very stiff competition, Lord Nelson Restaurants took just a few years to make their mark both in the area and on the rarely impressed élite who use them.

An executive club-like atmosphere has been created with classically elegant decor – a setting which encourages the very highest expectations for true *haute cuisine*. The four restaurants average 220 covers a day and have six day operations. The average spend on food and beverages is £40.00 per person.

Lord Nelson Restaurants Ltd spend 4–5 per cent of total revenue on promotions. Given below are last year's promotional expenses in percentages:

Direct mail	3
Brochures	4
Newspaper advertising	40
Radio advertising	20
Special evenings	7
Press/critic invitations	2
Guide book advertising	5
Regular customers' cocktails	5
Competition survey	3
Subscriptions	1
Wall displays	5
Other	5

The following are quotes from brochures of hotels Ms Miller considers as competitors:

1   'Finest traditions of British hospitality and comfort with gracious and attentive service. The kitchens are under the personal supervision of Stefan Kaufmann, regarded as one of the world's finest chefs.'

2   'Traditions, service and dignity of the last century with the comfort of today.'

3   'Inviting, warm, easy luxury, and unique sense of home comfort and relaxation. Breathtaking views from the restaurants.'

4   'Everyone enjoys the same discreet and highly personalised service which recognises that during a visit they become an important and indispensable part of the Carlton.'

5   'You can be sure we understand the word "service". Ideally placed in London's most prestigious residential area, within easy reach of the city and the capital's tourist attractions.'

6   'A distinguished address. Distinguished, too, is its international reputation for elegant comforts and gracious amenities.'

7   'A city of hospitality, in Mayfair. It is luxurious, it is right in atmosphere, it is unique, and it is very British.'

8   'Creates an atmosphere in which gracious living and business activities combine in harmony. Magnificent panoramic views blend with quiet surroundings.'

9   'Unique Edwardian atmosphere, in the centre of fashionable Knightsbridge. Combining the ambience of an aristocratic country house with the discreet atmosphere of an exclusive private club, the Wellington Hotel prides itself on its unique blend of good taste, tranquility and gracious living. The quality of service throughout is such that patrons are able to treat the Wellington as a home away from home.'

10 'London's best location. Designed for unobtrusive luxury and modern comfort.'

11 'We don't believe in mass-produced hospitality. An elegant and efficient place to stay. A place to live rather than a trade centre. The atmosphere is calm, the place is comfortable.'

12 'Location alone does not make a great hotel. The great British tradition of service, brought to life by a superbly trained staff, is blended by Sakura International skill with the most modern facilities. A magnet for international business, a prime convention and meeting centre of London, a mecca for the gourmet and a warm, hospitable home away from home.'

13 'With an enthusiastic and experienced staff who provide a truly five-star service. A beautiful view across the park.'

14 'Steeped in the finest traditions of the English way of life and embodies aristocratic luxury with excellence of service. Character all of its own.'

In general most brochures attempted to highlight aspects such as good food, quality of service, location and views, British traditions, homely atmosphere, modern facilities and comforts.

Some relevant information regarding the advertising and merchandising of Lord Nelson Restaurants Ltd are as follows:

1   Only the individual restaurant names are given in all advertisements but the company name appears on all menu cards and letterheads.
2   There is no annual advertising/promotion plan. Advertisements are scheduled as and when revenue level comes down or when a competitor restaurant starts an advertising campaign.
3   Communication share analysis is not done as it is not practical to carry out such an analysis for the great number of restaurants in London.
4   There is no permanent advertising agency serving the company.
5   Advertising agents are given a free hand in developing the key message and in selecting media for advertising.
6   Blackboards and illuminated wall displays are the only type of merchandising used.
7   Direct mail flyers with the latest news are posted to all regular customers every three months.

Ms Miller has asked you to spend a day in each restaurant and the head office and submit a report with your suggestions to improve advertising and merchandising of Lord Nelson Restaurants. Appointment to the post will depend on the quality of your report.

CHAPTER 5

AIMS, POLICIES AND STANDARDS

The main objective of the present chapter is to provide a comprehensive background for Chapter 6. It is important to remember that, before any budgets are prepared, we should be absolutely clear about the major aims as well as the specific objectives of the business. It is for this reason that food and beverage directors of most large hotels spend a great deal of time on the statement of basic aims that should guide their departments. Such stated aims are of paramount importance because they explain the *raison d'être* of the food and beverage department and provide a base – a starting point – for all departmental strategic and operational planning and budgeting.

Food and Beverage Operations: Major Aims

Two points should be noted before we examine the major aims in detail. First, different organisations will place a different emphasis on the major aims. All hotels expect the food and beverage department to make at least a reasonable contribution to overall profits. However, whilst some will stress the element of profitability, others will emphasise the importance of customer satisfaction. Secondly, when discussing the major aims, it is not always easy to distinguish between the aims of the food and beverage operation as such and the major aims of the hotel as a whole. These are clearly matters that demand a lot of clear thinking.

PROFITABILITY

Hotels and restaurants are, with very few exceptions, privately owned commercial enterprises, and their fundamental long-term aim is profitability. All revenue-producing departments of the hotel – rooms, food, beverage, telephone, guest laundry, etc. – should therefore be expected to make a satisfactory contribution to overall profitability.

It is, however, important to realise that profits in some departments will always be higher than in others. Thus the rooms department will always tend to show a high percentage of departmental profit. In most European countries, room sales will produce a departmental profit of rather more than 70 per cent. What we are selling here is a service. There is no cost of sales and the operation of a rooms department does not require a large amount of skilled labour.

A hotel food and beverage department can never hope to achieve such results. Food and beverage costs will account for some 30 per cent of departmental sales. Wages, salaries and related expenses will absorb 35–40 per cent, and other departmental expenses will usually account for some 10 per cent of departmental sales revenue. The net outcome is a departmental profit of about 20 per cent. Where separate results are shown for food and beverages, it is always found that the profit on the beverage operation is significantly higher than that on food. Beverages are purchased in bulk and subsequently sold in small amounts. They require no processing, and the cost of labour incurred in the beverage operation is therefore considerably lower than in the case of food. It is the difference in the relative labour costs that is mainly responsible for the appreciably higher profitability of beverages.

In the case of restaurants, the absence of extensive departmentalisation makes profitability a less complex matter. The sale of food and beverages is the principal aim of the enterprise. It must produce not only a satisfactory net profit margin but also the right return on the capital employed.

CUSTOMER SATISFACTION

During the last decade or so the number of restaurants has grown very substantially. Also, it should be noted, culinary skills and standards of food and beverage service have shown a considerable improvement. Hotel and restaurant customers have, in consequence, a great deal of choice with regard to what kind of food they can eat and in relation to the actual choice of the establishment. In this situation we have a buyers' market, where customer satisfaction must be seen as a fundamental and critical aim of all food and beverage operations.

In spite of its undoubted importance, customer satisfaction does not lend itself to easy measurement. Whilst some customers will look for interesting, even adventurous, food, served in a friendly and professional manner, others may attach more importance to a whole host of elements such as hygiene, cleanliness, price range or parking facilities. What, ultimately, makes a customer visit a particular establishment on a given occasion is far from easy to ascertain.

Two points, however, are important in this context. First, whatever the nature of the food and beverage operation, it is always possible to observe and note the proportion of repeat business. The higher the proportion of repeat business, the greater the certainty that what we are offering to the customers meets with their approval. The important point to note here is this: customer satisfaction determines the level of repeat business, and hence the sales volume and, therefore, the profitability of the operation.

Secondly, it should be appreciated that customer satisfaction is very much dependent on the appropriate operating standards built into the preparation and service of food and beverages. Standard yields, purchase specifications, standard recipes – all have a major bearing on customer satisfaction and, ultimately, the success of the establishment.

Aspirations of Managers and Employees

A competent food and beverage director will not only strive to ensure the highest level of customer satisfaction; he or she will also look after the staff. This implies more than merely offering the employees a decent wage, hygienic working conditions and adequate meals on duty. Employees also, quite rightly, expect a friendly attitude and respect from managers and supervisors. These qualities are important and need not detract from the basic requirements of efficiency and discipline.

Consideration should always be given to the aspirations of managers, supervisors and trainees. All employees should be encouraged to improve their qualifications. Attendance at local colleges and in-company courses and seminars all demonstrate a healthy and responsible attitude to the employees. It is all these matters that tend to create a good team spirit and ensure a high degree of motivation, without which the provision of satisfactory levels of service is impossible.

Professional and Industry Obligations

Hotels and restaurants do not exist in complete isolation, and practically all of them have good personal and professional contacts. Such contacts take many different forms – from 'purely social' meetings (at which business is invariably discussed) to membership of professional bodies, meetings and seminars.

Most food and beverage managers recognise the importance of their professional contacts. In consequence a large number of conferences, meetings and seminars are held in different parts of the country. Such gatherings enhance the professionalism of those concerned and, at the same time, indicate the strength of their commitment to the hotel and catering industry. It is, more often than not, the more progressive and well-managed establishments that display a strong professional commitment to the industry. It is also such establishments that see their professional industry obligations as a major aim.

SOCIAL AND LEGAL OBLIGATIONS

As suggested above, hotels and restaurants do not exist in a vacuum, but constitute an integral part of a local community and, as such, are expected to observe the law of the land. Whatever the actual location of the establishment, there are certain clear obligations towards the local community. Such obligations relate to the employment of local people, public hygiene and waste disposal, as well as compliance with any local anti-pollution measures.

In addition hotels and restaurants – just as all businesses – must ensure that they comply with legal requirements with regard to work permits, hygiene, tax and insurance liabilities, etc.

Such social and legal obligations may not always have a great deal of immediate operational relevance. They are nevertheless of paramount importance.

EXAMPLE

A formal statement of aims for a food and beverage operation is not easy to draft. It requires a great deal of thought, extensive consultations and much fine-tuning. The example which follows is a suggested statement of aims for a large four-star hotel.

St Martin's Hotel
Major Aims
Food and Beverage Department

1 To recognise the importance of the hotel guest as a source of all our revenue, and to offer the highest level of service.
2 To provide good working conditions, offer fair rates of pay and encourage the professional development of all employees.
3 To ensure adequate profitability of the department, consistent with the highest standards of food and service.
4 To act as a responsible member of the community and observe the law of the land at all times.

It should be noted that the statement of aims is usually fairly brief. Also, in the case of hotels and restaurants it should display the right degree of market orientation. It is for this reason that we start the above statement of aims with the recognition of the importance of the guest. It is only after the completion of the statement of major aims that we can address ourselves to the specific objectives. These are now discussed in more detail.

Food and Beverage Operations: Specific Objectives

The specific objectives of a hotel or restaurant flow from its major aims. They are more clear-cut, concrete and precise than the major aims, and provide the necessary strong link between the fundamental, major aims of the establishment and its operating budget. Specific objectives may be categorised into those which are quantitative, such as planned sales volumes or number of covers, and those which do not lend themselves to precise measurement – which are described as qualitative objectives.

QUANTITATIVE OBJECTIVES

Sales Volume
The planned volume of food and beverage sales is, most certainly, one of the most important specific objectives. It has a direct impact on profit levels; it influences the cash flow of the establishment; it indicates the required numbers of staff; it determines the levels of variable costs. Indeed it is difficult to think of anything that has a stronger influence on all the major aspects of food and beverage operations. It will be readily appreciated that this particular objective is of paramount importance when we are preparing the budget.

Number of Covers
The sales volume is determined by two factors: the number of covers (NOC) and the average spending power (ASP). It is therefore essential to plan the sales volume in conjunction with the relevant NOC figures. The overall number of covers should first be determined for the forthcoming budget year, and then be appropriately subdivided to show the detailed NOC figures for each quarter, month, etc., as well as each selling outlet.

Average Spending Power

Average spending power is, for all practical purposes, as important as the number of covers, and should be determined on the basis of past trends as well as prospects for the forthcoming budget year. Separate ASP figures should be fixed for all selling outlets, as ASP levels will vary considerably from one outlet to another. Also, separate ASP figures should be shown for food and for beverages. Overall, total ASP figures may be misleading.

Gross Profit

Gross profit levels have always been regarded as strong determinants of profitabilty, and traditionally all food and beverage managers regard them as very important indeed. In all planning and budgeting, therefore, gross profit percentages feature as key specific objectives. As explained in Chapter 11, there is now a trend to pay attention not only to gross profit percentages, but also to cash gross profit (i.e. the amount of gross profit). When developing the specific objectives for any one period, we should therefore specify not only what gross profit percentages are to be aimed at but also what amounts of gross profit we wish to earn on food sales and beverage sales respectively.

Payroll

The labour intensive nature of food and beverage operations results in high levels of payroll. In most European countries total payroll and related expenses absorbs approximately 40 per cent of food and beverage revenue. In such circumstances it is essential to monitor payroll levels in all areas of the food and beverage operation. Of particular importance is the adjustment of payroll to the ever-changing level of sales. As all hotels and restaurants experience some degree of seasonal fluctuation, payroll control must be seen as an important specific objective.

Departmental Profit

This is defined and discussed in some detail in Chapter 7. As far as the specific objectives are concerned, departmental profit is clearly an objective of considerable importance. As may be seen from the examples given in Chapter 7, it is the size of the departmental profits that very largely determines the net profit of a hotel. Also, as most of the undistributed operating expenses tend to be fixed and uncontrollable, changes in the total of departmental profits have a strong and direct impact on net profit.

Net Profit

Net profit is, in fact, both a major aim and a specific objective. It is a major aim because ultimately we are in the business to earn a satisfactory return on the capital invested in the enterprise. It may be seen as an objective when the exact amount of profit for a particular budget period is the subject of detailed profit planning through changes in menu prices, gross profit margins, cost ceilings, etc.

QUALITATIVE OBJECTIVES

Quality Standards

Customer satisfaction, as a major aim, is quite impossible to achieve without a whole series of food and beverage operating standards. These are detailed standards built into the catering cycle to ensure the highest possible quality of food and service and hence customer satisfaction. They include standard purchase specifications, standard portion sizes and standard recipes – and all these, it will be appreciated, have direct relevance to food and beverage quality standards.

Quality of Service

We all know how important this is, especially in hotels and restaurants. At the same time, we all realise that this particular objective is difficult to define and measure. This difficulty does not, of course, detract from its critical importance, and if we use the right operating standards, provide thorough training and employ skilful supervisors, quality of service will hopefully follow.

Decor and Atmosphere

Hotel and restaurant guests do not purchase just quantities of food and drink, but a whole package – an eating experience – where the ambience, decor and atmosphere are critically important. This is particularly true of high ASP, or up-market, establishments where the guests expect not only high gastronomic standards and highly professional service, but all this provided in the right setting. The total package will not be satisfactory without an appropriate decor and atmosphere.

POLICIES

Once an establishment has determined its aims and objectives, it can start thinking about how it intends that they will be achieved. A number of hotels and restaurants have prepared policy statements in which they indicate what they will, or will not, do in pursuance of their aims and objectives. Such statements reflect the culture of the organisation and should be seen as statements of conduct. A few examples will make this clear:

1   A four-star hotel will only buy fresh meat and fish; no frozen meat or fish will be used.
2   A chain of up-market restaurants will only recruit junior managers who are graduates in hotel and catering management.
3   A city restaurant will offer only fixed-price menus.

Policies are not the same as plans or objectives. An aim or objective is a goal; a plan provides a framework of action for achieving goals; and policies state what the managers will do, or refrain from doing, in pursuing the stated goals.

Operating Standards

Operating standards are performance norms which show, in relation to different parts of the food and beverage operation, the results that should be achieved. Thus, a standard yield will show what percentage/amount of edible meat should be obtained from a given cut or joint. A standard portion cost will indicate the expected cost per portion of a given menu item.

Operating standards are basically of two kinds: ideal and attainable. Ideal standards are theoretical standards which, in practice, may never be achieved. They indicate what should happen under ideal conditions and thus tend to be impractical and unrealistic. Attainable standards, on the other hand, still aim at a high level of performance and efficiency, but allow for normal waste, losses and occasional mishaps in production and service.

STANDARD YIELDS

When we purchase foods such as coffee, butter or sugar, we have no waste problem: we can use every part of the commodity. With other goods – some of them quite expensive – we can only use a certain part of the total weight purchased (known as the 'yield'). The rest is unusable/inedible. Let us take a simple example.

EXAMPLE 1

We buy a cut of meat weighing 5kg at £6.00 per kg. The standard portion is 200g. Bone loss is 1.1kg and fat (which we cannot use for any purpose) amounts to 0.4kg. We find subsequently that cooking loss amounts to 0.75kg. Our yield calculations are shown below.

	kg	%
Weight as purchased	5.00	100
Less bone loss	1.10	22
	3.90	78
Less fat	0.40	8
Edible meat	3.50	70
Less cooking loss	0.75	15
Cooked meat	2.75	55

From the above information we can calculate a number of interesting figures, as follows:

(a) Ratio of edible to original weight:

$$\frac{3.5}{5} \times 100 = 70\%$$

(b) Ratio of cooked to original weight:

$$\frac{2.75}{5} \times 100 = 55\%$$

(c) Cost of edible meat per kg:

$$\frac{£30.00}{3.5} = £8.57$$

(d) Cost per portion of edible meat:

$$\frac{£8.57}{5(\text{portion/kg})} = £1.71$$

(e) Cost factor:

$$\frac{\text{cost of 1kg of edible meat } £8.57}{\text{cost of 1kg as purchased } £6.00} = 1.43$$

The cost factor shows by how much the 'as purchased' cost has to be increased to allow for bone loss, fat, trimming, etc. In this case the 'as purchased' cost per portion is (£6.00 ÷ 5) £1.20. This multiplied by the cost factor of 1.43 gives £1.71 – the cost per 200g portion, after allowing for bone loss and fat.

Most of the yield tests undertaken by hotels and restaurants are in respect of meat, and are commonly described as butchering tests. Readers should note, however, that yield tests may be carried out for a large variety of food items. The principal objectives of yield tests may be summarised as follows:

1   To determine the edible part of a food item, i.e. the 'standard yield'. This may be expressed as a percentage, weight of food or number of portions.
2   To establish the cost factor and assist in the costing and pricing of menu items.
3   To facilitate the conversion of edible or cooked quantities of meat into their raw material equivalents.

EXAMPLE 2

The purpose of this exercise is to determine the yield and ascertain the relevant costs in respect of a leg of lamb. We purchase a leg of lamb weighing 3.9kg at £4.10 per kg. Bone loss amounts to 0.6kg and trimming loss 0.85kg. Subsequently we ascertain that cooking loss amounted to 0.45kg. We may present the facts as follows:

	kg	%
Original weight	3.90	100.0
Bone loss	0.60	15.4
Trimming loss	0.85	21.8
Total	1.45	37.2
Edible meat	2.45	62.8
Cooking loss	0.45	11.5
Cooked meat	2.00	51.3

From the above test we may calculate a number of useful figures, such as:

(a)   Ratio of edible to original weight:

$$\frac{2.45}{3.9} \times 100 = 62.8\%$$

(b)   Ratio of cooked to original weight:

$$\frac{2}{3.9} \times 100 = 51.3\%$$

(c)   Cost of edible meat per kg:

$$\frac{(3.9 \times £4.10) \ £15.99}{2.45} = £6.53$$

(d)   Cost per 150g portion of edible meat:

$$\frac{£6.53 \times 0.15}{1} = £0.98$$

(e)   Cost factor:

$$\frac{\text{Cost of 1kg of edible meat } £6.53}{\text{Cost of 1kg as purchased } £4.10} = 1.59$$

With regard to beverages, standard yields do not really present a problem. Whatever we purchase – whether it is a bottle of sherry or a can of ginger ale – the size of the beverage item is always constant. Also there is no waste, and we are able to use every drop of the beverage. To sum up, there are no problems here on the supply side. All we have to do is establish the necessary portion size in relation to each beverage.

Standard Purchase Specifications

A standard purchase specification is, essentially, a means of communication between buyer and seller. To fulfil this function, it must contain a concise description of the commodity concerned. The main aims and advantages of purchase specifications are as follows:

1   They describe the essential characteristics of a food item in terms of its weight, size, age, grade, degree of preparation, etc.
2   From (1) above, it follows that having examined the purchase specification, the supplier cannot be in any doubt as to what exactly is required. Purchase specifications should therefore be seen as effective means of communication between the hotel/restaurant and its suppliers.
3   Purchase specifications are also an important means of communication within the hotel or restaurant. In this context, they are not only of great value to the purchasing manager, but also to the executive chef, the goods received clerk and the food and beverage controller. Once we have written a purchase specification for, say, the

'spring chicken', we no longer have to imagine what this is: we all 'see' the same standard product in terms of its age, weight, degree of preparation and yield.

4 Purchase specifications result in the establishment buying the exact foods required. This implies less waste and hence a more cost-effective operation.

A typical example of a purchase specification is given in Figure 5.1.

Standard purchase specification
Lamb cutlets – PS 0316

(a) *Description:* meat obtained from cutting between the ribs of a best end of lamb.

(b) *Grade:* Ex YM grade, New Zealand lamb carcasses.

(c) *Weight:* each cutlet to weight between 90 and 110g.

(d) *Preparation:* remove the chine bone and ensure that all cutlets contain a complete rib bone; remove the outer skin; 20mm of the end of the rib bone is to be cleaned of all fat and meat. Do not use a band saw.

(e) *Delivery:* all cutlets to be delivered frozen packed in batches of 10.

Figure 5.1 Purchase specification

Standard purchase specifications are not necessary and, therefore, are not used for beverages. The quality of each beverage is constant – in some cases over decades – and little purpose would be served by explaining to the supplier the product size, age, grade and other essential characteristics.

Standard Portion Sizes

The determination of standard portion sizes is an important task in all food and beverage operations for the following reasons:

1 Uniformity of portion sizes is essential if we are to achieve adequate food quality standards. If a guest is offered a 225g steak on the first visit and, on a subsequent occasion, one which weighs only 175g, he/she will not be impressed – particularly if in the meantime there has been upward revision of menu prices.

2 Strict adherence to predetermined portion sizes is essential for effective cost control. All food production and service personnel should therefore be familiar with the standard portions of the establishment.

3   Without effective cost control there is no satisfactory gross profit. Portion control should therefore be seen as something which can make a significant contribution to the gross profits of the business.

The implementation of standard portion sizes should be remembered at the buying stage of the control cycle, as this is an excellent opportunity to secure the uniformity of at least some portions of food. Many meat items, such as lamb cutlets and pre-portioned steaks, as well as other foods such as individual portions of butter and breakfast cereals, offer a great deal of scope in this context.

During the actual food preparation the kitchen crew should be conscious of portion control. The use of appropriate utensils, giving a fixed number of standard portions, slicing machines, as well as a high level of skill in the portioning of meat, poultry and fish are all essential. Finally, standard portion sizes should be remembered during the service of food – particularly with regard to expensive food items. Undue generosity at this stage of the control cycle can only lead to indifferent gross profit margins

With regard to beverages, portion control presents no problem. The use of optic measures is quite simple and in general use throughout the industry. Automatic drink dispensers are even easier to operate and produce consistently identical portions. In other situations we rely on the right glassware (frequently referred to as 'standard glassware'). Finally, the packaging of beverages is frequently such as to make the portion size quite obvious – for example a can of beer or a bottle of ginger ale.

STANDARD PORTION COSTS

Standard portion costs are of undoubted importance, particularly from the point of view of the profitability of the operation. Periodic standard portion costs are the basis of periodic revisions of menu and beverage prices; and the updating of standard costs and prices is of direct relevance to the establishment's gross profit control. In the UK, standard portion costs are usually determined in conjunction with standard recipes. Where, for example, portion costs are revised once a month, there should be a consequential monthly revision of menu prices. (The example given in Figure 12.13 on page 290 makes this quite clear.)

Our discussion of standards earlier in this chapter is of particular relevance here. Standard portion costs should reflect attainable rather than ideal portion costs. Whatever the nature of the food and beverage operation, we always have some waste, petty pilfering, bad portioning, leftovers, etc. This means that ideal standards are inappropriate. Ideal portion costs should therefore be increased by a given percentage to convert them into realistic, attainable portion costs. In other words the percentage is intended to cover the 'unproductive cost' of the operation.

In the case of a large banquet, where final numbers are known at least a week in advance, the amount of waste and leftovers will be minimal, and there is no need to add more than 3–4 per cent for unproductive cost. In the case of a small, up-market restaurant, offering an extensive menu, there will inevitably be a lot of waste resulting from the relatively heavy stocks of food that have to be carried to support the menu. In such circumstances even 10 per cent may not be enough to cover the unproductive cost of the food operation. As a general principle then, the larger the number of customers and the more limited the menu, the lower the percentage of unproductive cost, and vice versa.

EXAMPLE

A Christmas menu has been agreed with a customer for 100 covers and the relevant food costs are given below. Assume that unproductive cost is 4 per cent, the required gross profit 75 per cent and VAT $17\frac{1}{2}$ per cent. Calculate the selling price per cover.

	Food Cost £
Grapefruit cocktail	30.00
Filet de sole bercy	220.00
Dindonneau rôti au chipolatas	130.00
Pommes château	10.00
Boutons de choux de bruxelles	15.00
Charlotte russe	35.00
Café	15.00
Total cost of food	455.00
Portion cost – ideal	4.55
Add unproductive cost – 4 per cent	0.18
Portion cost – attainable	4.73
Add gross profit	14.19
Selling price – VAT exclusive	18.92
Add VAT at $17\frac{1}{2}$ per cent	3.31
Selling price – VAT inclusive	22.23

Beverage prices are characterised by relatively greater stability. Whilst the prices paid for foods – particularly fresh fruit and vegetables – tend to change from one week to another, beverages do not, as a rule, display such price volatility. The periodic updating of portion costs presents no problem. Readers should note that this stability of portion costs, coupled with the relatively easy control of portion sizes, means that beverage gross profits are invariably more stable than food gross profits.

Standard Recipes

A standard recipe is a written formula for producing a particular menu item. In Chapter 1 we discussed the concept of market orientation, and standard recipes are an excellent example of market orientation in action. No two steak houses or four-star hotels are identical, and they will always differ in important respects: size, location, range of services offered, and of course types of clientele. As far as standard recipes are concerned, the most important element is the type of customer. It is this rather than anything else that determines the nature of the menus offered, the decor and atmosphere, and the selection, size, shape and quality of the individual menu items. Standard recipes emphasise the market orientation of the establishment in a very practical way.

We may summarise the main objectives of standard recipes as follows:

1   Standard recipes predetermine the quantities and quality of the ingredients and therefore influence the quality of each menu item.
2   As they control the quantities of ingredients used, they also influence portion costs and thus make a significant contribution to cost control generally.
3   As standard recipes determine the quantities of ingredients, they are an important aid to internal requisitioning as well as purchasing.
4   One of the most important advantages of standard recipes is that they facilitate food preparation. Most standard recipes show, in addition to the necessary ingredients and their cost, the standard method of preparation. This ensures a consistently good product over a period of time, regardless of changes in the kitchen crew.

An example of a typical standard recipe is given in Figure 5.2. Essentially a standard recipe consists of three parts: (a) particulars of the ingredients, including their costs; (b) the standard method of preparation and (c) other relevant information, such as the standard batch, advice on cooking temperatures.

The preparation of standard recipes is a time-consuming process and one which has to be fitted into the daily routine of food preparation. In the case of new hotels and restaurants, it is useful to have a schedule for this

STANDARD RECIPE NO: 0036			
Menu item: *Blanquette d'agneau*		**Standard batch:** 10	
Ingredients	**Quantity**	**Unit Cost**	**Ingredient Cost**
		£	£
Shoulder of lamb – diced	1.8kg	3.25	5.85
Carrots – peeled and sliced	0.25kg	0.80	0.20
Onions – skinned and sliced	3	0.10	0.30
Sticks of celery – sliced	5	0.09	0.45
Bay leaves	2	0.05	0.10
Dried thyme	15ml	0.02	0.30
Salt and pepper	—	—	0.10
Stock	750ml	—	0.10
Butter	65g	2.90	0.19
Flour	120g	0.65	0.08
Yolks	3	0.09	0.27
Single cream	400ml	2.20	0.88
Parsley – fresh, chopped			0.10
Total cost of food			8.92
Cost per portion			0.89
Add unproductive cost – 10 per cent			0.09
Standard portion cost			0.98

Method of preparation
1　Put the meat, onion, celery, flavourings and seasonings in a large pan. Cover with stock and simmer for $1\frac{1}{2}$ hours. Remove bay leaves.
2　Blend together the butter and flour and, when mixed, add to the stew and stir until thickened. Simmer for 10 minutes.
3　Blend together the egg yolk and fresh cream, add to the stew and reheat without boiling. Garnish with parsley before serving.

Figure 5.2 A standard recipe

work, and channel it into slack periods. Just two recipes a week will, over one year, produce an impressive bank of essential standard recipes.

Standard recipes are not used for beverages and the only exception here are cocktails. 'Preparation' in this context means the process of mixing several drinks; and cocktail recipes will normally show only the amounts of the relevant ingredients. There is no need to show any costs, as these are, in any case, of little interest to the bar staff.

STANDARD GROSS PROFIT

An important standard, without which the purposeful conduct of a hotel or restaurant would be difficult, is standard gross profit. This is the planned level of gross profit which is required to ensure satisfactory overall profitability.

Standard gross profit is sometimes determined in a haphazard manner – for example by simply informing the head chef that he/she is expected to achieve a gross profit of, say, 65 per cent. This is a most unsatisfactory method as: (a) we want to achieve not only the right gross profit percentage, but also the right amount of gross profit (i.e. cash gross profit); (b) standard gross profit needs a lot of planning and a simple instruction will not usually produce the desired results; (c) the chef is not the only person with responsibility for gross profit.

The determination of standard gross profit entails a great deal of thought and necessitates a lot of planning. Some of the most important considerations that need to be taken into account are discussed below.

Standard gross profit is that gross profit which is necessary for the establishment to achieve a satisfactory net profit. Every underachievement in the level of gross profit has a direct effect on the net profit of the business. This is demonstrated in Table 5.1.

Table 5.1 Gross profit relative to net profit

	Month 1		Month 2		Month 3	
	£	%	£	%	£	%
F&B sales	50,000	100	50,000	100	50,000	100
Less F&B costs	17,000	34	18,000	36	19,000	38
Gross profit	33,000	66	32,000	64	31,000	62
Labour costs	13,000	26	13,000	26	13,000	26
Overheads	12,000	24	12,000	24	12,000	24
Total	25,000	50	25,000	50	25,000	50
Net profit	8,000	16	7,000	14	6,000	12

Standard gross profit should be expressed as a percentage of food and beverage sales; it should also be fixed as an amount of gross profit. The detailed reasons for this are discussed in Chapter 11 in the section on 'Menu Engineering'.

Standard gross profit has a strong and direct relevance to the establishment's pricing policy. Once the overall percentage of standard gross profit has been determined, it is necessary to develop the necessary differential gross profit margins. A full discussion of differential profit margins will be found in Chapter 11. The following example will suffice for the time being.

EXAMPLE

A restaurant has budgeted for food and beverage sales of £900,000. In order for the establishment to achieve a satisfactory net profit, it has to earn a standard gross profit of 64 per cent. Differential profit margins (i.e. different percentages of gross profit on different sections of the menu) might then be developed as follows:

	Sales mix		Differential profit margins	
	£	%	£	%
Soups and appetisers	90,000	10	67,500	75
Meat, fish and poultry	450,000	50	247,500	55
Vegetables	135,000	15	94,500	70
Desserts	135,000	15	94,500	70
Teas and coffees	90,000	10	72,500	80
Total	900,000	100	576,000	64

The intention to earn a particular level of gross profit must be supported by the right approach to pricing. In this particular case our standard gross profit is 64 per cent and £576,000. In order to achieve this gross profit, we must: (a) reach the right volume of food and beverage sales and (b) price all menu items in accordance with the differential profit margins. All soups and appetisers will attract a gross profit of 75 per cent, all meat, fish and poultry dishes 55 per cent, etc.

Gross profit levels are influenced by the skills and efficiency of many persons at all stages of the catering cycle. If we are to achieve the planned levels of standard gross profit, the performance of all the relevant departments: purchasing, stores and cellars, kitchen etc., should be monitored closely.

From our discussion on operating standards it will be appreciated that the standard gross profit on food sales will be more difficult to control than the gross profit on beverages. The perishability of food and instability of demand are responsible for this. Even in situations when the establishment uses standard yields, standard purchase specifications and standard recipes, the food operation will always be more vulnerable than the beverage operation. In terms of gross profit performance, this means that deviations from standard gross profit will tend to be significantly greater in the case of food than in the case of beverages.

QUESTIONS

1   Explain what you understand by 'aims' in relation to food and beverage operations.

2   How important are the following aims:

   (a) profitability;
   (b) customer satisfaction;
   (c) aspirations of managers and employees;
   (d) professional and industry obligations;
   (e) social and legal obligations?

   Which of the above do you regard as more important than others?

3   The London City Inn is a four-star hotel with 120 rooms and a successful food and beverage operation. The hotel is situated in central London. The restaurant of the hotel is open to non-residents; it seats comfortably 100 guests, most of whom are foreign business persons. The average spending power in the restaurant is £28.00.

   Assume that you have just been appointed Food and Beverage Manager of the hotel, and asked to write a 'statement of aims' for the food and beverage department. State clearly any assumptions you have had to make.

4   Distinguish clearly between the aims and the specific objectives of a food and beverage operation. Why are some objectives described as 'quantitative' and others as 'qualitative'?

5   Enumerate the principal specific objectives appropriate to a hotel food and beverage department. Explain the relevance of these objectives to the budgets of the hotel.

6   Explain what you understand by 'food and beverage operating standards'. Of what value are such standards in a practical situation?

7   Distinguish between 'ideal standards' and 'attainable standards'. What are their respective uses and advantages?

8   Write brief explanatory notes on each of the following:
     (a)   standard yields;
     (b)   standard purchase specifications;
     (c)   standard portion sizes;
     (d)   standard portion costs;
     (e)   standard recipes.

9   A restaurant buys a leg of lamb weighing 3.8kg at £3.90 per kg. Bone loss amounts to 0.6kg and trimming loss 0.8kg. Subsequently, it is found that cooking loss amounted to 0.8kg. You are asked to calculate:
     (a)   ratio of edible to original weight;
     (b)   ratio of cooked to original weight;
     (c)   cost of edible meat per kg;
     (d)   cost per 150g portion of edible meat;
     (e)   cost factor.

10   What are the objectives and advantages of standard purchase specifications?

11   Write a purchase specification for a cut of meat of your choice.

12   Explain the importance of standard portion sizes and suggest how they would vary from one type of customer to another.

13   Define 'unproductive cost'. How do we take it into account in arriving at standard portion costs?

14   A menu has been agreed with a client for 200 covers. Set out below are particulars of the cost of food. From experience we know that unproductive cost will amount to 4 per cent. The gross profit on this function is to be 75 per cent and VAT will be added at $17\frac{1}{2}$ per cent.

	Food Cost
	£
Starter	52.00
Main course	374.00
Dessert	54.00
Coffee	20.00

Calculate the price per cover in respect of the above.

15   Prepare standard recipes for the following:

(a)   Cream of Cauliflower Soup;
(b)   Sole Colbert;
(c)   Crème Caramel.

CHAPTER 6

BUDGETING

Budgetary control is now generally regarded as an important management tool – indeed a critical instrument of planning and control. Food and beverage budgeting, which is an integral part of the overall budgetary process, has three principal aims:

1 First and foremost it is a planning instrument. Food and beverage budgets are detailed plans of action which show what should be achieved in terms of food and beverage sales, sales mix, average spending power, cost ceilings and profit margins.

2 A food and beverage budget provides a basis for evaluating current results and is therefore an important means of performance evaluation. Actual sales volume, cost ceilings, profit margins, etc., are compared with the relevant budgeted figures, and an assessment of current performance is thus made possible.

3 Finally, the process of food and beverage budgeting involves a detailed review of anticipated trends in levels of activity. This should enable the budget committee to identify any slack periods and decide how to take advantage of any periods of spare capacity during the forthcoming budget period.

It is pertinent, at this stage, to indicate the importance and magnitude of food and beverage budgets. In restaurants and similar non-residential establishments, food and beverage sales constitute, so to speak, the 'bread and butter' of the operation. They typically account for at least 90 per cent of total sales revenue. Many large, up-market London restaurants have annual food and beverage sales budgets in excess of £1 million, and the same applies to restaurants in other parts of Western Europe. In hotels, food and beverage sales tend to represent 35–45 per cent of total revenue. Not infrequently, therefore, they amount to well over £2 million per annum. In a situation like this, it is clear that the food and beverage operation is an activity of considerable economic magnitude and one which enjoins detailed planning and strict controls.

The Budgeting Cycle

The complete cycle of food and beverage budgeting consists of five distinctly separate stages:

1 major objectives;
2 external environment;
3 own past performance;
4 budget preparation;
5 performance evaluation and control.

These are described in detail below.

MAJOR OBJECTIVES

Profit Target

The first and most critical step in the food and beverage budgeting process is to decide what one is trying to achieve during the forthcoming budget year. We obviously want to have satisfied customers and loyal and happy employees. Most certainly we want to ensure a good reputation for our operation. However, we can achieve all these aims and still fail if we do not earn a satisfactory net profit.

Profitability is of the utmost importance in all hotels and restaurants. This means that early in the budgeting process we have to fix a profit target. In the case of hotels, the appropriate profit target will be expressed as a percentage and amount of departmental profit. In the case of restaurants the profit target will be expressed as a percentage and amount of net profit – both in relation to total turnover and the capital employed. The practical examples given later in this chapter will make this clear.

Sales Volume

In all hotels and restaurants the sales volume is of critical importance. It is a powerful determinant of net profit. Moreover, changes in the level of sales have a direct effect on a large number of variable/controllable costs. The level of budgeted food and beverage sales must therefore be predicted with great care and accuracy. As far as food sales are concerned, it is necessary to predict separately:

1 the number of covers – for the operation as a whole as well as for the constituent sales outlets;
2 the average spending power – again a separate budgeted ASP figure is required for each individual sales outlet.

The statistical and graphic methods that may be used for such predictions are discussed in considerable detail later in this chapter.

Similar considerations apply in the case of the budgeted volume of beverage sales. A separate figure of budgeted ASP is required for each sales outlet. In the case of cocktail bars the calculation of NOC and ASP figures is generally difficult, as an individual guest will frequently order drinks for several people. The solution here is to budget for so many transactions (rather than covers) and so much per transaction.

Gross Profit

An objective which is always regarded as one of the most important is the level of budgeted gross profit. The level of budgeted gross profit has a direct and powerful impact on the level of departmental profit in hotels and net profit in restaurants, and it needs to be fixed after considerable thought and much reflection. Separate figures of budgeted gross profit will have to be determined for food and beverages. Also where there are several sales outlets in operation, there will usually be a different figure of budgeted gross profit fixed for each sales outlet. Our discussion of differential profit margins in Chapter 11 is relevant here.

Payroll

Payroll is a substantial expense and one which has shown a tendency to rise in recent years. It is essential, therefore, to plan the levels of wages, salaries and employee benefits for all areas of the operation. Whilst a large portion of the cost of payroll is fixed and, in practice, uncontrollable, that part of the expense which relates to part-time and casual labour should reflect the fluctuations in the food and beverage sales volume. This is of particular relevance to seasonal establishments as well as those which experience pronounced weekly fluctuations in their level of business.

Other Operating Expenses

Finally, we have to decide on the budgeted level of other operating expenses such as gas, electricity, repairs and maintenance, laundry and cleaning, and music and entertainment. Whilst some of these tend to be fixed and – at least in the short term – uncontrollable, others are semi-fixed and thus capable of being controlled through the budgetary process.

Qualitative objectives

All the objectives we have discussed so far are capable of being expressed in quantitative terms. For example we may budget for a sales volume of

£1,000,000, a gross profit of £650,000 and payroll of £300,000. In addition to such quantitative objectives there are others which – important as they are – do not lend themselves to easy quantification. Such qualitative objectives include:

1 Food and beverage quality standards. The importance of such standards was discussed in detail in Chapter 5. They are a matter of considerable operational significance and the budgetary process will never be complete unless it includes a detailed consideration of such standards. Matters which are relevant here are standard purchase specifications, standard recipes, available levels and repertoires of skills in the kitchen, as well as availability and condition of plant and equipment.

2 Quality of service. This, again, is difficult to define and measure, but we can all see the difference between food and beverage service which is competent, friendly and professional and that which is sluggish, amateurish and indifferent. When the quality of service is not considered satisfactory, provision should be made in the budget for remedial training.

3 Decor and atmosphere are also of undoubted importance. The total eating out experience includes several important elements including the decor and atmosphere of the restaurant/dining room. All the constituent ingredients here – furniture, wall coverings, carpeting, colour schemes – should be reviewed at least once a year to ensure that what we actually provide is wholly acceptable to the customers.

Readers will have noticed that no reference has been made to a food and beverage cost budget. The reason for this apparent omission is as follows. The vast majority of hotels and restaurants budget for food and beverage sales and food and beverage gross profits. If the necessary gross profits are achieved then it follows that food and beverage costs are at the right levels and a separate budget for food and beverage costs is not needed.

EXTERNAL ENVIRONMENT

The National Economy

The external environment is a major factor influencing most budgets, and especially the sales budgets of business organisations. Any prediction of food and beverage sales will therefore take into account all the factors external to the hotel/restaurant which have a bearing on consumer demand. Some of the most important points to bear in mind in this regard are:

1 The economic climate and the general condition of the national economy. Factors which are relevant here are: trends in employment/unemployment; movements in exchange rates (for example, when the pound is weak, we tend to have a greater influx of American tourists), as well as the relative degree of optimisim or otherwise amongst business people with regard to the future.

2 Corporate profits are also important. When businesses are earning satisfactory profits, they tend to spend more liberally on such things as travel, meetings and conferences, all of which stimulate the demand for hotel and restaurant facilities.

3 A large proportion of the business done by hotels and restaurants is dependent on disposable incomes – that is, incomes remaining after allowing for basic necessities such as rents, mortgages, clothing and food consumed in the home. Periods of economic recession – when many are out of work or fear unemployment – are associated with low levels of disposable incomes and a downward trend in eating out. As far as food and beverage sales budgets are concerned this means some decrease in the number of covers and, most probably, in average spending power.

Local Trends

Quite apart from the general trends in the national economy as a whole, local trends are a matter of considerable importance. When preparing the food and beverage sales budget, we should examine in considerable detail the fortunes of local industries, as local companies invariably generate a lot of business. Are new factories moving into the vicinity? Are businesses closing down? Are some new, dynamic industries taking on more employees? Questions such as these are of immense relevance to the hotel and restaurant industry. Finally, we must not forget local events such as exhibitions, conferences and festivals, some of which attract thousands of people from many parts of the world.

Competition

The third important factor that we should consider under the heading of external environment is competition. Our successes or otherwise depend not only on what we do, but also on what is done by our competitors. It is essential, therefore, that we know what our competitors are planning, for example in terms of new marketing programmes, new facilities or upgrading of existing facilities, as all these influence the level of service against which we have to compete.

Own Past Performance

Whatever happens during any one year must of necessity be influenced by events and happenings that have preceded that year. When preparing a food and beverage budget, therefore, we must be conscious of the importance of what has happened during the last four years. Budgeted sales volumes, ASP and NOC figures, as well as factors such as profit margins and cost levels, will therefore tend to reflect what has taken place during the most recent years of operation. Such figures will invariably play an important role in any predictions for the forthcoming budget year.

In order to facilitate the budgeting process, it is essential that we keep enough statistical data in relation to each trading period (week, month, quarter, year). Such statistics should be adequate (sufficiently comprehensive) for us to make predictions of: (a) total sales volume and its subdivisions as between food and beverages as well as by sales outlet and trading period; (b) the determinants of sales volumes – i.e. the relevant ASP and NOC figures; (c) operating costs – i.e. food and beverage costs, payroll and other expenses; and (d) profit margins – gross profit, departmental profit and net profit. Where there are sufficient statistical data, the preparation of budgets is considerably easier. This will be seen from the practical examples given later in this chapter.

Budget Preparation

The critical role of the sales level has already been emphasised. As far as budgeting is concerned, it is necessary to point out that, since changes in the volume of sales influence all variable and semi-variable costs, the very first step is to determine the volume of budgeted sales. In large hotels, where a number of different budgets would be prepared (including cash budgets and budgets for payroll, marketing and sales promotion, repairs and maintenance, etc.), it is the prediction of the budgeted sales volume that marks the start of the whole process of budgeting.

The actual determination of the budgeted figures is, typically, carried out as follows:

1 The first step is to ascertain the figures for the current year. Where the budget year runs from January to December, the compilation of the various budgets would usually start towards the end of October – before all the figures are available for the current year. However,

even if only ten months' figures are available, they constitute a sufficient base for predicting the immediate future.

2   The second step is to take into account: (a) the most recent trends and (b) prospects for the following year. This obviously requires a lot of knowledge and experience as well as the ability to project current trends into the future.

3   When we have considered all the matters relevant to (2) above, we have to commit ourselves and decide on appropriate percentage changes between the current year and the following year.

4   Finally we take the current figures, adjust them by appropriate percentages and thus arrive at the figures for the following budget year. A simple example is given below.

	This Year	Adjustment	Next Year
	£	%	£
Food sales	600,000	+5	630,000
Beverage sales	250,000	+4	260,000
Food cost	210,000	+5	220,500
Beverage cost	100,000	+4	104,000
etc.			

Limiting Factors

It is convenient at this stage to deal with an important operational aspect of food and beverage sales budgeting. When predicting the volume of food and beverage sales, we should consider the operation of any possible limiting factors. A limiting factor is something which limits the growth of the sales volume. Some of the principal limiting factors are described below.

1   *Seating capacity.* The seating capacity of practically all restaurants and hotel dining rooms is fixed. During peak periods this operates as a powerful limiting factor.

2   *Shortage of efficient labour.* In operations where the waiting staff are not properly trained, the speed of service will leave a lot to be desired. This, in turn, will have a negative effect on the volume of sales.

3   *Poor restaurant supervision.* Poor planning of waiters' rotas and incompetent supervision of the actual service will also have a negative effect on the volume of sales. Where there is a poor adjustment of the number of waiting staff to sales volumes, peak periods frequently witness indifferent service and low average spending power.

4   *Insufficient capital.* This may result in non-availability of essential plant and equipment and/or poor quality of such equipment – with a consequent negative effect on sales volumes.

In addition to some of the more common limiting factors described above, there are others peculiar to each different type of establishment and its special circumstances. In many hotels throughout the world, waiters find it difficult to communicate with guests because of insufficient linguistic skills. This results in their not being able to make appropriate recommendations (sell more profitable dishes, suggest desserts, wines, etc.) and leads to underachievement in terms of ASP figures and sales volumes. In self-service operations the speed with which customers choose their food and the cashier collects their cash both influence the volume of sales. Thus in each and every situation we should look for possible limiting factors and, having found them, take positive steps to remove their negative influences on the volume of sales.

PERFORMANCE EVALUATION AND CONTROL

Once the annual budgets have been prepared, it is essential to subdivide them into budgets covering shorter periods – weekly, monthly, quarterly, and so on. This is necessary in order to enable us to compare current performance against the budget target for a particular period.

Any differences between budgeted and actual figures – known as variances – will have to be ascertained and their causes investigated. Some practical examples relating to variances will be found later in this chapter.

FOOD AND BEVERAGE SALES FORECASTING

A forecast is a prediction of some event or happening during a future period. Forecasting is therefore the process of establishing what will occur at a future point in time or during a given future period. When we are forecasting we are simply – and disinterestedly – extending existing trends into the future. And so we might say: 'The number of covers last year was 20,000; this year we are likely to reach 22,000 covers – and so the number of covers next year will probably be 24,000.'

This disinterested forecasting has to be distinguished from budgeting, when our intention comes into play. To continue the above example, we might say: 'The number of covers last year was 20,000; this year we are likely to reach 22,000 covers, but we need to achieve at least 25,000 covers next year to achieve the right level of profit.' The 24,000 covers in the first quotation is a forecast; the 25,000 covers in the second quotation is a budgeted quantity. In practice we start with forecasting and then adjust the forecast figures to obtain the required budgeted figures.

In practical food and beverage sales forecasting we concentrate on the determinants of the sales volume: we forecast separately the number of covers and the average spending power (one multiplied by the other gives the sales volume). Two different methods are commonly used:

1   The first method relies on percentages. We ascertain the percentage change in, say, the number of covers from one year to another for several years and then decide on the most likely number of covers during the next budget period.
2   The second method – used by a large number of food and beverage managers – is graphic. We plot the relevant figures for the last few budget periods, and a 'line of best fit' (which cuts through the largest possible marked values) will then suggest what we should expect during the next budget period.

Finally, before we look at some practical examples, it is important to appreciate the difference between the forecasts of the number of covers and those of the average spending power. Trends in the NOC are influenced by a whole host of external factors (as discussed earlier in this chapter) and are invariably difficult to predict – particularly during periods of economic instability and market turbulence. Trends in the average spending power, on the other hand, though to some extent independent and uncontrollable, may be influenced by intelligent menu planning, waiters' recommendations and various methods of merchandising. In other words, we have considerably more influence over ASP figures than over NOC figures – a fact worth remembering when converting forecasts into budgeted figures.

EXAMPLE 1: PERCENTAGE METHOD

From the information given below you are required to prepare a food and beverage sales forecast for 1994. You are informed that:

1   the policy of the hotel is to adjust food and beverage prices in line with inflation – currently running at 7–8 per cent;
2   the Coffee Shop is new, having been opened at the beginning of 1991.

Figures for the last three years are shown in Table 6.1.

Explain what external factors you would take into account in preparing the final budgeted figures for the food and beverage department.

Table 6.1 Sales figures

		1991	1992	1993
Restaurant	NOC	18,000	18,760	17,820
	ASP	£10.00	£10.80	£11.56
	Sales	£180,000	£202,608	£205,999
Coffee Shop	NOC	14,000	16,240	18,510
	ASP	£7.60	£8.13	£8.78
	Sales	£106,400	£132,031	£162,517

When we use the percentage method, the first step is to calculate the percentage change from one year to another. We then look at the resulting trend and decide what is likely to happen during the following year. The calculations are shown below.

Table 6.2 The percentage method of budgeting

	1991		1992		1993		1994
Restaurant							
No. of covers	18,000		18,760		17,820		17,820
% Change		+4.2		−5.1		nil	
ASP	£10.00		£10.80		£11.56		£12.48
% Change		+8.0		+7.0		+8.0	
Sales volume	£180,000		£202,608		£205,999		£222,394
Coffee Shop							
No. of covers	14,000		16,240		18,510		21,287
% Change		+16.0		+14.0		+15.0	
ASP	£7.60		£8.13		£8.78		£9.48
% Change		+7.0		+8.0		+8.0	
Sales volume	£106,400		£132,031		£162,517		£201,801

The number of covers in the restaurant seems rather erratic, and the recent trend would suggest that no increase in the NOC should be expected in 1994. In view of the percentage increases which were obtained in the ASP over 1991–3, it is reasonable – other things being equal – to expect a rise of 8 per cent in 1994. As already explained, the budgeted average spending power is something that we can influence through appropriate price revisions, merchandising, etc. Finally it is important to stress that the forecasts for 1994 would normally have to be considered carefully in terms of the prevailing external environment before being approved by top management as the budgeted figures for 1994.

As far as the coffee shop is concerned, we have a greater degree of stability and this certainly facilitates the sales forecasting. In both cases – NOC and ASP – we assume that the external environment is such as to allow the trends during 1991–3 to continue into 1994.

EXAMPLE 2: GRAPHIC METHOD

A small restaurant is about to prepare its budget for 1994. Amongst other figures, the budgeted number of covers is required. The following past data are available:

Year	1990	1991	1992	1993
NOC	11,000	11,500	12,500	13,000

The first step is to plot the figures for 1990 to 1993. A forecast is then made to extend the existing trend into 1994. The forecast number of covers may be read off the vertical axis in Figure 6.1, and it would appear that in 1994 this will be approximately 13,700. Again, before this is approved as the budgeted NOC, due consideration would have to be given to the relevant external factors, as discussed earlier in this chapter.

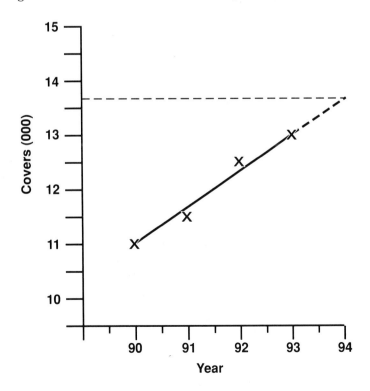

Figure 6.1 Forecast of number of covers

EXAMPLE 3: BUDGETING FOR SALES IN A LARGER HOTEL

Reference has already been made to the importance of statistical data. In larger hotels there will, typically, be several food and beverage sales outlets: à la carte restaurant, coffee shop, banqueting department, room service, etc. Where there are a number of sales outlets, sales budgeting is quite difficult as changes in the external environment will affect different sales outlets differently. An upward trend in employment and disposable incomes will tend to increase both the NOC and the ASP figures. However, the resulting gain from such trends will no doubt be greater in à la carte sales than sales volumes in the coffee shop and room service.

Conversely, a downward trend in employment and disposable incomes will result in fewer meetings and conferences as well as lower ASP figures on wedding receptions and similar functions. All such changes in the external environment make it essential that our food and beverage sales budgets are based on detailed and comprehensive statistical data. This is illustrated in the example below.

The Blue Lake Hotel is a medium-sized property with 150 rooms. Most of the guests are foreign tourists, and therefore the annual pattern of business is distinctly seasonal.

The hotel operates a system of budgetary control, and full food and beverage statistics for 1993 are given below. The notes which follow should be taken into account.

ASP and Inflation
Inflation is expected to average 7 per cent in 1994 and all menu prices will be adjusted accordingly.

Number of Covers
The restaurant has proved increasingly popular in recent years, and it is safe to assume that the number of covers will increase by 5 per cent in 1994.

The coffee shop has enjoyed a great deal of popularity during the last three years. However, its capacity is limited, and no increase in the number of covers should be expected during the six months May to October. Otherwise the Food and Beverages Manager is confident that it is realistic to assume an increase in the number of covers of 4 per cent.

Beverage Sales

Having regard to the projected increase in the number of covers and the necessary price adjustments in response to inflation, it is safe to assume that beverage sales will increase by 11 per cent in 1994.

You are required to prepare the hotel's food and beverage sales budget for 1994.

The figures for 1993 are given in Table 6.3. They have to be adjusted in accordance with the instructions outlined above.

Table 6.3 The Blue Lake Hotel food and beverage sales figures 1993

Month	Restaurant			Coffee Shop			Total food £	Beverage sales £	Total F&B £
	ASP (£)	NOC	£	ASP (£)	NOC	£			
Jan	16.20	1,400	22,680	9.20	2,900	26,680	49,360	18,350	67,710
Feb	16.10	1,500	24,150	9.15	3,200	29,280	53,430	19,450	72,880
Mar	16.15	1,600	25,840	9.15	3,500	32,025	57,865	20,350	78,215
Apr	16.10	1,800	28,980	9.10	3,800	34,580	63,560	22,550	86,110
May	16.05	1,900	30,495	9.05	4,100	37,105	67,600	23,700	91,300
Jun	16.00	2,200	35,200	9.00	4,700	42,300	77,500	26,450	103,950
Jul	15.95	2,400	38,280	8.95	5,100	45,645	83,925	28,650	112,575
Aug	15.90	2,600	41,340	8.90	5,400	48,060	89,400	30,600	120,000
Sep	15.95	2,400	38,280	8.95	5,000	44,750	83,030	27,500	110,530
Oct	16.05	2,000	32,100	9.00	4,200	37,800	69,900	24,550	94,450
Nov	16.00	1,300	20,800	9.10	2,800	25,480	46,280	16,300	62,580
Dec	16.10	1,100	17,710	9.15	2,400	21,960	39,670	14,400	54,070

The food and beverage sales budget for 1994, which is shown in Table 6.4, looks a most time-consuming exercise – which it is if completed manually. These days, however, practically all senior food and beverage employees are familiar with computer applications, and so the conversion of the 1993 statistics into budgeted figures for 1994 would present no major problem.

Table 6.4 Food and beverage sales budget 1994

Period	Restaurant			Coffee Shop			Food Sales	Bev. Sales	Total Sales
	ASP (£)	NOC	£	ASP (£)	NOC	£			
Jan	17.33	1,470	25,475	9.84	3,016	29,677	55,152	20,369	75,521
Feb	17.23	1,575	27,137	9.79	3,328	32,581	59,718	21,589	81,307
Mar	17.28	1,680	29,030	9.79	3,640	35,636	64,666	22,589	87,255
Apr	17.23	1,890	32,565	9.74	3,952	38,492	71,057	25,030	96,087
May	17.17	1,995	34,254	9.68	4,100	39,688	73,942	26,307	100,249
Jun	17.12	2,310	39,547	9.63	4,700	45,261	84,808	29,360	114,168
Jul	17.07	2,520	43,016	9.58	5,100	48,858	91,874	31,801	123,675
Aug	17.01	2,730	46,437	9.52	5,400	51,408	97,845	33,966	131,811
Sep	17.07	2,520	43,016	9.58	5,000	47,900	90,916	30,525	121,441
Oct	17.17	2,100	36,057	9.63	4,200	40,446	76,503	27,251	103,754
Nov	17.12	1,365	23,368	9.74	2,912	28,363	51,731	18,093	69,824
Dec	17.23	1,155	19,901	9.79	2,496	24,436	44,337	15,984	60,321
			399,803			462,764	862,549	302,864	1,165,413

In the case of beverage sales we have assumed an overall percentage increase. Frequently, however, a more analytical approach is called for. The number of transactions and the beverage sales per transaction would then be analysed separately.

We have now looked at three examples of budgeting for food and beverage sales. Our next step is to take a more comprehensive look at food and beverage budgeting. Example 4 deals with the food and beverage budget of a hotel. Example 5 is based on a medium-sized restaurant.

EXAMPLE 4: HOTEL FOOD AND BEVERAGE OPERATING BUDGET

The Green Valley Hotel has 75 rooms and boasts a successful food and beverage department. The Food and Beverage Manager has been asked to prepare a draft operating budget for his department for 1995. The attached schedule shows the operating results of the food and beverage operation for 1992, 1993 and 1994.

The following notes are relevant and should be taken into account.

NOC and ASP
It is expected that the upward trend in these figures will continue in 1995. Please assume that the trends in 1995 will be as good as the best during the last three years.

Gross Profit
The aim of the hotel is to achieve a gross profit of 67 per cent on food and 62 per cent on beverage sales.

Department Payroll
The General Manager insists that departmental payroll for 1995 should not exceed 37 per cent.

Departmental Expenses
He is also of the opinion – which is shared by the Food and Beverage Manager – that departmental expenses should be maintained at the level of 15 per cent of departmental turnover.

You are required to assume the role of the Food and Beverage Manager of the Green Valley Hotel and prepare the draft operating budget for 1995. State clearly any assumptions you have made.

Should the departmental profit resulting from your projections amount to less than £65,000, suggest ways and means of ensuring that the 1995 departmental profit shows an improvement of at least 5 per cent on the previous year. Table 6.5 gives the department's operating results for 1992–4.

As most of the budgeted figures – gross profit margins and cost ceilings – are related to the budgeted turnover, our first and most important step is to look at the determinants of the sales volume, the ASP and NOC figures. The necessary calculations are shown in Table 6.6.

As we expect the trends in 1995 to be as good as the best during 1992–4, it is fair to assume that the NOC and ASP figures will increase by 5 per cent. The appropriate calculations are shown below.

NOC
$32,760 \div 100 \times 105 = 34,398$

ASP
Food: $£8.74 \div 100 \times 105 = £9.18$
Beverage: $£3.06 \div 100 \times 105 = £3.21$

Table 6.5 Green Valley Hotel food and beverage operations 1992–4

	1992	1993	1994
No. of covers	30,000	31,200	32,760
ASP food	£8.00	£8.40	£8.74
ASP beverages	2.80	2.91	3.06
ASP total	10.80	11.31	11.80
Food sales	£240,000	£262,080	£286,322
Beverage sales	84,000	90,792	100,246
Total sales	324,000	352,872	386,568
Food cost	£79,200	£83,866	£94,486
Beverage cost	31,920	35,409	37,091
Cost of sales	111,120	119,275	131,577
GP food	£160,800	£178,214	£191,836
GP beverage	52,080	55,383	63,155
GP total	212,880	233,597	254,991
GP food	67.0%	68.0%	67.0%
GP beverage	62.0	61.0	63.0
GP total	65.7	66.2	66.0
Dept payroll	£123,120	£130,563	£146,896
	38.0%	37.0%	38.0%
Dept expenses	£42,120	£49,402	£46,388
	13.0%	14.0%	12.0%
Dept profit	£47,640	£53,632	£61,707
	14.7%	15.2%	16.0%

Table 6.6 Trends in NOC and ASP 1992–4

	1992		1993		1994
No. of covers	30,000		31,200		32,760
% change		+4.0%		+5.0%	
ASP food	£8.00		£8.40		£8.74
% change		+5.0%		+4.0%	
ASP beverage	£2.80		£2.91		£3.06
% change		+4.0%		+5.0%	

We are now able to prepare the department's draft budget for 1995. This is shown in Table 6.7.

Table 6.7 Green Valley Hotel food and beverage budget 1995

No. of covers	34,398
ASP food	£9.18
ASP beverage	3.21
ASP total	12.39
Food sales	£315,773
Beverage sales	110,418
Total sales	426,191
Food cost	£104,205
Beverage cost	41,959
Cost of sales	146,164
GP food	£211,568
GP beverage	68,459
GP total	280,027
GP food	67.0%
GP beverage	62.0
GP total	65.7
Dept payroll	£157,690
	37.0%
Dept expenses	£63,929
	15.0%
Dept profit	£58,408
	13.7%

The instruction to the Food and Beverage Manager is to ensure that the budgeted profit for 1995 is at least 5 per cent more than that for 1994. We should therefore budget for a departmental profit of (£61,707 ÷ 100 × 105) £64,792 – say £65,000. The profit in the draft budget is therefore approximately £6,500 short.

Several profit improvement strategies are possible. Budgeted payroll and departmental expenses amount to £212,619 and 52 per cent of the sales volume. A reduction of 3 per cent in these expenses would increase the budgeted departmental profit to the desired level. Another solution is to increase selling prices. These need only be raised by 1.5 per cent to increase the ASP to £12.58. The additional ASP (£12.58 – £12.39) of £0.19 multiplied by the budgeted NOC of 34,398 would produce an additional sales revenue of £6,536 and increase the departmental profit to the desired level. The third major solution is to increase the number of covers. This, however, is not normally easy to achieve without some additional expenditure on press advertising, merchandising, etc. The final decision on the budgeted profit target would have to explore all the major solutions available.

EXAMPLE 5: BUDGETING IN RESTAURANTS

Our last practical example relates to a medium-sized restaurant. It should be noted that – as in Example 4 – the first step here is to predict the volume of sales.

Table 6.8 shows the profit and loss account of the Ponte Vecchio Restaurant in respect of the year ended 31 December 1993.

Table 6.8 Profit and loss account of the Ponte Vecchio Restaurant

		£	%
Sales	food	300,480	72.7
	beverage	112,680	27.3
	total	413,160	100.0
Cost of sales	food	102,163	34.0
	beverage	50,706	45.0
	total	152,869	37.0
Gross profit .		260,291	63.0
Less operating expenses:			
Wages and salaries		102,464	24.8
Employee benefits		13,221	3.2
Direct operating expenses		21,071	5.1
Music and entertainment		7,850	1.9
Advertising and promotion		11,982	2.9
Gas and electricity		18,179	4.4
Administrative and general exps.		17,766	4.3
Repairs and maintenance		4,545	1.1
Rent		18,592	4.5
Depreciation		5,784	1.4
Total		221,454	53.6
Net profit		38,837	9.4

You are required to prepare the restaurant's budget for 1994, taking the following notes into account.

Food and Beverage Sales
The number of covers has shown a modest increase in recent years and this trend is expected to continue in 1994. The average spending power

(ASP) of the restaurant tends to reflect general inflationary trends. The following figures are available:

	1991	*1992*	*1993*
No. of Covers	22,734	23,802	25,040
ASP Food	£10.70	£11.32	£12.00
ASP Beverage	£4.00	£4.24	£4.50

Gross Profit Margins
The policy of the restaurant is to operate at gross profit margins of 65 per cent for food and 55 per cent for beverages.

Wages and Salaries
There will be no change in the number of employees, but wage rates and salaries will increase in accordance with current wage rates adjustments, which average 7 per cent. Employee benefits should not increase by more than 5 per cent.

Direct Operating Expenses
An increase of 8 per cent is expected.

Music and Entertainment
A new team of musicians and artists will be employed and this will entail an increase of 12 per cent on the expenses incurred in 1993.

Advertising and Promotion
It is considered that this should not exceed 2.4 per cent of sales revenue in 1994.

Gas and Electricity
From information available it is clear that this expenditure will not increase by more than 3 per cent.

Administrative and General Expenses
The proprietors are determined that this expenditure should be maintained at 4 per cent of the 1994 sales revenue.

Repairs and Maintenance
Past experience suggests that this will not cost more than £4,700 during the year to 31 December 1994.

Rent
This will show an increase of 6 per cent.

Depreciation
This will remain at the 1993 level of £5,784.

The proprietors insist that the restaurant must achieve a net profit of at least £50,000 during the year ended 31 December 1994.

The most relevant trends are shown below:

	1991		1992		1993
No. of Covers	22,734		23,802		25,040
% Change		+4.7%		+5.2%	
ASP Food	£10.70		£11.32		£12.00
% Change		+5.8%		+6.0%	
ASP Beverage	£4.00		£4.24		£4.50
% Change		+6.0%		+6.1%	

From the above analysis it is fair to assume that the number of covers will increase by 5 per cent and both ASP figures by 6 per cent. Therefore:

The number of covers will be   26,292
The ASP on food will be   £12.72
The ASP on beverage will be   £4.77

Table 6.9 Ponte Vecchio Restaurant operating budget for year ending 31 December 1994

		£	%
Sales	food	334,434	72.7
	beverage	125,413	27.3
	total	459,847	100.0
Cost of sales	food	117,052	35.0
	beverage	56,436	45.0
	total	173,488	37.7
Gross profit		286,359	62.3
Less operating expenses:			
Wages and salaries		109,636	23.8
Employee benefits		13,882	3.0
Direct operating expenses		22,757	4.9
Music and entertainment		8,792	1.9
Advertising and promotion		11,036	2.4
Gas and electricity		18,724	4.1
Administrative and general		18,394	4.0
Repairs and maintenance		4,700	1.0
Rent		19,708	4.3
Depreciation		5,784	1.2
Total		233,413	50.8
Budgeted net profit		52,946	11.5

Some Organisational Matters

Budget Committee

All hotels and restaurants which operate a system of budgetary control have a duly appointed budget committee. This consists of several senior executives with, frequently, the general manager or managing director acting as chairman. All the major departments would be represented on the committee, and therefore the food and beverage manager is invariably invited to join the budget committee.

An important task of the committee is to oversee the general operation of this system of budgetary control. Its main function is to prepare each year draft budgets for submission to, and final approval by, the board of directors. Where the budget year runs from January to December, most of the meetings of the budget committee would take place during the three months October to December, as that is the time when the budgets are being prepared for the forthcoming budget year.

Budget Review Period

Once the annual budget has been prepared it is necessary to subdivide it into budgets covering short trading periods. This is in order to allow frequent checks on the progress of the business. At the end of each week, month and quarter we should compare actual performance with budgeted results.

Different organisations choose different budget review periods, but most of them tend to incline towards one of the three possibilities illustrated in Figure 6.2.

The first possibility (Figure 6.2a) is to divide the annual budget into twelve parts, each representing a calendar month. This procedure is favoured by many food and beverage managers, because the budget periods correspond with normal calendar months. The one major difficulty is that, when weekly reports are prepared, they do not fit into the calendar months.

Many organisations divide the budget year into thirteen lunar months (of four weeks each), as in Figure 6.2b. This offers the advantage of months of equal length and ensures that all weekly reports fit into the budgeted monthly periods. A disadvantage of this arrangement is that the thirteen months do not correspond with ordinary calendar months.

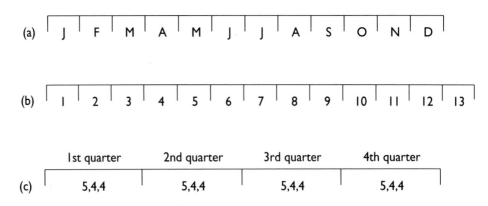

Figure 6.2 Alternative budget periods

Finally, many of the large hotel companies divide the annual budget into four quarterly budgets which, in turn, are divided into three months of five, four and four weeks (Figure 6.2c). This facilitates the preparation of weekly reports, but unfortunately results in monthly control periods of unequal length.

Budget Reports

As explained earlier in this chapter, it is of paramount importance to have the progress of the business under continual review. It is for this reason that the annual budget is subdivided into short (weekly, monthly, quarterly) budget periods. This enables frequent and therefore more effective monitoring of our food and beverage sales, cost of sales, profit margins, etc.

In the remainder of this chapter, we show three budget reports: a weekly, monthly and a quarterly report. Readers will notice that the content of these reports varies with the length of time under review. During a short period such as a week or month it is unlikely that costs such as rents, rates, insurances and depreciation will show much change. There is no point in reviewing such fixed and uncontrollable costs at frequent intervals. Instead we take the opportunity to concentrate on items which are of a variable/controllable nature as well as items which have a strong impact on the profits of the establishment. As far as food and beverage operations are concerned, weekly and monthly reports will emphasise sales volume, sales mix, NOC and ASP figures, cost of sales, gross profits and, more often than not, payroll.

A quarterly or half yearly report on the other hand, will tend to show practically all the items of expenditure. Indeed it will not differ materially from the annual profit and loss account. Let us now look at the three practical examples.

EXAMPLE 1: WEEKLY REPORT

This is a report suitable for a large hotel with several sales outlets. The subject matter of this particular report is food and beverage sales. It is for this reason that a great deal of prominence is given to the determinants of turnover – i.e. NOC and ASP figures. There would of course be other reports dealing with the cost of sales, gross profits and departmental payroll.

From the weekly report we may see that all three restaurants have done well in terms of numbers of covers. This has clearly contributed to the

Table 6.10 New City Hotel food and beverage department budget report, week 22

	Budget	Actual	Variance
French restaurant			
No. of covers	400	420	20
ASP food	£16.00	£16.10	£0.10
ASP beverage	6.20	6.40	0.20
ASP total	£22.20	£22.50	£0.30
F&B sales	£8,880	£9,450	£570
Japanese restaurant			
No. of covers	350	380	30
ASP food	£18.00	£17.60	(£0.40)
ASP beverage	6.30	6.50	0.20
ASP total	£24.30	£24.10	(£0.20)
F&B sales	£8,505	£9,158	£653
Indian restaurant			
No. of covers	260	290	30
ASP food	£9.00	£9.20	£0.20
ASP beverage	3.00	2.80	(0.20)
ASP total	£12.00	£12.00	—
F&B sales	£3,120	£3,480	£360
Total F&B sales	£20,505	£22,088	£1,583
	100.0%	107.7%	7.7%

very satisfactory volume of food and beverage sales, which is 7.7 per cent in excess of the budgeted figure. However, the ASP figures suggest that, with the exception of the French Restaurant, there is underachievement – something that would have to be investigated and watched carefully in subsequent weeks.

EXAMPLE 2: MONTHLY REPORT

This budget report has been designed to control, on a monthly basis, all the key determinants of the food and beverage departmental profit. NOC and ASP figures are not shown, as this would produce excessive

Table 6.11 Central Hotel food and beverage department budget report, January 1994

		Budget	Actual	Variances	
		£	£	£	%
Sales					
Grill Room	food	50,000	50,900	900	1.8
	beverage	16,000	15,800	(200)	(1.3)
Coffee Shop	food	25,000	26,100	1,100	4.4
	beverage	9,000	9,200	200	2.2
Total sales		100,000	102,000	2,000	2.0
Cost of sales					
Food cost		26,250	28,490	(2,240)	(8.5)
Beverage cost		10,000	9,750	250	2.5
Total		36,250	38,240	(1,990)	(5.5)
Gross profit £					
Food		48,750	48,510	(240)	(0.5)
Beverage		15,000	15,250	250	1.7
Total		63,750	63,760	10	—
Gross profit %					
Food		65.0	63.0	—	(2.0)
Beverage		60.0	61.0	—	1.0
Total		63.8	62.5	—	(1.3)
Payroll £		35,000	34,200	800	2.3
Payroll %		35.0	33.5	—	(1.5)
Dept expenses £		14,000	14,500	(500)	(3.6)
Dept expenses %		14.0	14.2	—	(0.2)
Dept profit £		14,750	15,060	310	2.1
Dept profit %		14.8	14.8	—	—

detail. Of course separate supporting schedules could be produced to show any additional information, including NOC and ASP figures for the month under review.

As may be seen, food and beverage sales were 2 per cent above budget. The resulting benefits of the enhanced sales volume were offset by higher than budgeted cost of sales figures. As a result actual cash gross profit is practically equal to the budgeted amount. The actual total of payroll and departmental expenses is not materially different from the corresponding budgeted total. Hence the final figure of actual departmental profit is not significantly different from that budgeted.

EXAMPLE 3: QUARTERLY REPORT

Our specimen quarterly report is suitable for a smaller restaurant. Readers will note that we are not showing the NOC or ASP figures. These, if required, could be shown in a separate supporting schedule. We do, however, show the full range of operating costs and arrive at the net profit figures.

Table 6.12 Kingfisher Restaurant budget report, quarter ended 30 June 1994

	Budget		Actual	
	£	%	£	%
Food sales	115,000	71.9	112,000	70.9
Beverage sales	45,000	28.1	46,000	29.1
Total sales	160,000	100.0	158,000	100.0
Food cost	40,250	35.0	40,880	36.5
Beverage cost	18,000	40.0	18,860	41.0
Cost of sales	58,250	36.4	59,740	37.8
Gross profit	101,750	63.6	98,260	62.2
Payroll	43,200	27.0	43,450	27.5
Employee benefits	4,000	2.5	4,110	2.6
Administrative & general	8,160	5.1	7,425	4.7
Marketing	3,520	2.2	3,790	2.4
Music & entertainment	7,200	4.5	6,480	4.1
Direct operating expenses	6,560	4.1	6,320	4.1
Gas & electricity	5,600	3.5	5,370	3.4
Repairs & maintenance	2,880	1.8	2,055	1.3
Depreciation	4,480	2.8	4,480	2.8
Total expenses	85,600	53.5	83,480	52.8
Net profit	16,150	10.1	14,780	9.4

Restaurant operators are accustomed to controlling their operations through percentages. It is for this reason that percentage, not quantitative, variances are shown in the example. From the report we see that actual sales were somewhat less than budgeted. Also the actual cost of sales in relation to actual sales was 1.4 per cent higher. Both these factors are responsible for the shortfall in cash gross profit of (£101,750 − £98,260) £3,490. The total of actual operating expenses was (£85,600 − £83,480) £2,120 less than budgeted, resulting in a net profit £1,370 less than that budgeted.

QUESTIONS

1 The Surrey Hotel is a privately owned 75-bedroomed hotel. It operates several restaurants, including the Wellington Restaurant. The Food and Beverage Manager of the hotel maintains detailed records for all the food and beverage sales outlets. Table 6.13 gives the sales statistics of the Wellington restaurant for 1994.

Table 6.13 Wellington Restaurant sales statistics 1994

Month	No. of covers	ASP food	ASP bev.	Food sales	Bev. sales	F & B sales
		£	£	£	£	£
Jan	1,000	12.00	4.00	12,000	4,000	16,000
Feb	1,100	11.90	3.95	13,090	4,345	17,435
Mar	1,200	11.85	3.80	14,220	4,560	18,780
Apr	1,400	11.80	3.75	16,520	5,250	21,770
May	1,600	11.70	3.75	18,720	6,000	24,720
Jun	1,800	11.75	3.70	21,150	6,660	27,810
Jul	1,900	11.60	3.65	22,040	6,935	28,975
Aug	1,700	11.70	3.75	19,890	6,375	26,265
Sep	1,500	11.80	3.80	17,700	5,700	23,400
Oct	1,300	11.90	3.90	15,470	5,070	20,540
Nov	1,100	12.00	3.95	13,200	4,345	17,545
Dec	900	12.10	4.05	10,890	3,645	14,535
				195,890	62,885	257,775

You have been asked to prepare the food and beverage sales budget for the Wellington restaurant for 1995. The following information is to be taken into account.

(a) All menu prices will be revised to secure an increase in ASP figures of 8 per cent.

    (b) Beverage prices will also be revised to give an overall increase in ASP for beverages of 5 per cent.

    (c) The restaurant tends to be quite full during the summer months. The Food and Beverage Manager is of the opinion that the number of covers will show an increase of 5 per cent next January–March and October–December. No increase in NOC figures should be expected during the six months April–September.

State clearly any assumptions you have to make.

2   Give an outline of the principal aims of food and beverage budgeting.

3   Explain what is meant by the 'cycle of food and beverage budgeting'.

4   What are 'limiting factors'? What limiting factors are likely to operate in restaurants?

5   What are 'budget review periods'? What purpose do they serve?

6   A busy city hotel is operating a cocktail bar. The hotel relies heavily on foreign tourists and this is reflected in the pattern of business, shown in Table 6.14.

Table 6.14 Cocktail bar sales Jan–Dec 1994

Month	No. of transactions	ASP per transaction	Sales
		£	£
Jan	600	6.50	3,900
Feb	650	6.60	4,290
Mar	750	6.60	4,950
Apr	850	6.70	5,695
May	1,050	6.70	7,035
Jun	1,300	6.60	8,580
Jul	1,550	6.80	10,540
Aug	1,650	6.70	11,055
Sep	1,450	6.80	9,860
Oct	1,250	6.70	8,375
Nov	1,050	6.60	6,930
Dec	800	6.60	5,280
			86,490

You are required to prepare a sales budget for the cocktail bar for 1995. The following information is available.

(a) The hotel expects a modest increase in its room occupancy in 1995; and this is likely to increase the number of cocktail bar transactions by 4 per cent.

(b) All beverage prices will be revised with effect from 1 January 1995. This will raise the ASP per transaction by 5 per cent.

The General Manager of the hotel is confident that changes (a) and (b) above will for the first time raise the sales volume of the cocktail bar to at least £100,000. Should this not be the case, state what increase in the ASP per transaction is required to achieve the required volume of sales. Assume that the number of transactions cannot be increased beyond the 4 per cent already assumed in (a) above.

7 Set out in Table 6.15 is the profit and loss account of the Rose and Crown restaurant in respect of the year ended 31 December 1994.

Table 6.15 Rose and Crown Restaurant profit and loss account

		£	%
Sales	food	360,575	72.7
	beverage	135,215	27.3
	total	495,790	100.0
Cost of sales	food	122,595	34.0
	beverage	60,845	45.0
	total	183,440	37.0
Gross profit		312,350	63.0
Less operating expenses:			
Wages and salaries		122,955	24.8
Employee benefits		15,865	3.2
Direct operating expenses		25,285	5.1
Music and entertainment		9,420	1.9
Advertising and promotion		14,380	2.9
Gas and electricity		21,815	4.4
Administrative and general exps.		21,320	4.3
Repairs and maintenance		5,455	1.1
Rent		22,310	4.5
Depreciation		6,940	1.4
Total		265,745	53.6
Net profit		46,605	9.4

You are required to prepare the restaurant's budgeted profit and loss account for the year ending 31 December 1995. The notes which follow should be taken into account.

Food and Beverage Sales
The owner is confidently expecting an increase in both food and beverage sales of 6 per cent.

Gross Profit
The policy of the restaurant is to operate at gross profit margins of 65 per cent for food and 55 per cent for beverages.

Wages and Salaries
No change in the number of employees is expected, but a rise of 4 per cent in the rates of pay should be allowed for. Employee benefits should show an increase of 5 per cent.

Direct Operating Expenses
An increase of 6 per cent is expected.

Music and Entertainment
This is expected to show only a modest increase of 3 per cent.

Advertising and Promotion
This should be equal to 2.6 per cent of the turnover in 1995.

Gas and Electricity
An increase of only 3 per cent is expected.

Administrative and General Expenses
The owner is determined that this should not be allowed to increase above 4.2 per cent of the sales turnover in 1995.

Repairs and Maintenance
This will amount to £5,500 during 1995.

Rent
An increase of 6 per cent is expected.

Depreciation
This will remain at the same level as in 1994; £6,940 should be budgeted for.

8   Trident Catering is operating three restaurants in Central London. The company maintains detailed records of all sales statistics. Table 6.16 gives the relevant information in respect of the three units from 1991 to 1994.

Table 6.16 Trident Catering sales statistics 1991–4

	1991	1992	1993	1994
ASP food:	£	£	£	£
Restaurant A	20.00	21.00	22.26	23.60
B	16.00	16.80	17.47	18.00
C	14.00	14.84	15.73	16.83
ASP beverage:	£	£	£	£
Restaurant A	7.50	7.88	8.43	8.94
B	5.60	5.82	6.00	6.24
C	5.10	5.45	5.89	6.30
No. of covers:				
Restaurant A	19,000	19,760	20,945	22,200
B	24,500	24,990	25,740	26,250
C	14,600	15,470	16,245	17,380

You are required to prepare the food and beverage sales budget for 1995, showing the budgeted sales figures both for the three individual restaurants and for the operation as a whole. The layout of the budget is left to your discretion, but you should ensure adequate clarity as well as simplicity of presentation. Take the following notes into account:

Restaurant A has made good progress in recent years. Both NOC and ASP figures for 1995 should reflect the best performance in recent years.

Restaurant B has been moderately successful during the last four years. The directors of the company assume that 1995 will reflect average performance for 1991–4.

Restaurant C has made significant progress in recent years; both NOC and ASP figures have been consistently good. These trends should continue in 1995.

State clearly any assumptions you have to make in completing the above exercise.

9 The Orchard Restaurant Co. owns three restaurants. The Food and Beverage Controller of the company has done some preliminary work on the budget for 1995. Some of the key budgeted figures are shown in Table 6.17.

The directors insist that each restaurant should earn a net profit of at least 10 per cent of its turnover. You are required to:

(a) Calculate the budgeted net profit for each restaurant as well as total budgeted net profit.

Table 6.17 Orchard Restaurant Co.

	Apple Restaurant	Peach Restaurant	Cherry Restaurant
No. of covers	20,600	25,700	30,400
	£	£	£
ASP food	20.00	16.00	14.00
beverage	7.00	5.50	4.50
	%	%	%
Gross profit food	70.0	65.0	60.0
beverage	65.0	60.0	55.0
	£	£	£
Wages & salaries	133,500	143,650	141,800
Operating expenses	122,300	105,100	112,100
Fixed charges	75,400	42,700	47,300

(b) Comment on the profitability of the company, as indicated by your budgeted figures.

(c) Comment in particular on the projected profitability of the Cherry Restaurant. What would be the effect of a 10 per cent increase in ASP figures here on the budgeted net profit for 1995?

CHAPTER 7

PROFITABILITY

In Chapter 5 we dealt with the fundamental aims and specific objectives of hotels and restaurants. We explained then that one of the most important aims of such establishments is to ensure satisfactory profitability. Our present task is therefore to look at all the relevant aspects of food and beverage profitability and this we will do in some considerable detail.

A food and beverage manager may employ the most competent staff, ensure high quality standards, secure an excellent reputation for the establishment and achieve a high volume of sales. Nevertheless if he/she fails to achieve a satisfactory profit, then it is doubtful that we can regard him/her as a good, effective manager. In the final analysis profitability is of paramount importance.

Cost Concepts

THE ELEMENTS OF COST

Both in this chapter and throughout the present volume we make frequent references to various cost, revenue and profit concepts. All such concepts need to be clearly understood in the context of food and beverage profitability. Our first task, therefore, is to explain all such concepts before moving on to some more complex problems later in this chapter.

The total cost of operating an establishment may be divided into several different cost categories, depending on our choice of cost concepts. A traditional approach to cost classification is to segregate costs according to their nature. From this point of view we may distinguish the following:

1 Cost of sales – sometimes described as the 'cost of food and beverage sold' or 'materials'. This includes food cost, beverage cost and the cost of cigars, newspapers, etc., consumed.
2 Labour costs – often described as 'payroll'. Included here are the actual wages and salaries as well as a variety of benefits supplied to

the employees, such as meals on duty, contributions to employees' pensions, staff parties, outings, etc.

3   Other costs – which are frequently described as 'overheads'. These are all the costs of the establishment other than the cost of sales and labour costs.

EXAMPLE

Table 7.1 shows the profit and loss account of Richmond Restaurant.

Table 7.1 Richmond Restaurant profit and loss account for year ended 31 December 1994

	Sales	Cost of sales	Gross profit
	£	£	£
Food sales	360,000	126,000	234,000
Beverage sales	140,000	56,000	84,000
Total	500,000	182,000	318,000
Less Operating expenses:			
Wages and salaries		132,500	
Employee meals		8,500	
Employee benefits		5,000	
Administrative & general expenses		24,000	
Sales promotion		12,000	
Guest entertainment		13,500	
Laundry and cleaning		11,000	
Gas and electricity		16,000	
Repairs and maintenance		18,500	
Depreciation		19,500	260,500
Net profit			57,500

The elements of cost of the restaurant would be calculated as shown in Table 7.2. Readers should note that each element of cost is expressed as a percentage of total sales. This is the generally accepted procedure throughout the hotel and restaurant industry.

The cost classification shown in Table 7.2 will look rather different in a hotel food and beverage department. The cost of sales and labour costs will be calculated in the same manner as in restaurants. The 'other expenses', however, will only comprise the departmental controllable expenses such as laundry and dry cleaning, losses of equipment, contract

Table 7.2 Elements of cost

	£	£	%
Cost of sales			
Food cost	126,000		
Beverage cost	56,000	182,000	36.4
Labour costs			
Wages & salaries	132,500		
Employee meals	8,500		
Employee benefits	5,000	146,000	29.2
Other costs (overheads)			
Administrative & general	24,000		
Sales promotion	12,000		
Guest entertainment	13,500		
Laundry & cleaning	11,000		
Gas & electricity	16,000		
Repairs & maintenance	18,500		
Depreciation	19,500	114,500	22.9
Total cost		442,500	88.5

cleaning, and any music and entertainment. The three cost categories will therefore be:

1   Cost of sales;
2   Labour costs;
3   Departmental expenses.

FIXED AND VARIABLE COSTS

From the point of view of cost behaviour we may distinguish wholly different cost categories. These are described below.

1   Fixed costs. These are described as 'fixed' because they do not respond to changes in the sales volume. Thus the cost of insurances, rent, rates and any loan interest payable will remain unaltered irrespective of the number of covers achieved.
2   Variable costs. These are costs which, for all practical purposes, vary in proportion to the volume of sales. The best examples of variable costs are food cost and beverage cost, but there are others, as explained below.
3   Semi-fixed costs. These are sometimes described as semi-variable costs. Semi-fixed costs are neither fully fixed nor fully variable. They move in the same direction as the volume of sales, but not in proportion.

Let us look at the example of kitchen fuel:

Day	NOC	S-F cost
Monday	400	£10
Tuesday	800	£14

From Monday to Tuesday the number of covers increased by 100 per cent. The resulting increase in the cost of kitchen fuel was 40 per cent.

A semi-fixed cost consists of two elements: a fully fixed element and a fully variable element (which is why some people describe semi-fixed costs as 'mixed costs'). Let us look at another example. The cost of labour in the food and beverage department is normally a semi-fixed cost. If we look at it closely, we will see that some parts of it – for example salaries paid to the food and beverage manager, executive chef and restaurant manager – are clearly of a fixed nature. Other parts of the cost of labour – for example wages paid to banqueting waiting staff and other part-time and casual labour – are a wholly variable cost.

It is desirable to analyse all semi-fixed costs and segregate them into fully fixed and fully variable elements. This enables us to divide the total cost into these two cost categories. This, in turn, facilitates all kinds of calculations, profit projections, etc.

EXAMPLE

Let us revert to the Richmond Restaurant and show how it is possible to divide the total cost of £442,500 into the two separate cost categories.

Table 7.3 Fixed and variable costs of the Richmond Restaurant

	Total cost £	Fixed cost £	Variable cost £
Food cost	126,000		126,000
Beverage cost	56,000		56,000
Wages & salaries	132,500	95,000	37,500
Employee meals	8,500	6,000	2,500
Employee benefits	5,000	4,000	1,000
Administrative & general	24,000	21,000	3,000
Sales promotion	12,000	12,000	
Guest entertainment	13,500	13,500	
Laundry & cleaning	11,000	9,000	2,000
Gas & electricity	16,000	12,000	4,000
Repairs & maintenance	18,500	18,500	
Depreciation	19,500	19,500	
	442,500	210,500	232,000

Whilst it is clear that food and beverage costs are a wholly variable cost, all other costs would have to be scrutinised and analysed to decide (at least approximately) on the respective proportions of their fixed and variable elements.

From the above analysis we can show the composition of the total cost:

	£	%
Fixed cost	210,500	47.6
Variable cost	232,000	52.4
Total cost	442,500	100.0

In relation to the sales volume the above percentages would of course look rather different:

	£	%
Fixed cost	210,000	42.1
Variable cost	232,000	46.4
Net profit	57,500	11.5
Sales	500,000	100.0

Let us assume that during the year to 31 December 1994 the restaurant achieved 31,250 covers. On a 'per cover' basis the results for 1994 may be shown as in Table 7.4.

Table 7.4 Costs per cover of the Richmond Restaurant

	£	%
ASP Food	11.52	72.0
ASP Beverages	4.48	28.0
ASP Total	16.00	100.0
Food cost	4.03	25.2
Beverage cost	1.79	11.2
Other variable costs	1.60	10.0
Total variable costs	7.42	46.4
Fixed cost	6.74	42.1
Total cost	14.16	88.5
Net profit	1.84	11.5

SOME OTHER COST CONCEPTS

Several other cost concepts are routinely used in hotel and restaurants. These are detailed below.

Controllable Costs

These are costs which we are able to influence. Thus the cost of part-time and casual labour is wholly controllable in that we decide whether or not to employ such labour – and, if so, how much of it. Other costs such as rent, rates and depreciation are uncontrollable in that from one week/month to another we are not in a position to influence them. Of course, the longer the period of time, the more controllable all costs. As soon as the contract for window cleaning expires, we may decide not to extend it for another year but do the work ourselves. What was an uncontrollable cost is now controllable.

Budgeted and Estimated Costs

These were fully explained in Chapter 6. They should, however, be clearly distinguished from historical costs – i.e. costs which have already been incurred. All past costs are historical costs, and whenever we project costs into future periods, it is important to remember that historical costs may change quite significantly even during relatively short periods of time.

Marginal Cost

Sometimes described as 'incremental' cost, this may be defined as the increase in total cost resulting from one more unit being produced. Marginal cost may also be defined as total variable cost, divided by the number of units produced. Total cost, on the other hand, consists of a fixed as well as a variable element. To revert to our 'per cover' calculations above, marginal cost in this example is £7.42 and total cost is £14.16.

Revenue Concepts

In the section which now follows we will describe various revenue concepts and suggest in what circumstances they are relevant.

TOTAL SALES

This is the sum total of the sales in all the revenue producing departments. Alternative terms which are used include 'total turnover', 'total sales revenue' and 'total sales receipts'. As explained elsewhere in this volume (particularly in Chapters 2 and 11) the sales volume is a most powerful determinant of profitability. Responsibility for food and beverage profitability therefore necessitates continual monitoring of total sales as well as the composition of total sales.

Sales Mix

The term 'sales mix' refers to the composition of total sales. Thus the sales mix of a restaurant might be:

	£	%
Food sales	325,000	65.0
Beverage sales	145,000	29.0
Other sales	30,000	6.0
Total	500,000	100.0

A fairly typical sales mix in the case of a hotel would be:

	£	%
Room sales	1,120,000	56.0
Food sales	530,000	26.5
Beverage sales	220,000	11.0
Telephone sales	80,000	4.0
Other sales	50,000	2.5
Total	2,000,000	100.0

We may also show a more detailed sales mix for each revenue producing department. In the case of food sales, the sales mix might be:

	£	%
Grill room	225,000	45.0
Coffee shop	160,000	32.0
Banqueting	75,000	15.0
Room service	40,000	8.0
Total food sales	500,000	100.0

Finally, it is possible to show the sales mix for a particular sales outlet. An example is shown below.

	£	%
Starters	25,000	10.0
Meat, fish & poultry	135,000	54.0
Vegetables	35,000	14.0
Desserts	30,000	12.0
Teas and coffees	25,000	10.0
Total	250,000	100.0

Sales mix figures are important primarily because each element of the sales mix attracts a different rate of profit. Thus the percentage of gross profit on teas and coffees is often in excess of 80 per cent. The corresponding figure for meat, fish and poultry is frequently in the region of 60–65 per cent. Similarly, the gross profit on spirits is generally in excess of 75 per cent, whilst, at the same time, the gross profit on beers and minerals is usually less than 50 per cent. An example is shown in Table 7.5.

Table 7.5 A sales mix example

	Period 1				Period 2			
	Sales mix		Gross profit		Sales mix		Gross profit	
	%	£	%	£	%	£	%	£
Starters	11.7	35,000	70.0	24,500	10.0	30,000	70.0	21,000
Meat and fish	50.0	150,000	60.0	90,000	60.0	180,000	60.0	108,000
Vegetables	15.0	45,000	70.0	31,500	13.3	40,000	70.0	28,000
Sweets	13.3	40,000	75.0	30,000	10.0	30,000	75.0	22,500
Teas and coffees	10.0	30,000	80.0	24,000	6.7	20,000	80.0	16,000
	100.0	300,000	66.7	200,000	100.0	300,000	65.2	195,500

The overall volume of food sales and the percentage gross profit margins on the various elements of the sales mix are exactly the same during both periods. What has changed from period 1 to period 2 is the sales mix – with the result that in period 2 we have a lower overall percentage gross profit and a lower cash gross profit.

AVERAGE SPENDING POWER (ASP)

This is also referred to as 'average spend', and is calculated by dividing total food and/or beverage sales by number of covers, as illustrated below.

$$\frac{\text{F\&B sales } £20,000}{\text{No. of covers } 1,000} = £20.00 \text{ (ASP)}$$

ASP figures, because of their direct effect on sales volumes, have a strong impact on profitability, and therefore need to be monitored closely. Also, separate ASP figures should be calculated for all the different sales outlets operated by the establishment. An example illustrating the importance of ASP figures is shown in Table 7.6.

Table 7.6 An example of ASP

	Month 1	Month 2	Month 3
No. of covers	2,500	2,500	2,500
	£	£	£
ASP Food	15.00	15.75	16.54
ASP Beverage	5.00	5.25	5.51
ASP Total	20.00	21.00	22.05
F&B Sales	50,000	52,500	55,125
F&B Gross profit (60%)	30,000	31,500	33,075
Operating expenses	25,000	25,000	25,000
Net profit (£)	5,000	6,500	8,075
Net profit (%)	10.0	12.4	14.6

In the example in Table 7.6 all the figures are unchanged over the three months – with the exception of the ASP figures. These increase by 5 per cent in month 2 and then again by the same percentage in month 3, with the result that the net profit of the establishment shows a very significant improvement. Indeed the net profit for month 3 as a percentage of the original profit in month 1 is 161.5 per cent. The impact of ASP figures on profitability is not sufficiently recognised, and it is probably true to say that generally, throughout the hotel and catering industry, insufficient attention is paid to this powerful determinant of profitability.

NUMBER OF COVERS

The number of covers (NOC) is an important tool for measuring operating performance in hotels and restaurants. It is for this reason that detailed NOC figures are commonly maintained for budgeting, control and other purposes. This may be seen from the practical budgeting examples given in Chapter 6.

SEAT TURNOVER

'Seat turnover' is a measure of restaurant occupancy; it relates the number of covers to the seating capacity of the restaurant. Where seating capacity is 100 and we achieve 150 covers, seat turnover is:

$$\frac{\text{No. of covers } 150}{\text{Seating capacity } 100} = 1.5$$

This result means that on average each seat in the restaurant was sold 1.5 times during that particular day. The higher the seat turnover, the greater the degree to which we exploit the fixed facilities (space, furniture, equipment, atmosphere, etc.) of the establishment.

Where a restaurant opens for so many hours for lunch and then for dinner, seat turnover should be calculated separately for each service, as the combined or averaged daily figures may be misleading. Let us look at an example:

Seating capacity: 100
Service: twice a day – lunch and dinner
No. of covers: lunch 70; dinner 150

The average daily seat turnover is:

$$\frac{\text{No. of covers } 220}{\text{Seating capacity } (100+100)\ 200} = 1.1$$

The calculation of separate seat turnover figures for lunch and dinner would disclose a considerable difference between lunch (0.7) and dinner (1.5). Where there are several sales outlets, separate seat turnover figures should be calculated for each one.

SALES PER WAITER

This is simply food and beverage sales divided by the number of waiting staff. Where part-time staff are employed, two part-timers are generally regarded as equivalent to one full-time member of staff. The formula here is:

$$\frac{\text{F\&B sales } £25,000}{\text{No. of waiters } 20} = £1,250$$

Sales per waiter statistics are frequently used as a measure of productivity: the higher this particular ratio, the greater the productivity of the waiting staff. Many hotels and restaurants, particularly those in the USA, calculate 'sales per waiter' figures routinely on a weekly basis, in order to assess the performance of the individual members of the waiting staff. Where there is underachievement in terms of the sales effort – and thus significantly below-average results – the waiting staff are encouraged to 'sell' more starters, desserts and beverages.

A word of warning is necessary at this stage. High sales per waiter figures are not necessarily an unqualified blessing, as sometimes they are the result of a poor adjustment of the number of waiting staff to the number of covers. Where too few waiters are employed there is usually insufficient time to 'sell' starters, desserts and beverages – with the result that high sales per waiter figures are secured at the expense of below-average ASP figures. The saving of labour costs, due to fewer waiters being employed, is usually more than offset by losses in terms of customers' spending power.

Table 7.7 Waiters' sales analysis

	Adam		Sam		Paul	
	£	%	£	%	£	%
Starters	160	7.3	190	8.3	130	6.5
Main dishes	850	38.6	820	35.6	810	40.5
Vegetables	180	8.2	170	7.4	160	8.0
Desserts	210	9.5	250	10.9	170	8.5
Teas & coffees	150	6.8	160	6.9	140	7.0
Wines & spirits	650	29.6	710	30.9	590	29.5
Weekly total	2,200	100.0	2,300	100.0	2,000	100.0
No. of covers	120		118		114	
Waiter ASP	£18.33		£19.49		£17.54	

Table 7.7 shows a 'waiters' sales analysis' designed to provide an assessment of the individual sales effort of each member of the waiting staff. From this analysis we can see that Sam achieved not only the highest volume of food and beverage sales but also the most favourable sales mix. He has sold a high percentage of starters, desserts and beverage, and these are the elements which tend to attract an above-average percentage of gross profit. He clearly makes the effort to sell, and this has resulted in the highest ASP of £19.49, which is 11.1 per cent higher than that achieved by Paul. Readers should note that in many practical situations the differences in individual waiter ASPs are frequently considerably bigger than in the above example.

In the second example, shown in Table 7.8, we illustrate a fairly typical situation in which the number of waiting staff employed is not sufficiently adjusted to the weekly pattern of business.

If we look at the 'Covers per waiter' column, we will see that the average waiter was expected to serve exactly twice the number of customers on Saturday as he did on Monday. The steady rise, over the working week, in

Table 7.8 Waiters' sales analysis (b)

	F & B sales	No. of covers	No. of waiters	Covers per waiter	ASP	Sales per waiter
	£				£	£
Mon	700	113	4	28	6.19	175.00
Tues	750	120	4	30	6.25	187.50
Wed	800	130	4	33	6.15	200.00
Thurs	820	132	4	33	6.21	205.00
Fri	900	149	4	37	6.04	225.00
Sat	1,300	224	6	56	5.80	216.00
Sun	1,400	248	6	41	5.64	233.33
	6,670	1,116	32	35	5.98	208.44

the 'Covers per waiter' figures is accompanied by a downward trend in the ASP. When waiters are too busy, the sale of starters, desserts, teas, coffees, wines and spirits tends to suffer – and so does the general level of service.

In the last column we show the 'Sales per waiter' figures. These rise throughout the week. Whilst this in itself is welcome, we must realise that this is achieved at the expense of ASP figures, which show a substantial decrease towards the end of the week.

SALES PER EMPLOYEE

This is a similar concept to that of 'sales per waiter/ess', except that here total food and beverage sales are divided by the total of all employees. This is a useful measure of operating efficiency, and is particularly valuable in hotel and restaurant chains.

SALES PER OPENING HOUR

The inflow of sales revenue per opening hour is an important control concept used in many types of business – both in the hotel and catering industry and elsewhere. It is useful *per se* as an indicator of the level of activity. It is also valuable as a determinant of the establishment's opening hours. Where the volume of food and beverage sales is subject to pronounced fluctuations, sales per opening hour plus the relevant variable cost levels will indicate the times during which the business operates profitability as well as those when revenue inflows are insufficient to cover the resulting variable costs.

SALES PER AVAILABLE SEAT

An important operating characteristic of hotels and restaurants is their fixed capacity, and this includes all restaurants, various eating and drinking areas, banqueting rooms, etc. 'Sales per available seat' is an indicator of the degree of exploitation of such fixed capacity. In larger hotels it is a useful measure of the relative contribution of each sales outlet to total food and beverage sales. It is therefore a useful yardstick for the allocation of floor space to the various sales outlets operated by the hotel.

Profit Concepts

In this section we examine the most common concepts of profit and take the opportunity to suggest which profit concepts are relevant in particular situations.

GROSS PROFIT

Gross profit has always been regarded as a most important measure of operating efficiency in hotels and restaurants. Traditionally, however, caterers have tended to place too much emphasis on the percentage of gross profit and rather underestimated the importance of cash gross profit. As explained in Chapter 11, we cannot pay wages or expenses with percentages. Ultimately, whatever the percentage of gross profit, the important thing is cash gross profit. In the example which follows, it is clear that week 3 – although it produced the lowest percentage of gross profit – was the most profitable week.

	Week 1	Week 2	Week 3
	£	£	£
F&B sales	50,000	60,000	70,000
Less cost of sales	19,000	24,000	29,400
Cash gross profit	31,000	36,000	40,600
Percentage gross profit	62.0%	60.0%	58.0%

We are not advocating here a complete abandonment of percentages. In all kinds of control work in food and beverage operations percentages are useful in indicating what results should be achieved and, subsequently, pointing to deviations from planned results. When, however, we deal with profitability and have to assess the adequacy of profits, cash gross profit is invariably a more meaningful indicator than the gross profit percentage.

DEPARTMENTAL PROFIT

Departmental profit is a concept of profit we use in hotels. It may be defined as sales less: (a) cost of sales (if any); (b) departmental payroll and (c) departmental controllable expenses. A full example illustrating the concept of food and beverage departmental profit is shown in Table 7.9.

It should be noticed that in the example in Table 7.9 we regard food and beverage as one department, and therefore show one figure for food and beverage departmental profit. Some hotels regard food and beverage as

Table 7.9 An example of departmental profit

Kandy Hotel Food and Beverage Department		
	£	%
Food sales	850,000	68.0
Beverage sales	400,000	32.0
Total	1,250,000	100.0
Food cost	297,500	35.0
Beverage cost	120,000	30.0
Cost of sales	417,500	33.4
GP Food	552,500	65.0
GP Beverage	280,000	70.0
GP Total	832,500	66.6
Wages & salaries	412,500	33.0
Employee benefits	87,500	7.0
Total	500,000	40.0
Laundry & cleaning	17,500	1.4
China, glassware & linen	20,000	1.6
Contract cleaning	6,250	0.5
Other dept. expenses	81,250	6.5
Total	125,000	10.0
Departmental profit	207,500	16.6

two separate departments. In such cases, of course, it is necessary to separate all the wages, salaries, employee benefits, laundry and cleaning, etc., before we can arrive at the separate figures of departmental profits for food and for beverage operations.

NET PROFIT

Net profit may be defined as total sales less total expenses. Hence,

$$\text{total sales} - \text{total expenses} = \text{net profit}$$

In the case of restaurants we may also define net profit as total gross profit (plus any other income) less operating expenses. Hence,

$$\text{total gross profit} - \text{operating expenses} = \text{net profit}$$

In the case of hotels we use the concept of departmental profit. If we add all the departmental profits of the revenue-producing departments and deduct the operating expenses, we will arrive at the net profit of the hotel. Hence,

$$\text{total departmental profits} - \text{operating expenses} = \text{net profit}$$

The concept of net profit in relation to a restaurant is illustrated in the profit and loss account of the Richmond Restaurant, shown earlier in this chapter (page 117). The total gross profit of £318,000, less operating expenses of £260,500, gives the restaurant's net profit of £57,500.

Table 7.10 A hotel profit and loss account

Department	Net sales	Cost of sales	Payroll rel. exp.	Other exp.	Dept profit
	£000	£000	£000	£000	£000
Rooms	2,770	—	490	180	2,100
F&B	2,610	930	1,040	280	360
MOD	320	110	70	30	110
Total	5,700	1,040	1,600	490	2,570
Less undistributed operating expenses:					
Administrative & general				480	
Marketing				220	
Guest entertainment				50	
Energy costs				220	
Property operation & maintenance				100	
Fixed charges				650	1,720
Net profit					850

In Table 7.10 we show a specimen example of a hotel profit and loss account. As may be seen, we arrive at the net profit of the hotel in two stages. The first step is to arrive (in the upper section of the profit and loss account) at the departmental profit of each revenue-producing department. The next step is to deduct from the total of departmental profits (£2,570,000) all the operating expenses (£1,720,000), and thus arrive at the net profit of the hotel.

Gross Profit per Cover

This may be defined as total cash gross profit divided by the number of covers. This particular concept emphasises the importance of earning the best profit in relation to each customer. As already discussed earlier in this chapter, the performance of the waiting staff is considerably influenced by their ability to sell starters, desserts, wines and spirits. The greater the effort they make in this direction, the higher the 'sales per waiter figures', the higher the relevant ASP figures and the higher the gross profit per cover. It should be noted that ultimately – as we are in business to earn a profit – cash gross profit per cover is more important than the corresponding sales per waiter and ASP figures. It should also be noted that cash gross profit per cover figures are particularly important during slack periods, when the number of customers is limited and the waiting staff have ample opportunity to 'sell'.

Gross Profit per Waiter

Gross profit per waiter may be defined as total cash gross profit divided by the number of waiting staff employed. This is an important indicator of operating efficiency, and should be monitored carefully from one period to another. Earlier in this chapter we discussed the concept of 'sales per waiter', and readers will appreciate that as our ultimate objective is profitability, gross profit per waiter is the more critical indicator.

Gross Profit per Employee

This is a similar concept to that of gross profit per waiter, except that here it is a measure of the operating efficiency of the establishment as a whole. Gross profit per employee figures are frequently used for assessing the relative performance of individual establishments within a group of restaurants.

GROSS PROFIT PER AVAILABLE SEAT

This is defined as total cash gross profit divided by the seating capacity of the establishment. When using this particular profit concept, we recognise that the seating capacity of the establishment is fixed, but also costly, and that therefore each available seat should make a fair contribution to overall profitability. Where a hotel operates a number of sales outlets, cash gross profit per available seat will be seen as an important guide to periodic re-allocations of space as between the various sales outlets. The higher this ratio, the stronger the claim of the sales outlet concerned for a more generous allocation of space.

CONTRIBUTION

We now come to our last concept of profit, that of 'contribution'. This may be defined as sales less variable cost. It is frequently expressed as a percentage and then described as a P/V (profit to volume) ratio.

Let us assume that the ASP of a restaurant is £20.00 and that the food and beverage cost per cover is £7.00. The gross profit per cover will therefore be:

	£	%
ASP	20.00	100.0
Less F & B Cost	7.00	35.0
Gross profit	13.00	65.0

In addition to food and beverage costs there are always other variable costs, such as energy, laundry and linen, etc. Let us assume that these, on a per cover basis, amount to £0.50. The contribution per cover will therefore be as follows:

	£	%
ASP	20.00	100.0
Less variable cost	7.50	37.5
Contribution	12.50	62.5

The concept of contribution is very useful in the context of food and beverage operations because it facilitates all kinds of calculations and projections and, above all, helps in management decisions. Let us look at the following example.

EXAMPLE

A hotel has several rooms within its banqueting department, but only one large room capable of accommodating functions for up to 100 persons. Two clients have approached the hotel, and your task now is to decide which function should be accepted.

Function 1: This is a banquet for 100 persons. The menu would cost the client £17.00 per cover and the relevant food cost would amount to £6.00. Beverage sales are estimated at £4.00 per cover, with a beverage cost of £1.50 per cover. Additional staff required would be: 10 waiters @ £10.00 each. Finally, floral decorations would cost £25.00.

Function 2: This is a smaller banquet for 80 persons. The client would choose a menu for £22.00 per cover, and the relevant food cost would amount to £8.00 per cover. Beverage sales are estimated at £7.00 per person with a beverage cost of £2.50 per cover. Additional waiting staff would be 9 waiters @ £10.00 each. There would be no need for floral decorations.

In all short-term decisions of this nature, the decision-maker should have regard to three elements:

1   The additional sales revenue.
2   The additional variable cost and the resulting contribution.
3   The fact that, in the short term, fixed costs will remain fixed. They should therefore be kept in the background.

Quite clearly, whether we choose one function or another, the fixed costs (cost of space, management salaries, depreciation of equipment, etc.) will not in any way be affected. The decision should be made by reference to the contribution that would be earned from each function. The calculations shown in Table 7.11 overleaf make it clear that we should accept function 2 as it would produce a better contribution than function 1.

THE BREAK-EVEN POINT

An important application of the concept of contribution is in the calculation of the break-even point. The break-even point is a situation in which total cost is equal to total sales revenue – when, of course, there is no profit or loss. The example at the bottom of page 134 will make this clear.

Table 7.11 A contribution comparison

Function 1	£
Food sales: 100 covers @ £17.00	1,700.00
Beverage sales: 100 covers @ £4.00	400.00
Total sales	2,100.00
Variable costs:	
Food cost: 100 covers @ £6.00	600.00
Beverage cost: 100 covers @ £1.50	150.00
Additional staff: 10 waiters @ £10.00	100.00
Floral decorations	25.00
Total variable cost	875.00
Hence, contribution	1,225.00

Function 2	£
Food sales: 80 covers @ £22.00	1,760.00
Beverage sales: 80 covers @ £7.00	560.00
Total sales	2,320.00
Variable costs:	
Food cost: 80 covers @ £8.00	640.00
Beverage cost: 80 covers @ £2.50	200.00
Additional staff: 9 waiters @ £10.00	90.00
Total variable cost	930.00
Hence, contribution	1,390.00

EXAMPLE

A restaurant has fixed costs of £9,000 per month. Its ASP is £10.00 and variable costs amount to 25 per cent of sales revenue. The monthly number of covers varies from 800 to 1,400. We may express this information in tabular form as follows:

No. of covers	Sales	Fixed costs	Variable costs	Contribution	Profit (loss)
	£	£	£	£	£
800	8,000	9,000	2,000	6,000	(3,000)
1,000	10,000	9,000	2,500	7,500	(1,500)
1,200	12,000	9,000	3,000	9,000	—
1,400	14,000	9,000	3,500	10,500	1,500

From this table we see that the break-even point is reached when the restaurant serves 1,200 covers. This ensures equality between total sales revenue (£12,000) and total cost (£9,000 + £3,000 = £12,000).

Also, it should be noticed, the break-even point is reached when contribution is equal to fixed costs. Any excess of contribution over fixed costs is net profit; conversely, any excess of fixed costs over contribution is net loss. The formula for the calculation of the break-even point is given below.

$$\frac{\text{Fixed costs}}{\text{Contribution per unit}} = \text{BEP}$$

Hence, in relation to the table above,

$$\frac{£9,000}{£7.50} = 1,200 \text{ (covers)}$$

The 'unit' in the above formula means one cover or customer. In other situations it may mean something different, for example an occupied room or £1.00 of sales revenue.

Finally it should be noticed that the restaurant operates at a P/V ratio of 75 per cent, as shown below.

	£	%
ASP	10.00	100
Less variable cost	2.50	25
Contribution and P/V ratio	7.50	75

The higher the P/V ratio the more profitable each addition to the sales revenue. In this particular case – after the restaurant has reached its break-even point – 75 per cent of each addition to total sales goes into net profit.

BREAK-EVEN CHARTS

The technique of break-even analysis is relatively simple, but has numerous applications within the general field of food and beverage operations. It presumes an understanding of cost behaviour (dynamics of fixed, variable and semi-fixed costs), and a knowledge of the concept of contribution. Two examples are given below as well as the necessary explanations and comments.

EXAMPLE 1: RESTAURANT

The Pot Pourri Restaurant incurs fixed costs at the rate of £30,000 per month. During October 1995, the restaurant served 3,000 covers and achieved an ASP of £20.00. Variable costs were equal to 25 per cent of the sales volume. The break-even chart would be prepared as shown in Figure 7.1.

The break-even chart is prepared as follows. The first step is to plan the axes to ensure that the break-even chart will accommodate all the relevant data. The restaurant's sales in October were (3,000 × £20.00) £60,000. The vertical axis was drawn accordingly. The horizontal axis was also drawn to allow it to accommodate 3,000 covers.

The fixed costs of the restaurant are represented by a straight line, parallel to the horizontal axis; whatever the number of covers, the fixed costs remain unchanged. Variable costs are then placed on top of the

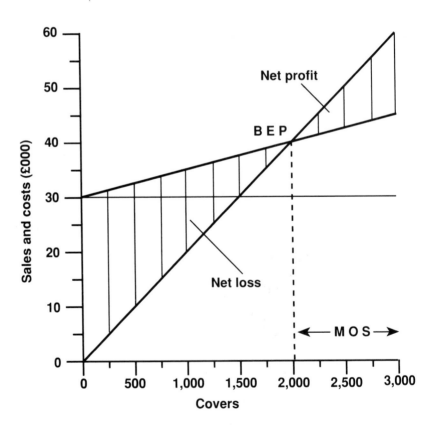

Figure 7.1 Restaurant break-even chart

fixed costs to give the total cost line. Finally we draw the sales line – from the point of origin – and this gives an intersection of the total cost and sales lines, denoting the break-even point. It is at this point that there is no profit or loss. Some calculations are shown below.

Contribution and P/V Ratio

	£	%
Sales	60,000	100.0
Less variable cost	15,000	25.0
Contribution and P/V ratio	45,000	75.0

On a 'per cover' basis, the results are:

	£	%
Sales	20.00	100.0
Less variable cost	5.00	25.0
Contribution and P/V ratio	15.00	75.0

We may now calculate the break-even point, using the formula with which we are already familiar.

Break-even Point

$$\frac{\text{Fixed cost } £30,000}{\text{Contribution/cover } £15} = 2,000 \text{ (covers)}$$

The restaurant needs 2,000 covers per month to break even. It is at this level of business that total cost is equal to total sales revenue. Also, it is at this level of business that contribution (75 per cent of £40,000, i.e. £30,000) is equal to fixed costs. Finally, it should be noted that the restaurant has a fairly wide margin of safety (MOS). This is a measure of profit stability: the wider the MOS, the more stable the profits of the business, and vice versa. Where the margin of safety is narrow, a relatively small loss of turnover will convert the net profit into a net loss. In the case of the Pot Pourri Restaurant, quite substantial fluctuations in the sales volume may occur before the restaurant starts incurring losses.

EXAMPLE 2: HOTEL FOOD AND BEVERAGE DEPARTMENT

The following information was extracted from the records of the Excelsior Hotel in respect of the year ended 30 September 1995.

Food and beverage sales	1,200,000
Food and beverage costs	400,000
Payroll fixed	420,000
variable	60,000
Direct expenses fixed	80,000
variable	40,000

In order to prepare a break-even chart for the hotel's food and beverage department (see Figure 7.2), it is first necessary to divide all the departmental costs into fixed and variable.

Departmental fixed costs are as follows:

	£
Payroll	420,000
Direct expenses	80,000
Dept. fixed costs	500,000

Departmental variable costs are as follows:

	£
Food and beverage costs	400,000
Payroll	60,000
Direct expenses	40,000
Dept. variable costs	500,000

The contribution and P/V ratio of the food and beverage department would be calculated as shown below.

	£	%
Food and beverage sales	1,200,000	100.0
Less variable costs	500,000	41.7
Contribution + P/V ratio	700,000	58.3

As we know nothing about the number of covers served, our 'unit' here is £1.00 of food and beverage sales. Out of every £1.00 of our sales we require £0.417 to cover the variable costs, and we are left with a contribution per unit of £0.583. Our break-even point is therefore:

$$\frac{\text{Fixed costs £500,000}}{\text{Contribution/unit £0.583}} = 857,633$$

Hence 857,633 units of £1.00 are required for the food and beverage

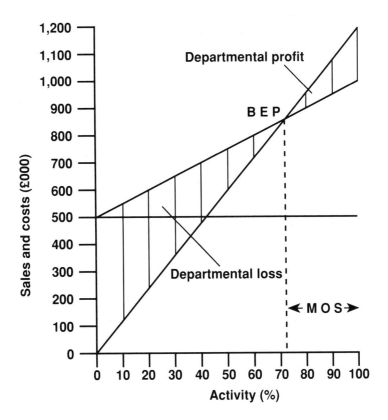

Figure 7.2 Break-even chart for a hotel F & B department

department to break even. As a percentage of the current volume of food and beverage sales, this represents:

$$\frac{£857,633}{£1,200,000} \times 100 = 71.5\%$$

Comments on Break-even Chart

Readers will have noticed that in the break-even chart we show 'departmental profit' and 'departmental loss', rather than 'net profit' and 'net loss'. The reason for this is as follows. Our break-even chart shows only departmental controllable expenses. It excludes fixed costs such as general administration, marketing, depreciation of premises, etc. Such costs are difficult to apportion and are, therefore, usually excluded from departmental break-even charts.

Secondly, we show that our break-even point is £857,633 of food and beverage sales. This is only true if the sales mix of the food and beverage department remains unchanged. Over a period of months quite significant changes in the sales mix may occur. Between October and April the hotel is likely to do considerably more banqueting work than otherwise. Where a hotel operates several restaurants, their popularity may well change quite appreciably over a period of time. All such changes will influence the break-even point to some extent. When there is more emphasis on the sale of high gross profit items the break-even point may be nearer £845,000. With less favourable sales mix the break-even point may well be nearer £870,000.

Productivity in Food and Beverage Operations

Productivity is a matter which has engaged the attention of senior managers in the hotel and catering industry for many years. Whilst we all agree that high levels of productivity are desirable, we realise that its measurement presents a number of intractable problems.

Let us start with a definition. Productivity is a measure of the relationship between the output of goods/services and the input of the relevant resources. It may thus be defined in terms of a simple formula:

$$\frac{\text{Output}}{\text{Input}} = \text{Productivity}$$

In the hotel and catering industry – both in Europe and elsewhere – we understand productivity as 'labour productivity', simply because the cost of labour is high and tends to rise over a period of time.

High labour productivity is important for several reasons. As far as the national economy is concerned, high productivity leads to high wages and contributes to higher living standards. This is quite evident from variations in productivity throughout the world. With regard to the individual hotel or restaurant, productivity is equally important. High labour productivity is associated with efficient and profitable operations; conversely, low productivity invariably leads to poor results in terms of bottom-line considerations.

SOME MEASUREMENT PROBLEMS

In the case of food and beverage operations the measurement of productivity poses several problems. Such problems are, however, present in all service industries, where the 'product' sold is to some extent intangible. Thus if we measure the productivity of the waiting staff in terms of 'covers per waiter', we immediately realise that:

1 It does not measure the quality of service. Waiter B may serve the same number of covers as waiter A but offer a more professional and friendly service, which is likely to lead to more repeat business.
2 It does not measure the revenue generated by the covers actually served. The waiter who sells more starters, desserts and beverages will generate more sales revenue than one who serves the same number of covers but makes no effort to sell.
3 This indicator of productivity does not measure the cash gross profit from the covers served.

EXAMPLE

A restaurant employs four waiters. Given below is a schedule setting out their typical weekly performance.

Waiter	Hours worked	Covers served	F&B sales £	Gross profit %	Gross profit £
Andy	40	115	2,875	64	1,840
Bill	42	127	2,794	59	1,648
Charles	42	114	3,078	65	2,000
David	40	110	2,530	62	1,569

You are required:

1 To calculate:

    (a)   The productivity index;
    (b)   F&B sales per hour;
    (c)   £ Gross profit per hour;
    (d)   Waiter ASP;
    (e)   £ Gross profit per cover.

2 To rank the waiters in terms of their relative performance.

The solution is given overleaf.

Waiter	Productivity index*	F&B sales per hour	£ GP per hour	Waiter ASP	£ GP per cover
		£	£	£	£
Andy	2.9	71.88	46.00	25.00	16.00
Bill	3.0	66.52	39.24	22.00	12.98
Charles	2.7	73.29	47.62	27.00	17.54
David	2.8	63.25	39.23	23.00	14.26

*Obtained by dividing covers served by hours worked

From the above table it is clear that whilst the highest productivity index is achieved by Bill, all the other indicators suggest that it is Charles who performs best. Bill has the lowest ASP, which would imply that he is not making the effort to sell items other than the main course. His low ASP also results in the lowest cash gross profit per cover.

QUESTIONS

1 How important in your opinion is profitability in the context of the food and beverage manager's responsibilities?

2 Explain what you understand by the elements of cost.

3 The figures given below were extracted from the records of the Tamarisk Restaurant at 31 December 1995.

Food sales	423,000	Gas & Electricity	19,200
Beverage sales	167,000	Laundry & Cleaning	13,300
Food cost	151,600	Marketing	16,900
Beverage cost	67,000	Office expenses	28,800
Wages and salaries	29,000	Employee meals	10,100
Depreciation	23,500	Employee benefits	4,500
Repairs & Maintenance	22,400		

(a) You are required to:
  (i) calculate the restaurant's elements of cost;
  (ii) express each element of cost as a percentage of sales;
  (iii) calculate the restaurant's net profit.
(b) You are informed that during 1995, the restaurant served 32,765 covers, and asked to calculate:
  (i) the average spending power;
  (ii) cash gross profit per cover.

4   Explain what is meant by:

    (a) fixed cost;
    (b) variable cost;
    (c) semi-fixed cost.

5   Explain what you understand by 'sales mix' and give three examples of assumed sales mix figures from different types of food and beverage operation.

6   The information in Table 7.12 was made available by a restaurant at the end of the first quarter of 1995.

You have been asked to comment on the performance of the restaurant in terms of:

    (a) food and beverage sales;
    (b) cash gross profit;
    (c) % gross profit;
    (d) number of covers;
    (e) ASP;
    (f) cash gross profit per cover.

State which month you regard as the most successful, giving your reasons.

Table 7.12 Restaurant profitability

	Month 1	Month 2	Month 3
	£	£	£
Food sales	80,000	88,000	84,000
Beverage sales	34,000	37,000	35,000
Total sales	114,000	125,000	119,000
Food gross profit	48,000	54,500	53,000
Bev. gross profit	22,000	23,000	21,500
Total gross profit	70,000	77,500	74,500
	%	%	%
% GP Food	60.0	61.9	63.1
% GP Beverage	64.7	62.2	61.4
% GP Total	61.4	62.0	62.6
No. of covers	4,950	5,600	5,250
	£	£	£
Cash GP per cover	14.14	13.84	14.19
ASP	23.03	22.32	22.67

7 The information given in Table 7.13 was extracted from the record of Weggis Restaurant. Complete the table and explain, with reasons, which was the most profitable week.

Table 7.13 Restaurant profitability

	Week 1	Week 2	Week 3
Sales	£	£	£
Food	4,000	4,400	4,200
Beverage	1,700	1,850	1,750
Total	5,700	6,250	5,950
Sales Mix	%	%	%
Food	....	....	....
Beverage	....	....	....
Total	....	....	....
Cost of sales	£	£	£
Food	1,600	1,675	1,550
Beverage	600	700	675
Total	2,200	2,375	2,225
Cash gross profit	£	£	£
Food	....	....	....
Beverage	....	....	....
Total	....	....	....
% Gross profit	%	%	%
Food	....	....	....
Beverage	....	....	....
Total	....	....	....

8 Explain what you understand by 'productivity' in the context of food and beverage operations. How can we measure the productivity of food and beverage personnel?

9   The information given in Table 7.14 was extracted from the records of Hertenstein Restaurant at the end of week 8 of 1995.

You are required to:

(a)   complete the table;
(b)   explain the significance of the figures you have calculated.

Table 7.14

	Tue	Wed	Thu	Fri	Sat	Sun
Opening hrs	12–15	12–15	12–15	12–15	12–15	12–15
	18–23	18–23	18–23	18–23	18–24	18–24
Seat capacity	150	150	150	150	150	150
No. of waiters	4	4	4	5	6	6
Sales:	£	£	£	£	£	£
Food	480	740	900	1,750	1,800	1,100
Bev.	360	550	680	1,050	1,450	820
Total	840	1,290	1,780	2,800	3,250	1,920
No. of covers	40	60	75	115	150	90
ASP	....	....	....	....	....	....
Sales/seat	....	....	....	....	....	....
Sales/Op. hr	....	....	....	....	....	....
Seat turnover	....	....	....	....	....	....
Sales/waiter	....	....	....	....	....	....

10   The Old Bridge Restaurant averages 2,500 covers per month. The average spending power is £8.00, and variable costs are equal to 40 per cent of the sales revenue. Fixed costs are incurred at the rate of £10,000 per month.

You are required to:

(a)   prepare the restaurant's break-even chart;
(b)   calculate the margin of safety;
(c)   calculate the break-even point.

11 Table 7.15 summarises the operating results of the London Restaurant for March 1995.

In April there will be no change in the operating costs or the number of covers, but there will be a 10 per cent increase in menu prices.

You are required to:

(a) prepare a break-even chart for March, which additionally shows the effect of the increased prices in April;

(b) calculate for both months the break-even point, margin of safety as well as the percentage increase in net profit from March to April.

Table 7.15 Results – March 1995

NOC		1,000
ASP		£15.00
Sales		£15,000
Less variable costs:		
F&B costs	£6,000	
Other costs	1,000	7,000
Contribution		8,000
Less fixed costs:		
Labour	£4,000	
Other costs	2,000	6,000
Net profit		£2,000

12 Explain the meaning and significance of the following:

(a) sales turnover;
(b) sales per waiter;
(c) sales per employee;
(d) sales per opening hour;
(e) sales per available seat.

13 Explain how important you regard the following concepts of cash gross profit:

(a) per cover;
(b) per waiter;
(c) per employee;
(d) per available seat.

14 In what circumstances would you use the concept of cash gross profit in preference to that of percentage gross profit?

Table 7.16 Profit and loss account

Department	Net sales		Cost of sales		Gross profit	
	£	%	£	%	£	%
Food						
	480,000	66.7	144,000	30.0	336,000	70.0
	240,000	33.3	108,000	45.0	132,000	55.0
	720,000	100.0	252,000	35.0	468,000	65.0
Less operating expenses:						
Payroll and related expenses			160,000			
Administration and general			43,200			
Gas and electricity			9,200			
Advertising and sales promotion			10,000			
Repairs and maintenance			10,000			
Rent and rates			80,000			
Depreciation			32,000		344,400	47.8
Net profit					123,600	17.2

15   Table 7.16 gives the profit and loss account of the Arusha City Restaurant in respect of the year ended 30 June 1995.

You are required to:

(a)   prepare the restaurant's break-even chart;
(b)   calculate the P/V ratio, the precise break-even point, margin of safety and contribution per cover.

You are informed that:

(a)   the 'operating expenses' of the restaurant are fixed, with the exception of 'payroll and related expenses' of which £140,000 should be regarded as the fixed element and the balance of £20,000 as fully variable;
(b)   the restaurant served 40,000 covers during the year to 30 June 1995.

CHAPTER 8

FOOD PRODUCTION OPERATIONS

Chefs and Kitchens

The executive chef or the *Maître chef de cuisine* of a hotel has an important position in the organisation, certainly a very special position within the food and beverage department. Nowhere else in a hotel is the opportunity for creativity, imagination and self-expression greater than in the kitchens, particularly if the hotel still holds to the traditions of *haute cuisine* first founded and built upon many years ago by the great French chefs such as Brillat, Savarin and Escoffier. It is upon the skill of the head chef that much of a hotel's reputation rests, and whilst their skill is now much aided by technological advances in food processing and production, at the final reckoning it is the chef's skill and imagination that determine whether good food, imaginatively served, comes from their kitchen. Cooking in a hotel today is a combination of artistic ability, practical skills and technical knowledge. If wages are any measure of the importance of a profession, there should not be any doubts as to the importance of the chef. Most chefs receive a wage and institutional benefits that rank second only to those of the general manager.

From purchasing through to service stage, the chef's role is always vital in ensuring a good food product. They act like a consultant during the initial four stages of the food production process – purchasing, receiving, storing and issuing. The food production process is as shown in Figure 8.1.

Chefs should be considered an exception to the general rule of the high labour turnover of hotel executives. The present executive chef at the Ritz is the eighth person to hold that position since 1906. This indicates that executive chefs remain at the Ritz for an average of eleven years. This is a remarkable length of service in comparison to the general pattern of mobility in the industry.

It is essential that modern-day chefs are good administrators. The chef de cuisine in the large establishment is much more a departmental manager than a working craftsman. They will be selected for the position and will

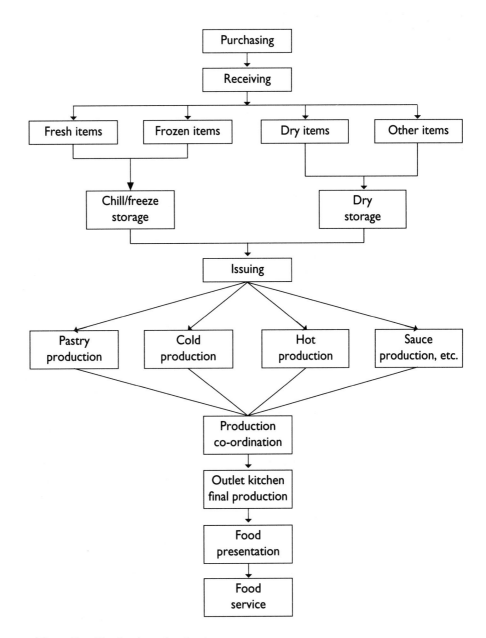

Figure 8.1 The food production process

retain it more for organising and executive abilities than for their
culinary skills, though it is obvious that they should have such skills and a
good appreciation of fine cookery as a part of their background.
Nevertheless, their principal function is to plan, organise and
superintend the work of the kitchens. The fundamental functions of

management which have to be undertaken by the chef de cuisine as a departmental manager may be summarised as follows:

1 **Planning**
They must determine the course of action in a given set of circumstances.

2 **Organising and co-ordination**
They must allocate work amongst the various parties and sections. At the same time they must establish and foster sound working relationships in the midst of satisfactory working conditions. They should also co-ordinate with other departments and win their support.

3 **Motivating**
Encouraging the working groups to achieve the objectives required by the plan is also a function of the chef de cuisine. They must give leadership, inspiration, direction and example to the chefs de partie and their teams.

4 **Controlling**
What is achieved or produced must be evaluated against the requirement of the plan. In controlling, the chef de cuisine will be taking such corrective steps as are necessary to ensure that the result will be as planned.

One of the most respected chefs in the United Kingdom explained his functions in the kitchen:

> On a normal day, first thing I do at work is to go round and shake hands with every member of my staff. At 10.00 a.m. I meet my sous chefs in the private dining room adjoining my office. We discuss the events of the previous day, plan for the day ahead, and other kitchen matters. The bulk of my administrative work is attended to by me then; and I normally delegate most office work to my secretary. This enables me to spend time in the kitchen cooking and supervising the work for about four or five hours a day. I work in the kitchens until every guest in the restaurants and special banqueting functions have consumed their dinner. I have a brigade of nearly one hundred, including six sous chefs and twelve chefs de partie to prepare a daily average of 1,000 meals. But still I continue to cook.

He is a great believer in experience – he is always happy to help one of his staff find a job elsewhere, and he likes to see them return when they have gained that extra experience. With a staff of about one hundred, there are four applications a day from people wanting to join his kitchens.

Another well-known hotel chef stated:

> Simplicity, precision and perfection are the basis of my art. Take the
> ingredients, cook them to perfection and present them with simplicity. The
> whole secret of successful cooking – more, the very essence of culinary
> perfection – is, or should be, simplicity.

During the interviews with famous chefs, it was felt that they shared
similar views about the quality of staff and team work. All of them
identified 'team work' as an essential component in successful kitchen
operations. Most of the executive chefs met their sous chefs every
morning in a formal meeting, and the entire brigade at least once a
month in a formal meeting, apart from the day-to-day working
relationships

Another reputed chef stated:

> We believe in freshness in all food items, and we don't have any can openers in
> our kitchen. We use deep freezers only to store ice cream. We make our own
> preservatives to be sure of the quality. Just to make that little bit of difference
> we have to really work hard, and pay attention to every minor detail. The
> freshest possible ingredients, cooked for the minimum amount of time, and
> simply but beautifully presented in small portions, is my concept of good food,
> but this demands total dedication and hard work.

Some of the hotels in which we carried out our research use quite a lot of
wines and spirits in their cooking, mainly because the chefs are keen to
continue preparing traditional dishes in the traditional manner. Some
hotels spend as much as £4,000 a month on liquor used in cooking. In
one month alone, one hotel used 475 bottles of wine and 276 other
bottles of liquor for cooking.

Menus

Some hotels feel that menus should not be written in French. A former
banqueting manager of the Savoy said, 'I do not see any logic in writing
the menus in French, when the majority of our guests [in food and
beverage outlets] are English. Often it complicates the operation and
confuses them, as obviously most of them cannot read French'. However,
this issue seems to be complicated with contrasting views of the practising
hoteliers, academics, food critics and other interested parties. Another
comment made was:

> Whether in fact more modest establishments should base their cooking on the
> French tradition and whether their menus should continue to be composed in
> French has been hotly debated within the hotel and catering industry for many

years. Few would dispute, however, that cuisine at the international tourist level is unlikely to relinquish its tradition of menu composing in French in a hurry because this tradition is rooted, not in mere convention, but in the whole art of professional cookery.

Mr Egon Ronay once wrote:

> Never one to avoid sticking his neck out, let me make a suggestion about the language of menus, even if it is bound to cause consternation at catering colleges and among chefs of the old school. I call for breaking the mould of British menus and am in favour of proportional representation of languages. There is no logical reason why menus should be either totally French or completely English. They should be written in such a way that customers understand instantly what every item means. For instance, at the otherwise excellent Indigo Jones in London, I find it ridiculous that, as there are no established names for most dishes, the English Chef and proprietors explain the delicious but non-classical concoctions in French, and yet their clientele is English: it could be done just as well in English.

Kitchen Organisation

Most older hotels are designed in such a manner that supervision and control of the staff often becomes a difficult task. For example in most older hotels the chef has to cope with sections of the kitchen being on two floor levels.

A major variable in hotel kitchen facilities is the extent to which they are centralised. Some hotels have one central kitchen serving all food outlets; in others, separate kitchens serve each restaurant, and there may even be separate kitchens for room service and functions. The scale and diversity of the food operations are usually the main determining factors but much also depends on the operating preferences and philosophies of hotel managements. One central kitchen makes it easier to supervise food production and may also lead to high utilisation of equipment and staff. But where meals are produced for several outlets, it may become more difficult to separate costs of food production attributable to each area of the operation. Kitchen staff specialising in various aspects of the culinary art are shown in Table 8.1.

Nowadays some of the traditional job titles are no longer used. What is more common is grouping the operation and organising the kitchen:

1   according to the main area of activities (some duties are combined for practical reasons);

Table 8.1 Traditional kitchen brigade titles

	Main area	French titles
1	Administration	*Chef de cuisine* (executive chef) *Sous chefs* (executive assistant chefs)
2	Pastry	*Pâtissier* (head pastry cook) and under him/her • *Tourier* (pastrymaker) • *Confisseur* (confectioner) • *Glacier* (ice cream cook) • *Boulanger* (baker)
3	Larder	*Chef garde-manger* (larder cook) and under him/her • *Chef de froid* (cold buffet cook) • *Boucher* (butcher) • *Hors-d'oeuvrier* (hors-d'oeuvre cook) • *Saladier* (salad hand)
4	Sauce	*Chef saucier* (sauce cook)
5	Others	*Chef poissonier* (fish cook) *Chef de nuit* (night cook) *Chef rôtisseur* (roast cook), who may be responsible for *grillardin* (grill cook) *Entremeteur* (vegetable cook) *Chef tournant* (relief cook) Breakfast cook, who may also act as *communard* (staff cook)

2   according to the destination (e.g. coffee shop kitchen or Chinese restaurant kitchen) of the final product;

3   according to the kitchen hierarchy. This means levels of each section or partie (a sectional chef is designated chef de partie) as shown below:

(a)   chef de partie (CP)
(b)   demi (assistant) chef de partie (DCP)
(c)   first commis (senior cook)
(d)   second commis (cook)
(e)   third commis (junior cook)
(f)   apprentice.

In the organisation charts of the modern kitchen, the following are also observed:

1   In large kitchens a 'generalist' second in command is designated executive sous chef.

2 Pastry is kept on a higher level than the chef de partie (in some hotels even at the level of executive sous chef if the pastry chef is very senior).

3 In very large kitchens a 'generalist' third in command is designated sous chef and often the function of chef tourant is combined in this post. This means he/she acts for the chefs de partie during their off days and overlooks their sections with the help of demi chefs de partie. Exception to the rule is the pastry. This is owing to the highly specialised nature of the pastry kitchen operation. In fact, pastry still remains the weakest area of expertise for most executive chefs.

Figure 8.2 shows a typical organisational chart for a modern kitchen with a large operation.

A chef de partie of a restaurant is similar to a production manager of a particular brand and the restaurant manager is similar to a product manager. Only in very large hotels will the executive chef have the luxury of a separate secretary. In most hotels the executive chef uses the food

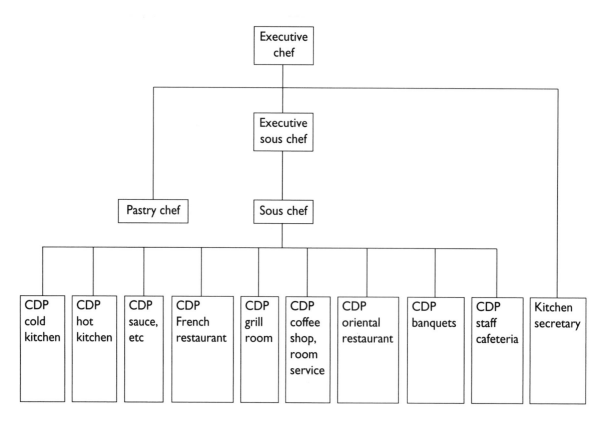

Figure 8.2 The organisation of a large kitchen

and beverages secretary or the banquet secretary or the pool secretary shared by other department heads such as laundry manager and chief security manager.

It is unwise for a small kitchen to have over-specialised jobs. With minimised specialisation kitchen operations become more efficient. This involves parties or sections, each fulfilling clearly defined roles so as to produce high standard dishes, efficiently and expeditiously, to meet demands of both à la carte and table d'hôte guests. In recent years the partie system has undergone many modifications, mostly prompted by labour-saving and technological advances.

With these modifications many of the parties or functions have been amalgamated or have disappeared altogether owing to the development of food processing and bulk food industries (e.g. ice cream, bread, pastry). At the beginning of the century many chefs prepared their own bread, sugar confectionery, jams and preserves, and a wide range of other subsidiary commodities. Escoffier, too, associated himself even more intimately with factory production of food. The fifty-page *A few recipes by Mons. Escoffier of the Carlton Hotel, London* was designed to promote and give guidance on pre-prepared foods. In Escoffier's own words: 'To bring the results of my work within the reach of all I have arranged for the preparation under my personal supervision of a series of soups and sauces in preserved form. Most recipes begin with a phrase such as "empty the contents of the bottle or can into a saucepan".'

Such was Escoffier's realistic attitude towards cookery and food for operations lacking the resources of his own Carlton kitchens. In his hotel work he did not hesitate to recognise the kitchen system and himself made it quite plain in the preface to his principal opus, *A Guide to Modern Cookery*, that he expected that his recipes would soon be out of date and that a new collection would be necessary in a few years.

Changes in technology have an obvious impact on kitchen operations. Generally kitchens have become smaller in staff numbers and size owing to advancement of machinery and equipment.

Operational Links in a Large Hotel

The executive chef in a hotel with large food production activities should have very good communication skills, the ability to co-ordinate, and tact. This is due to the complexity of the total operation and the high dependency of various other departments and sections providing supporting services. It is less complicated to manage a kitchen situated in

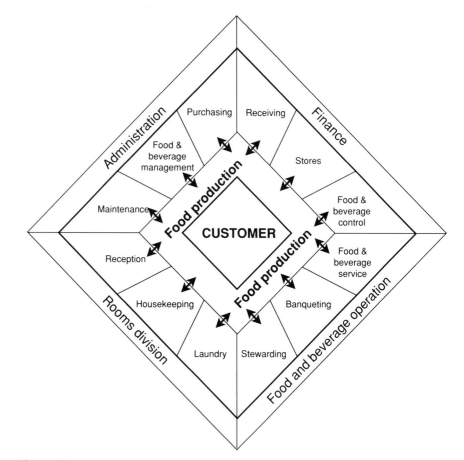

Figure 8.3 Food production – operational links in a large hotel

a small hotel or the kitchen of an individual restaurant, as the executive chef will certainly be dealing with fewer people (with some influence over production of food).

The food and beverage director, as the divisional head, will not usually interfere with the kitchen operation unless there are major problems.

Most food and beverage managers (especially those with little or no kitchen experience) are extra careful in handling the executive chef. Communicating with the other departments through the food and beverage director will be necessary only with regard to policy decisions and major changes or problems. The executive chef will be totally in charge of the day-to-day operation of the whole kitchen department. In some small hotels the executive chef still reports to the general manager and has lateral communication with the food and beverage manager, who will be at the same level in the hotel hierarchy. In our example we have looked at the earlier mentioned type of operation where the executive chef reports to the food and beverage director. In such a hotel with a large food and beverage operation the executive chef and his/her brigade may have to deal with as much as twelve other departments/sections or individuals over whom they will not have any authority. This is explained briefly below:

1 **Purchasing**
Purchasing food items according to the agreed specifications.

2 **Receiving**
Checking the quality, quantity and quoted price.

3 **Stores**
Maintaining the minimum stock levels and ensuring storage at correct temperatures.

4 **Food and beverage controls**
Co-ordinating stocktaking and calculating the food cost on daily basis.

5 **Food and beverage service**
Providing a quick service to the customers ensuring warm and well-presented food as per specifications.

6 **Banqueting**
Co-ordinating with the kitchen with regard to practical menu planning and timely service.

7 **Stewarding**
Issuing kitchen utensils, co-ordinating the service of kitchen equipment, washing the kitchens daily and keeping all kitchen areas clean throughout.

8 **Laundry**
Laundering uniforms.

9 **House-keeping**
Issuing uniforms.

10 **Reception**
Providing guest information such as groups, a number of guests, meal plans to the kitchen.

11 **Maintenance**
Attending to repairs, servicing of equipment and carrying out planned preventive maintenance programmes.

12 **Food and beverage management**
Co-ordinating administration, personnel, budgets and cost
controlling.

Quality in Food Production

'Quality is never an accident, it is always the result of intelligent effort' –
John Ruskin.

'Excellence lies not in doing one thing well but in doing everything
superbly' – Anon.

A relatively new hotel in Park Lane uses the above sayings in their
brochure to focus attention on their high standards. As expressed above,
a lot of effort is needed and attention should be paid to every respect of
an operation to ensure consistently high quality.

Quality cannot be assured in food production in a badly planned
kitchen. The following dimensions are recommended for 'back of house'
service facilities during the preliminary planning stage of a project:

Kitchen for dining room and coffee shop (exclusive of stores)	60 per cent of dining room and coffee shop or $0.9m^2$ to $1.0m^2$ per seat.
Kitchen for coffee shop only	45 per cent of coffee shop or $0.6m^2$ per seat.
Food, liquor and china storage	50 per cent of the kitchen or $0.5m^2$ per seat in dining room and coffee shop; or $0.3m^2$ per seat where coffee shop only.
Kitchen or pantry banquet rooms	20 per cent of banquet facility or $0.24m^2$ per seat
Banquet storage	8 per cent of banquet area or $0.05m^2$ per seat.

Recommended dimensions for service areas are given in Chapter 9.

In the case of food production in hotels, the first step in assuring quality
and high standards is good purchasing. Purchasing may be defined as 'a
function concerned with the search, selection, purchase, receipt, storage
and final use of a commodity in accordance with the catering policy of
the establishment'. The catering policy of most hotels provides guidance

on the quality of food and beverage to be purchased. If purchasing is done efficiently a sound foundation will be laid for producing quality food products at the minimum cost consistent with the policy of the establishment. Most hotels actively use standard purchase specifications describing the quality, size and weight, or count, of food items.

Purchase specifications and other matters pertaining to food are often determined by a committee comprising the food and beverage manager, executive chef, food and beverage controller and purchasing manager. Many chefs spend a considerable amount of time advising those involved in supplier selection, market surveys, quality control at receiving bays and portion size decisions. Since the freshness of the ingredients is seen as a vital aspect of improving and maintaining high quality dishes, many hotels purchase perishables on a daily basis, direct from the producers. At the five-star level, some chefs have rejected the use of frozen, canned and bottled food (with the exception of a few items such as caviar and *foie gras*) in their kitchens.

By and large, food is the most important component of the total hotel operation and it is largely responsible for creating enduringly pleasant memories for many of the guests. A past President of the Hotel, Catering and Institutional Management Association once wrote: 'We all have fond memories of hotels. I remember a marvellous steak I was served at a hotel in the North on the night before I got married; the poached egg on smoked haddock they served for breakfast at a seaside hotel when I was a child, and a superb mushroom soup, home-made at a restaurant outside Carlisle.' Egon Ronay's organisation gives priority to the standards of food when grading and listing the best restaurants of Great Britain and Ireland, and explains the main criteria for evaluation by stating that, 'We only include restaurants where the cookery comes up to our minimum standards, however attractive the place may be in other respects.'

It is also quite normal for a committee comprising the food and beverage manager, assistant food and beverage manager, banqueting manager, food and beverage controller and bar manager to meet once a month to determine a stock policy and all other matters pertaining to the purchase of wines and spirits, stock policy of vintage wines, beverage sales mix, pouring brands of spirits, house wines, and cellarkeeping.

In food production the following basic guidelines will be helpful:

1 Develop a proper attitude towards cooking. Food must be treated creatively in order to bring out its best qualities.
2 Use standard recipes.
3 Use the right techniques and equipment when cooking.

4   Train employees to perform required tasks in each kitchen.
5   Ensure that employees are properly supervised.
6   Maintain production equipment.
7   Schedule food production according to needs.
8   Have a limited variety of dishes on menus.

Most chefs feel that their responsibility does not end at the service counter of the kitchen once the food is picked by service staff. Some chefs pay special attention to buffet set-ups. The following suggestions may be useful in this connection.

The position of the buffet must be selected with care in order to be seen from the entrance of the restaurant, to be within easy reach of the guests, and to be close to the kitchen (if replenishing is regular).

Through its presentation and composition, the buffet must be given an impression of abundance and freshness. Different levels of presentation should be foreseen. Tablecloth and skirting must be perfectly clean. Use of artificial plants or polystyrene props should be avoided. Whenever necessary, lighting can be reinforced with concealed spotlights.

For the display of dishes, local handicrafts such as pottery or basketwork should be used rather than traditional hotel-ware.

Some tips on enhancing the presentation of food are given below:

Fruit juices
Beside classical fruit juices (orange, grapefruit) exotic juices should also be served. They should be presented in carafes or pitchers with an engraved name-tag, in a cooler with crushed ice.

Fresh fruits
Seasonal, exotic, original fruits should be served – some of them pre-cut. The presentation should be backed up by a large basket or cornucopia.

Fruit compotes
Should be presented in large bowls and backed up by large glass jars with mosaics of fruits.

Cereals
Whenever possible, unattractive individual packs should be avoided and preference given to large glass bowls.

Cheese
Should be presented on a wooden board, in earthen terrine for cottage cheese. A presentation of whole cheeses should be made.

Croissants, brioches

Should be displayed in large baskets together with a presentation of large decorative loaves.

Jams, honey

Beside individual glass jar, display of large jars and honeycomb.

Eggs

Whenever possible, a cook should be present in order to prepare egg-orders in front of the guests. Display eggs on straw, in a large basket.

Cold cuts

To be presented on a wooden board – whole products (ham, sausages, etc.) should be displayed.

Chafing dish

Hot preparations should be presented in reduced quantities and replenished as often as necessary in order to avoid overcooking.

Coffees and teas

Should be displayed in linen sacks and wooden boxes. There could be a mosaic of different roasts of coffee on a large tray.

Menu Planning

Menu planning is another important function of an executive chef. To design a menu is not an easy task; menus must suit the style, the elegance and the prestige of the restaurant itself. Each dish is carefully selected, tasted and priced, remembering that to succeed in this highly competitive field one must cater for an immense variety of customers. Some restaurants have made a name just because of one particular dish or a chef's simple speciality. The following must be taken into consideration:

1 Type of customer;
2 Cost;
3 Season and availability;
4 Plant and equipment;
5 Menu balance.

However, a good chef cannot ignore vital factors such as the capabilities of his/her brigade and the business promotion aspect of the menu. Some restaurants are blessed with a kitchen that puts out good food day after day. Some restaurants also have a menu that can be trusted from top to bottom. The chef in such establishments is inventive and creative, and has the talent, background and courage to try new dishes. Gradually he/she develops a menu that is unique and successful.

Kitchen Stewarding

The kitchen stewarding section provides a very useful service to both kitchen and food and beverage service. The main duties of an executive kitchen steward and his/her team will be as follows:

1 Handling stocks of small operating equipment (cutlery, crockery, glassware, kitchen equipment, etc.);
2 Cleaning, washing of all such operating equipment;
3 Washing and cleaning of entire kitchen and 'back of house' areas (of food and beverage department);
4 Co-ordinating the servicing of kitchen equipment with the maintenance department.
5 Planning the requirement lists and purchasing orders for all small operating equipment and helping the food and beverage manager with the budget in this area;
6 Garbage clearance operation from all food and beverage areas;
7 Ordering chemicals, washing liquid, polishing liquids, etc.;
8 Handling polishing and buffing of silverware;
9 Minimising the breakages and losses of all small operating equipment;
10 Kitchen pot-washing operations.

This is often a neglected and underrated area. However, poor attention paid to this section often causes operational delays (e.g. in banquets owing to wet plates, uncleaned teaspoons) which bring down the efficiency of the entire food and beverage department. This may lead to guest dissatisfaction, decrease of sales and a lowering of departmental profits. Some hotel corporations believe that all trainee food and beverage managers should gain a few months' experience in handling kitchen stewarding. An issue of the *Savoy Standard* a few years ago highlighted this: 'For each banquet meal served at the Savoy, there are eleven dirty plates, ten pieces of cutlery and four glasses to be washed up. The averages of ten thousand covers a month in all three rooms meant a mighty big monthly clean up of some two hundred and fifty thousand pieces.' This is a good indication of the size and the importance of kitchen stewarding.

Table 8.2 gives the equipment-cleaning schedule of a 300-room hotel with ten outlets.

Table 8.2 Equipment-cleaning schedule

Equipment	Location	Frequency	Standard time
Main kitchen			
Hood	Hot range	Weekly 10.00 p.m.	$1\frac{1}{2}$ hr
Filters	Hot range	Weekly 11.00 p.m.	1 hr
Ovens	Hot range	Daily 2.30 a.m.	$\frac{1}{2}$ hr
Salamander	Hot range	Daily 2.30 a.m.	$\frac{1}{2}$ hr
Chinese kitchen			
Hood	The fish kitchen	Weekly 10.00 p.m.	1 hr
Filters	The fish kitchen	Weekly 11.00 p.m.	1 hr
Tilting pan	Production	Every time after using	
Soup area			
Hood	Production	Weekly 10.00 a.m.	
			1 hr
Filters	Production	Weekly 11.00 p.m.	1 hr
Steam kettles	Production	Every time after using 8.00 p.m.	$\frac{1}{2}$ hr
Steamer	Production	Every time after using 8.00 p.m.	$\frac{1}{2}$ hr
Oven	Production	Daily 9.00 p.m.	$\frac{1}{2}$ hr
Baking oven	Production	Daily 9.00 p.m.	$\frac{1}{2}$ hr
Cold kitchen			
Espresso machine	Pantry	Daily 1.00 p.m.	$\frac{1}{2}$ hr
Deep freezers	Pantry	Weekly 9.00 a.m.	1 hr
Coffee urn	Pantry	Weekly 9.00 a.m.	1 hr
Butcher shop			
Potato peeler	Butcher	Daily 10.00 p.m. After every use	
Mixing machine	Butcher	Daily 10.00 p.m.	$\frac{1}{2}$ hr
Vegetable washer	Staff cafeteria	Daily 10.00 p.m.	15 min
Dish-washing area			
Glass-washing	Main kitchen	2 to 3 times a day 2.30 p.m. to 11.30 p.m.	$\frac{1}{2}$ hr
Dish-washing machine	Main kitchen	2 to 3 times a day 7.00 a.m./2.30 p.m./11.30 p.m.	$\frac{1}{2}$ hr
Machine curtains	Dish washer	-Do-	$\frac{1}{2}$ hr
Scrap trays	Dish washer	-Do-	$\frac{1}{2}$ hr
Spray arms	Dish washer	-Do-	$\frac{1}{2}$ hr

Safety and Hygiene

Safety precautions are of the utmost importance and the basic guidelines should always be displayed in the kitchen. Every member of staff should be aware of the importance of the guidelines. Such as:

1 Know the uses of different kinds of fire extinguishers.
2 Label containers of detergents and disinfectants.
3 Wear double-breasted jacket made of absorbent but fire-resistant material. Tuck apron string ends under the turned-down apron top.
4 Carry knives point downwards; arrange them all facing one way on the workbench.
5 Ensure that all equipment is turned off before closing down at night.
6 Use the leg muscles rather than the back muscles when lifting heavy objects.

Shown on Table 8.3 is an overview of foodborne illnesses.

Proper refrigeration is very important in the prevention of food poisoning. Table 8.4 shows the optimum storage temperature and relative humidity. Figure 8.4 shows the temperatures critical to bacterial reactions.

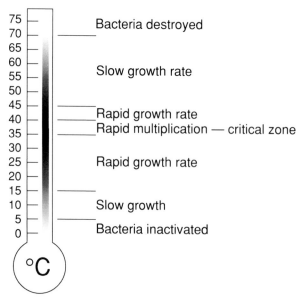

Figure 8.4 Bacterial reactions to temperatures

Table 8.3 Foodborne illnesses

Main type	Type of illness	How people become infected	Foods commonly associated with this illness	How this illness can be prevented
Chemical	1 Chemical poisoning	Eating food poisoned by chemicals from: • Insecticides. • Empty poison containers. • Food utensils containing soluble metals.	• Any food accidentally poisoned. • Especially acid food in containers or utensils.	• Carefully wash all fresh fruits and vegetables before using. • Keep all chemicals away from food. • Throw out chipped enamelware.
Bacterial	2 Staph poisoning	Eating food infected by careless food handlers: • Germs from cuts. • Coughing or sneezing around food.	Potentially hazardous food that is high in protein content: • Custard and cream dishes. • Meat dishes (especially ham, poultry, and meat salads).	• Careful food handling habits. • School food service employees free from infections. • Thorough cooking of food followed by immediate serving or refrigeration.
	3 Botulism	Eating food containing poison from bacteria.	Canned goods which are not processed properly such as beans, corn, meat, and fish.	• Careful processing of canned foods. • School food service personnel should not use home- or school-processed canned goods.
	4 Sam poisoning	Eating improperly cooked foods contaminated by: • The organism. • Contact with faecal material (often from rodents).	Foods high in protein content, especially: • Meats. • Poultry. • Eggs and egg products. • Baked products with cream fillings.	• Good personal habits of food handlers. • Thorough cooking and immediate serving or refrigeration of foods. • Good food storage practices.
	5 Clostridium perfringens	Eating food contaminated by: • Food handlers. • Insects.	Foods high in protein content, especially: • Meats. • Poultry. • Sauces, soups, and gravies made with meat and poultry.	• Thorough cooking and immediate serving or refrigeration of foods. • Good food storage practices. • Good personal habits of food handlers.

Table 8.3 *Continued*

Main type	Type of illness	How people become infected	Foods commonly associated with this illness	How this illness can be prevented
Bacterial (*continued*)	6 Strep	Eating foods contaminated by: • Coughing or sneezing. • Dust, dirt from clothing, facility air.	Foods high in protein content, especially: • Milk, milk products. • Egg products. • Meats and poultry.	• Good personal habits of food handlers. • Pasteurisation of milk. • Thorough cooking and immediate refrigeration of foods.
	7 Trichinosis	Eating pork products which are contaminated.	Pork and pork products.	• Cook pork and pork products thoroughly (66°C or 150°F) minimum in centre). • Local, state, federal pork inspection.
	8 Tuberculosis	Eating food infected by food handlers who carry the disease.	Foods high in milk or milk products.	• Milk pasteurisation. • Proper sanitation of all eating, drinking, and cooking utensils. • Careful food handling. • Routine health exams for school food service employees.

Correct storage of food is essential. Failure to ensure satisfactory temperature and humidity will affect the quality of the food and the reputation of the organisation. Food should be cooked to an internal temperature of 75°C for a minimum of 10 minutes. If not used immediately the cooked food should be cooled quickly and held at 3 to 7°C in separate (from raw foods) refrigerators so as to avoid the possibility of cross-contamination.

Table 8.4 Storage temperature and humidity

Product	Temperature °C	Relative humidity
Dairy produce	3 to 5	70 to 80
Meat & poultry	3 to 6	80 to 85
Fish	1 to +1	90 to 95
Vegetables	1 to 3	90 to 95
Cooked meat	3 to 7	75 to 80

Ensuring a cost-effective standard of hygiene to avoid food-poisoning is a primary duty of executive chefs and the responsibility of food and beverage managers.

QUESTIONS

1 'Nowhere else in a hotel is the opportunity for creativity, imagination and self-expression greater than in the kitchens.' Comment on this statement.

2 Explain the food production process with the help of a chart.

3 Compare and contrast the traditional and modern kitchen brigade titles.

4 Suggest organisational charts for the kitchen of a 50-room hotel with one restaurant, and the kitchen department of a 500-room hotel with ten restaurants and a large banqueting operation.

5 Discuss the operational links between a kitchen and other departments/sections of a large hotel.

6 'Quality cannot be assured in food production in the absence of various prerequisites.' Identify such prerequisites and discuss this statement.

7 Quote examples of good food presentations in restaurants to enhance the quality of the food product.

8 What are the main duties of a kitchen stewarding department? List and explain.

9 'Paying inadequate attention to kitchen stewarding can result in operational delays which reduce the efficiency of the entire food and beverage department.' Discuss this statement.

10 Write short notes on the following:

(a) Safety precautions in kitchens;
(b) Foodborne illnesses;
(c) Storage temperatures for basic foods;
(d) Bacterial reactions to temperatures.

Case study: the Victory Hotel, Portsmouth

The Victory Hotel has been owned and managed by the Watkin family since 1931. Present owner, manager and accountant Mr Joe Watkin lives in the hotel. His wife Mary works as the receptionist and housekeeping manager. The outsiders who work in the hotel as executives are yourself (assistant manager – catering), Mr Bruno Bazzani, restaurant and bar manager, and Mr Giovanni Giachetti, the new chef. The organisational chart is given in Figure 8.5.

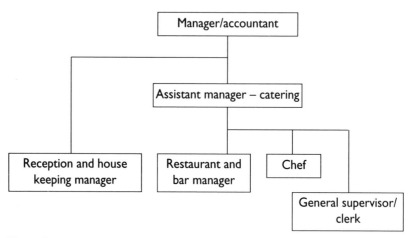

Figure 8.5 Organisation chart – Victory Hotel

Apart from the weekend break business and few business travellers who patronise the hotel during weekdays, the main income comes from the food and beverages sold at the restaurant, bar, ice cream counter (closed during the winter) and the banquet room, which can accommodate 100 persons for a sit-down function. The hotel is located near the harbour and the famous ship HMS Victory. It has 50 rooms and two souvenir shops.

Mr Giovanni Giachetti, who joined the hotel two months ago, has seven years kitchen experience in restaurants and four-star hotels in Milan, Rome and Brighton. He is 25 years of age and lives with his girlfriend in Cosham. He has no formal qualifications but is considered a good cook, especially in the hot kitchen area.

The Victory Hotel has one small kitchen with a brigade of ten, the kitchen structure is given in Figure 8.6.

Since joining the hotel, Mr Giachetti has shown great interest in improving the quality of food and the standards of kitchen hygiene. He has attempted to introduce an exclusive Sunday brunch, which failed on three consecutive

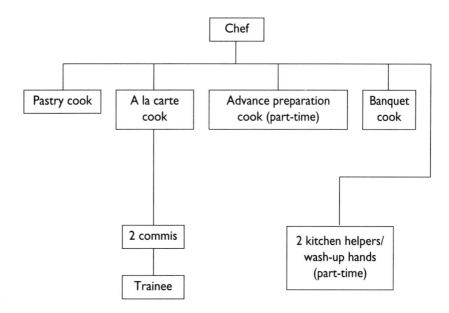

Figure 8.6 Kitchen structure – Victory Hotel

weeks. He was not happy with the speed of work and the commitment to quality of most members of his brigade. Mr Bazzani advised him about the shortcomings of the food and beverage service areas and requested him to plan simple banquet menus and thus avoid elaborate service. Mr Giachetti was of the opinion that service was not his concern. He is only interested in creating a name for the hotel and himself for good food in Portsmouth.

Today for a banquet for 75 persons Mr Giachetti planned a seven-course menu at the cost of 56.5 per cent. The host was delighted with everything up to the time of the function. The waiters did not know the menu and could not arrange all the tables owing to inadequate stocks of cutlery. More seriously, the food was not ready as only Mr Giachetti was in the kitchen. The rest had walked out at 6 p.m. complaining of long working hours for two days (14 hours on each day), lack of kitchen equipment and harassment by the hot-tempered chef. Mr and Mrs Watkin are on holiday with the family in Cornwall and Mr Bazzani has been off sick since yesterday. The time is 7 p.m. and the banqueting hall is gradually becoming full. At this moment, the host of the function calls you and demands quick action.

1 What will you do to solve the problem?
2 What will you do to avoid similar problems in the future?
3 How will you (in writing) inform the manager about the problem, your solution and your suggestions for the future?

CHAPTER 9

SERVICE CONCEPTS

Food and beverage service is the climax of the relationship between a customer and a caterer during a meal experience. The actual contact with the customer is made at this stage of the food and beverage operation. In the presentation of food and beverages to the customer, the food and beverage service staff, in fact, represent the whole organisation. They deliver to the customer the product which was:

1 planned by the management;
2 costed by finance;
3 assured by marketing; and
4 produced by the kitchen.

A restaurant concept begins with an overview of the marketing mix, and market orientation is the key to success. The main factors to be considered are:

1 **The site** is top priority as it determines the degree of contact or exposure to market.
2 **The size** of the food and beverage operation determines the desired impact on the market.
3 **The menu** is a fundamental aspect of the early decision-making process aimed at satisfying customer expectations.
4 **Pricing policies** determine the average spend and affect the sales volume.
5 **Service**, in conjunction with the type of restaurant, menus, customers, and seating arrangement.
6 **Opening hours**, days according to marketing strategies and customer requirements.
7 **Decor and music**, for a pleasant environment which contributes to customer satisfaction.
8 **Standards and quality**, according to customer requirements.
9 **Advertising and merchandising**, to appeal to the target market segments.
10 **Meal functions** are subdivided into breakfast, morning snacks, midday meal, afternoon snacks, evening meals, etc., according to the anticipated and identified market demands.

A clear understanding of various operational problems that occur in restaurants is essential. These problems should be understood by the management. The other departments providing support services as well as the other sections of the food and beverage department (such as kitchen and stewarding) are equally important. It is essential that the department and the entire hotel work as a team. A restaurant which is a 'front of house' area can also be identified as a sales outlet with a captive audience. By implementing suitable merchandising (as explained in Chapter 4), by training food and beverage service staff in personal selling, and by proper motivation, a food and beverage manager can achieve a considerable increase in revenue as well as the average spend.

It is also important to create the 'right' ambience in a food and beverage service outlet. A specific restaurant atmosphere should blend well with the customer expectations and image of the whole organisation. The following factors help to create the 'right' ambience:

- Welcome
- Design
- Decor
- Lighting
- Music
- Furniture, equipment, etc.
- Friendly and courteous service
- Menu and choice of food and beverages
- Staff product knowledge
- Technical skills of staff
- Good food and beverages
- Efficient management

Customers patronising restaurants do so for various reasons and to satisfy different needs. It will be wrong to assume that all customers visit restaurants because of hunger. This can be a main need but it is important to note that some customers visit restaurants for other reasons such as:

- To be entertained
- To be seen around (in gourmet restaurants, etc.)
- To discuss business
- To relax in a preferred ambience
- To experience something new or adventurous

The four main categories of restaurants are as follows:

1   Gourmet – expensive, fashionable and reputed

2 Ethnic/personality – mostly owned individually
3 Reliable brand names – identifiable chains
4 Necessity feeding – fast food outlets with limited service or self-service

If the customer is dissatisfied with the product delivered, the food and beverage service staff will be the first to know it and will be expected to handle the situation with a view to eventually satisfying the customer. The food and beverage service staff should be well trained, well motivated and properly directed. Their performance will either enhance or lower the values of the food and beverages they serve and the reputation of the organisation they represent. A well-performed food and beverage service will increase the value for money in the minds of customers.

Food and Beverage Service Standards

Many elements contribute to the quality of food and beverage service in different five-star hotel restaurants.

Apart from the quality of food and beverage, longer operating hours, better quality linen, cutlery, crockery, glassware, design, wider choice of food and beverage items, better quality print of menu cards and beverage lists, more tasteful decor, better operating equipment, better tailored uniforms and better calibre of staff (in general) can be noticed in restaurants situated in five-star hotels in comparison with hotels of lower grades. The food and beverage service in five-star hotels has become more complex and challenging owing to the important fact that this class of clientele certainly pay much more money and in return expect a different and better service/product.

Many customers see waiter service as adding value to their meal experience. They are spared chores which they may have to face when eating at home and they are also undergoing a pleasurable experience in which they are cosseted and made to feel wanted. The service should be seen as adding value to the meal experience by the management as well as the food and beverage service staff.

A survey carried out a few years ago revealed that waiting staff thought that expert serving techniques were the most important features of their work. The customers surveyed, on the other hand, indicated that what they valued most in a waiter was a smiling, agreeable, welcoming blend of social qualities. This does not mean that techniques are not important, since many guests appreciate a high level of practical skills and expect a fully professional service. However, the waiting staff who merchandise a 'meal experience' must cultivate friendliness, good manners and the relevant social skills.

In the past, many successful hoteliers instilled a customer-oriented attitude in their employees with the slogan 'the customer is always right'. A more modern version recognises that employees have minds of their own. The customer may not always be right but he/she is never wrong. The more enlightened approach eliminates the question whether the customer is right or wrong because it doesn't matter. The objective is to retain goodwill and future business.

Words like 'high standards', 'good service', and 'fair value for money' mean totally different things to different people and are therefore meaningless until they are defined in clear, precise terms. Yet expensive hotel investments and crucial marketing decisions are based on these phrases.

Potential quality can be affected by technical and behavioural factors within organisations and from the environment. It is important to determine the variables which can be manipulated to control these factors, such as design of service process, selection, training, supervision, communication, peer relationships and rewards.

The quality of food and beverage service is a combination of predictions and characteristics on which an individual assesses whether it will give satisfaction each time it is used, based on the guest's own set of values. A quality standard in food and beverage operations is a combination of characteristics accepted by the consensus of market segments as being appropriate to provide satisfaction for their particular purposes. Therefore it is important to base policy decisions with regard to quality standards of food and beverage service in a hotel or an individual restaurant on identified and anticipated specific customer needs through research, as shown in Figure 9.1.

During our research a number of characteristics were identified by sixty practising hoteliers in the UK as most essential for quality food and beverage operations in hotels. The most prominent are listed in order of popularity:

1 Personalised service;
2 Well-trained, experienced, professional and efficient staff;
3 Excellent food prepared with fresh, best quality ingredients;
4 Well-chosen wine list;
5 24-hour room service;
6 Banqueting, conference and small function facility;
7 Tasteful decor;

173

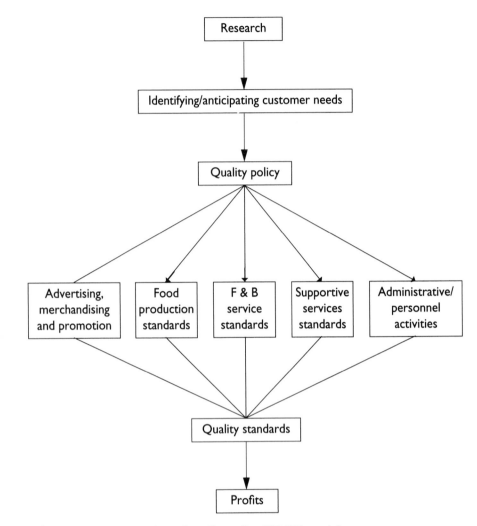

Figure 9.1 Customer-oriented quality policy (COQP) model

8   At least one high class restaurant;
9   Good coffee shop or a general popular-priced restaurant;
10   Good bar and mini-bar facility.

Most of those interviewed shared similar views regarding the characteristics listed above.

Whenever possible, logical space standards should be used as guidelines. Suggested figures for preliminary plans for food service areas are:

Dining rooms (luxury) $1.7m^2$ to $1.9m^2$ per seat
Coffee shops/Restaurant standard $1.3m^2$ per seat

Lounge and bar	1.1m^2 to 1.4m^2 per seat
Banquet	0.9m^2 to 1.3m^2 per seat
Staff canteens	0.7m^2 to 0.9m^2 per seat

Recommended dimensions for 'back of house' areas are given in Chapter 8.

It is also important to analyse customer complaints and take corrective action. Given below are some common complaints:

1   An inadequate reservation system.
2   Regular guests are not recognised by name.
3   Inappropriate service language, such as 'What do you all want?'
4   Service employees are not knowledgeable about the menu, or they use improper service procedures or make errors on guest checks.
5   Long waits for food and beverage servers to receive guest checks and change returned.
6   Employees are poorly groomed, improperly dressed, and/or wearing dirty uniforms.
7   Poor housekeeping such as the presence of dust, dirt, or equipment in disrepair.
8   Dining service that appears rushed and disorganised.
9   Dining service employees who talk excessively to one another, smoke, eat food, show indifference and inattention.
10   Hot food served cold and cold food served lukewarm.

Standard Specifications

This is of the utmost importance in standardising an operation. We suggest the following guidelines for standard room service breakfast as an example.

CONTINENTAL BREAKFAST COMPOSITION

	1 person	2 persons
• Fresh fruit juice 15cl	1	2
• Croissant	1	2
• Bread roll	1	2
• Brioche or local bakery	1	2
• Butter roll or patty on crushed ice	4	8
• Jam (in glass jar – 35g min)	2	3
• Wrapped sugar lump (3 pieces)	4	6
• Hot beverage (coffee, tea) with necessary side serving (milk, hot water)	1 pot	2 pots

Special Remarks

- Choice of jam for 1 person: 1 yellow – 1 red
  2 persons: 1 yellow – 2 red
- Honey on request
- Toasts on request on the basis of 6 half-toasts per person.

Quality of Products

- Fruit juices must be fresh.
- Croissants, rolls and brioche must be of top quality and whenever possible served warm.
- Unless there is a specific regulation against this, butter is to be served in rolls or patties on crushed ice.
- Jam and honey should be presented in glass jars in their original wrapping and should be of the best quality.
- Hot beverages should be of good quality and served hot.

Tray Presentation

The general presentation and set-up of the trays must be done in accordance with the specifications manual.

Equipment (linen – china – glass and silverware) to be used must comply with the specification.

Particular attention should be paid to the following points.

- The linen must be in perfect condition and properly ironed (tray cloth and napkin in linen).
- The tray cloth must completely cover up the tray.
- Chinaware, glassware and silverware must be clean and in perfect condition.

Special Attentions

- Special attention to good quality such as: candies, chocolates, fresh seasonal fruit or fruit compote.
- Fresh flower(s) in the bud vase.
- Newspaper: local or international according to the country;
  whenever possible: choice of newspapers on the doorknob;
  in the absence of newspapers: copy of fax news.

Order Taking

The guests will order either by using the doorknob or by phone.

- Time indicated on doorknob should be strictly respected.
- When ordering by phone, the guest should be advised of the time needed for the service.

Removal of Trays

- Equipment should be available in sufficient quantities in order to avoid staff having to ask guests for the tray.
- Removal of trays should take place when the guest is leaving his/her room.
- Room service should regularly inspect the floors and offices to clear them of empty trays.

Menu Presentation

The more common styles of menu are as follows:

À la carte

This style of menu is used in the majority of restaurants, and literally translated means 'from the card'. The customers are given the menu from which they may select as many courses in whichever order they desire. Each dish on the menu is individually priced.

This style of menu is generally more expensive and has a longer waiting time between courses as dishes are cooked only when ordered. This may also necessitate a larger number of staff (both cooking and service) with a higher range of skills.

Table d'hôte

Literally translated means 'table of the host'. The host may be the manager or chef of the establishment, but is more often the person paying for the function; that is, in the case of a wedding, the bride's father would select the menu for his guests. The menu in every case includes a set number of courses which are offered at a set price.

The number of courses may vary from three to seven and a choice is sometimes offered within each course. This style of menu allows pre-preparation of some of the dishes and therefore quicker service using fewer staff. Customers are usually served at the same time.

Set menu

This style of menu is mostly used at large functions. As the term implies, all items of the meal have been predetermined, which means that the customers have no choice of dishes.

The set menu allows pre-preparation of all the dishes and a set price is charged per person.

The quality of menu presentation is important and attention should be paid to the following:

1   Size of menus;
2   Menu illustration;
3   Quality of paper;
4   Graphic character;
5   Wording;
6   Terms used.

There are no hard and fast rules about menu presentation, but the following general guidelines may be useful in understanding some of the trends.

Quality in the presentation of restaurant menus is essential to preserve the image, not only for the outlet concerned but also for the entire hotel. The restaurant menu is a promotional and sales tool. It does not only give information but should also motivate the customers.

The menu is the restaurant's showcase; through its presentation the guest pre-judges the quality of the meal.

For these reasons, the conception of a new menu should be handled with particular care and should be part of the management concern rather than left to one individual's decision.

Whenever necessary, help should be sought from a professional designer in order to obtain new ideas and see the problem from a different perspective to that of the hotel executives.

The different menus of the various outlets of one hotel are not always standardised. However, some basic principles should be followed. These are outlined below.

1   **Size**
    Oversized menus should be avoided, being unpleasant for the guest, difficult to handle and as a result not easy to keep in good condition. However, the format should be sufficient so that the menu remains easy to read, clear and with a limited number of pages (in order to avoid a tariff-style presentation).

2   **Illustration**
    Any illustration should be light, tasteful and in harmony with the company image, match the restaurant and table decor, and be in line

with the concept of the restaurant. Caricature or heavy illustrations should be avoided. Pastel colours in harmony with the environment should be given preference.

The menu should be part of the restaurant decoration with the exception of privately owned restaurants for which the menu can be personalised. There should be some harmony among the menus of the various outlets.

3 **Quality of paper**
The paper used for the cover should be selected according to the type of restaurant either:

- in a strong, heavy-duty and easy-to-clean cardboard for outlets such as cafés with a large volume of business; or

- in a lighter, soft cardboard for brasserie-type and quality restaurants.

Any insert should be in the same quality of paper, but lighter. The insert must be perfectly integrated in the menu by the use of a multi-purpose glue.

4 **Graphic character**
The typeface must be clear, easy to read, in the same tone as the menu, but darker. Tariff-style type should not be used; similarly, there should be no dotted line between item and price. The type-size for prices should be no larger than for the dishes.

Whenever possible, rounded prices should be used. Prices are important for guests, but should not be oversized.

5 **Wording**
The different categories of items should be listed in the normal sequence of a meal, each category being separated by a blank space.

Headings should be avoided.

Daily suggestions should be placed on the upper part of the right-hand side (this part of the menu being the one guests will look at first).

6 **Terms used**
Names of dishes and their composition must remain simple, concise and understandable for all guests. 'Escoffier' or fancy terms should be avoided. Whenever necessary, the composition of the dish should be listed underneath in small characters.

- A limited choice of fixed dishes will allow a clear and airy presentation.

- Avoid characters which are too small or difficult to read.

- Wording and terms should remain clear and simple to allow guests an easy choice.

- Any insert for daily specials must be perfectly integrated in the menu. The text must be clear, easy and pleasant to read.

Altogether the menu must be harmonious, attractive and appetising.

Food and Beverage Service Methods

There are various methods of food and beverage service. In most hotels it is now common to have different methods of service in different food and beverage outlets. Very simply the objective of food and beverage service is 'to provide the food or/and beverage items produced/dispensed in a kitchen or a bar to a customer as desired by him/her'.

There are fourteen main methods of food and beverage service which can be broadly grouped into two categories as shown in Figure 9.2.

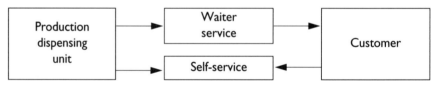

Figure 9.2 Food and beverage service methods

The waiter service methods are:

1 American – plated service (explained below)
2 French – silver service (explained below)
3 Russian – served in front of the guests, who help themselves
4 English – portioned in front of the guests
5 Guéridon – show cooking in front of the guests
6 Drive-in – served to the vehicles
7 Room – trolley service offered to guest rooms of hotels

The self-service methods are:

1 Cafeteria – one entry, one exit line
2 Buffet – guests help themselves to foods of their choice
3 Carvery – main course selected from carvery counter

4 Freeflow, cafeteria – separate counters
5 Carousel – roundabout server
6 Vending – vending machines
7 Take-away – food taken out of the restaurant

The basic principles of waiter service are:

1 If food is served at the table from a salver onto a plate, it is from the left side of the guest.
2 Pre-plated food/soup is served at the table from the right side of the guest.
3 If soup is served at the table from a tureen onto a soup cup, it is from the left side of the guest.
4 Soiled crockery is cleared from the table from the right side of the guest.
5 Empty crockery is placed at the table from the right side of the guest.
6 All beverages are served from the right side of the guest.
7 Ladies are served first.
8 Service is done clockwise. (In some restaurants champagne is served anticlockwise.)
9 Reaching across a guest is not done.
10 All items and equipment on the right of the guest are placed from right side of the guest, and that of the left, from the left.

The above are not strict rules, and in some organisations these principles are not followed. What is important is that food and beverage service staff in one organisation should be trained to provide the service in whatever agreed style throughout, without ad hoc changes in style. However, experience shows that these ten principles are practical and more convenient to the guests.

Once the standards and styles are decided upon by the food and beverage management, it is important to prepare training manuals and train all food and beverage service staff. Staff joining a hotel or a restaurant with food and beverage service experience elsewhere should be given a good 'refresher' training in order to ensure that service standards acceptable to the organisation are maintained.

Handling Complaints

Some complaints can be prevented before they occur, by giving the required information and explanations to the guests right from the beginning.

Handling complaints is an art. Most complaining guests can be converted to satisfied guests by handling complaints with tact and courtesy. Arguments should be avoided at all costs and the guest's point of view should be respected.

A basic procedure for handling complaints is as follows:

1 **Listen**
   Pay attention, listen to the details of the complaint patiently and show sincere keenness in solving the problem. Apologise at an early stage. Quickly analyse the motive of the complaint and the exact need of the guest. Make notes.

2 **Repeat**
   Show the guest that you understood the complaint by repeating the main points of the complaint briefly. But do not interrupt when the guest is talking.

3 **Agree**
   Do not disagree, contradict or give excuses. Put yourself in the customer's shoes in looking at the complaint. Agree with the guest and put the guest on your side.

4 **Action**
   Act fast. Do something to show your concern (e.g. replacing a dish, offering an extra item free of charge, offering a flower, etc.). Inform the immediate superior. Pay special attention during the rest of the meal. Ensure that the guest leaves the hotel/restaurant in a happy mood. Analyse the problem, improve the operation and avoid such complaints in the future.

Food and Beverage Service Organisation

An example of a sectional chart of a medium-sized international hotel is given in Figure 9.3.

Among various duties of the restaurant manager, the following are of importance.

1 Develop, with department head assistance, operating budgets and monitors budget to control expenses.
2 Supervise, schedule, and train staff.
3 Provide required information needed by food and beverage controller.
4 Review all operating reports with food and beverage manager;

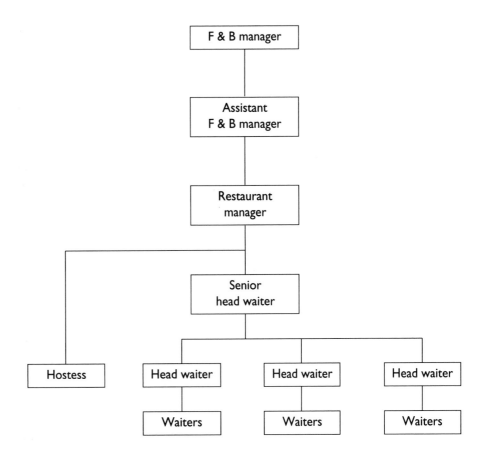

Figure 9.3 Typical organisation chart of a medium-sized international hotel

conduct regular and ad hoc meetings to correct operating problems.
5   Meet with clients.
6   Audit source documents to ensure that all moneys due have been collected.
7   Delegate miscellaneous administrative tasks to assistant.
8   Work on special problems as assigned by food and beverage manager and assistant food and beverage manager.
9   Be available to provide assistance as needed during peak periods.

A restaurant manager should be supported by his/her assistant and other staff. Having a good staff and team spirit are two pre-requisites for successful restaurant management. Chapter 13 gives a practical method of calculating staffing levels of restaurants.

ROLE OF WAITING STAFF

The role of the waiting staff is as follows:

1 **Requirements or expectations**
   Guests: customer perception of service levels and style varies with the style and expense of the venue, but they will always expect prompt, friendly attention.

   Colleagues: co-workers will expect open communication and co-operation

   Company: employers depend on front-of-house staff to provide appropriate food service and to communicate the company image or style to the general public.

2 **Honesty**
   In all dealings with guests, staff and company property.

3 **Personality**
   A warm, friendly nature, good manners and plenty of common sense.

4 **Good health/ability to work hard**
   Time constraints and food service delivery requirements mean that a great deal of effort is required at peak times. Ill health and food service do not mix.

5 **Punctuality, efficiency and excellent personal hygiene**
   These three qualities are essential.

6 **Sales/product knowledge**
   Everyone needs to know what they are eating and drinking, and possibly how it might differ from another restaurant or café. Basic sales techniques are highly successful, and when properly used to market daily specials and desserts, increase customer satisfaction and the average bill.

7 **Industry trends, current affairs and general knowledge**
   Food style and service trends are continuously evolving. In a competitive market place, the front-of-house staff are vital contributors toward the customer's decision to return. It is important to keep up with these changes.

A broad general knowledge and an awareness of current affairs makes communicating with people easier and more interesting. These skills develop confidence, which is valued by customers and employers.

Restaurants should have job assignment sheets where the restaurant manager will indicate the special duties of his/her staff daily (on rotation). A sample job assignment sheet taken from a city hotel is shown opposite:

Figure 9.4 Job assignment sheet

Date	House count:
Previous day's sales:	Above/Below target by:
Month of date sales:	Day's special dish/drink:
Forecast:	

Table layout
Clean table tops/Cover layout/Table Nos/Group menu tent card/Napkin folding

Side station
Dessert plate underliners/Soup underliners/B & B plates for extra covers/Tea cups/
Tea saucers/Demi tasse cups & saucers/Sugar bowls/Tooth pick holders/Mustard/
Sauce bottles/Chilli paste/Soya sauce/Lime wedges/Finger bowls/Tea strainer & drip
bowls/Ash trays/Boxes of matches/Capt. order pad/Straws/Bill folders/Water jugs/
Table mop/Beverage & bussing trays/cutlery

General mise-en-place
Service trolley set up/Linen exchange/Bread baskets/Table water/Check dinner plates
– soup cups – food dishes which are needed for service in the hot cupboard/Wine
buckets & stands/Wine baskets/Clean pdr. requisitions/Check back of the house

Inventories (weekly)
Cutlery (AP cutlery/Dessert cutlery/Soup spoons/Teaspoons/Fish cutlery/B & B
knives/Service spoon)/Cruet sets/Tooth pick holders/Wine buckets & stands/Wine
baskets/Water jugs/Ash trays/Tea strainer & drip bowls/Table cloth/Napkins/
Glasscloth

Maintenance
Fused bulbs/Tables/Chairs/Cushions/Doors/Walls/Other equipment

Buffet set up/Refilling cruet sets/Wine cellar

Special assignments if any

Shift captain's duties
Maintaining books/Update registers/Clean telephones/Telephone cards/Check
reservations and place reserved tags/Briefing points/Filing/Flowers/Drink cards/Menus

Senior captain's duties
Get non-available items/Check cleanliness of restaurant/Lights/Music/Air condition/
Pantry area/Check service equipment for service/Write log books/Release staff for
breaks/Note down comments, complaints and suggestions/Staff cleanliness/Write
requisitions/Lock up restaurant.

Staff on duty

Station one:	Shift captain:
Station two:	Senior captain:
Beverage waiter:	Maitre d':

QUESTIONS

1 Why do customers visit restaurants? Explain with emphasis on ambience.

2 'If the customer is dissatisfied with the product, the food and beverage service staff will be the first to know it and will be expected to handle the situation.' Discuss this statement.

3 Explain the food and beverage service operational links in the context of a restaurant in a large hotel.

4 What is 'quality standard' in food and beverage service? Discuss the importance of a research-based, customer-oriented quality policy and suggest guidelines for a standard lunch buffet.

5 Identify common customer complaints in restaurants and suggest practical means of solving those problems.

6 Write a standard specification for breakfast service in a hotel restaurant.

7 Discuss the more common menu styles.

8 'Quality of menu presentation is important and attention should be paid to various relevant factors.' Discuss this statement.

9 Write an essay on the main methods of food and beverage service.

10 Draw an organisational chart for a small individual restaurant and list the main duties of three members of staff.

CASE STUDY: THE GABLES

The Somerset Hotel is a 300-roomed five-star hotel managed by a leading American hotel corporation based in Boston, USA. You were recruited as the restaurant manager of the new restaurant, The Gables, a month ago.

When a new luxury restaurant opens its doors on the London scene and quickly, yet discreetly, establishes a widespread reputation for offering the very best in food, service and atmosphere – the message is clear. Its standards are such that those who have experienced them are eager to pass on their recommendation to others – and what better advertisement is there than the word of a satisfied customer! From its inception in 1976, the Somerset Hotel's primary restaurant, the William's was situated on the first floor. The hotel earlier closed down a restaurant in the basement in which they served British food surrounded with typical medieval decor and atmosphere. The theme seemed novel, but a basement without any windows or interesting views was not the right location for the restaurant. The hotel converted the space to a sauna recently. Since this closure, the William's has been a fairly successful operation. However, the Somerset's management believed that the premier hotel restaurant should be easily accessible to resident as well as non-resident guests without going through the reception and the public areas of the hotel. In this context a new restaurant was planned to be constructed at the ground floor of the hotel to replace the William's. This restaurant was opened last month and many competitors feel that the theme and the concept may result in a complex operation.

The Gables, the new restaurant at the Somerset Hotel, is an interesting new addition to London's stock of five-star restaurants. It is an up-market all-day dining operation, which has become the premier brasserie de luxe in Knightsbridge. It is a restaurant whose mood changes throughout the day and evening, reflecting the best characteristics of other establishments – the beauty of Lane's food display, Simpson's reputation for roast beef carved in the room, Scott's wine and oyster bar, afternoon tea at the Ritz, and a more formal West End à la carte dining experience at dinner service. The façade of the exterior enhances the hotel frontage; the elegant interior decor reflects an English Edwardian personality and contributes greatly towards endorsing the hotel's five-star image.

The layout of this restaurant offers a great deal of flexibility. On entering it from the hotel entrance, one is immediately confronted by a superb marble-topped buffet display bordered by a cathedral stained glass partition, adjacent to an elegant raised section of the restaurant, which itself is adorned with an intricate glass ceiling. The floor of this section of the restaurant has wall-to-wall carpeting, an abundance of wall-panelling, and brass fittings throughout. The centre section of this restaurant has, conversely, a marble floor, complemented by a marble top. Again, wood panelling is prevalent and an interesting feature of wine display is in evidence. This section of the restaurant is particularly bright, due to the beautiful glass conservatory roof and frontage. The restaurant is adorned by three magnificent trees, which instil a feeling of natural elegance. The far section of the restaurant is, in fact, the Champagne Bar which has three steps leading up to the entrance, a marble floor and stand-up stools with small tables. Clients using this bar can oversee the entire restaurant, whilst enjoying an aperitif. The pavement section of this restaurant is bordered by a natural plantation of shrubs and trees, and garden tables and umbrellas are used when the weather is suitable.

The marketing objectives of the restaurant were laid down well in advance.

The operation aims to attract a varied clientele, but especially the wealthy residents of Knightsbridge, local businessmen and their friends and acquaintances, local shoppers, especially those using the highly reputable stores of Harrods and Harvey Nichols, and of course the hotel guests.

Table 9.1 Profiles of five-star London hotel restaurants

Hotel		Restaurant	Quality of food (stars)	Degree of luxury (crowns)	Wine list	Average spend £	Cost of set lunch £	Cost of set dinner £	Seats
Milton Tower	1	Carlton Room	2	3	Above average	85	—	—	60
Western	2	Derby Room	2	1	Superior	43	22.50	22.50	70
Western	3	Pavilion 29	1	3	Superior	60	—	35.00	70
Norfolk	4	Norfolk Grill	1	3	Superior	85	—	—	70
Hamilton	5	Le Chateau	1	1	Outstanding	52	21.00	—	80
The John	6	John's Restaurant		3	Outstanding	60	30.00	33.50	90
Guildford	7	Surrey Restaurant		3	Outstanding	50	17.00	17.00	100
Green Park	8	Rainbow Room		2	Outstanding	62	20.00	—	80
Somerset	9	Williams		2	Superior	48	16.00	27.50	130

The Restaurant of the Year Award was given to the Derby Room of the Western. The most expensive restaurants are the Carlton Room and Norfolk Grill. Publicity gained by these restaurants certainly is advantageous to the overall image and success of the operation of those hotels.

Sales analysis is helpful in predicting the number of covers (NOC) as well as forecasting the choice of menu items. The average sales mix in the food and beverage department of the Somerset Hotel during last year was:

	%
Food	60
Beverages	35
Cover charges, rental etc.	3
Tobaccos	2

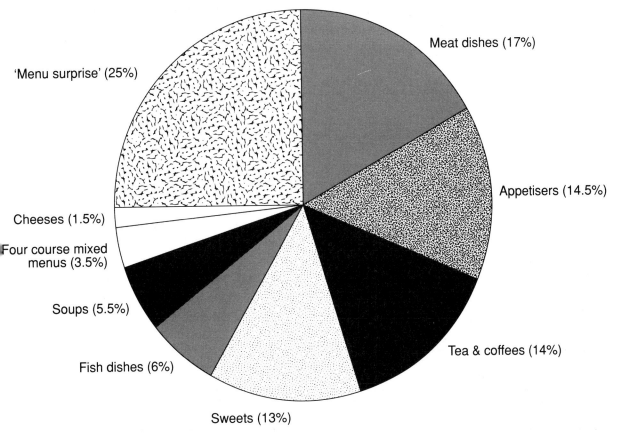

Figure 9.5 Detailed sales mix pie-chart for Gables Restaurant

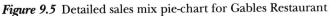

These percentages are more similar to the percentages of provincial hotels than the percentage of London hotels, where the beverage percentage is 30.7 per cent.

The menu sales mix of The Gables of the Somerset Hotel during the first month of operation is shown in Figure 9.5

Last month's sales at The Gables could also be analysed as follows:

	%	
Appetisers and soups	20.0	
Fish, meat and vegetables	51.5	(28.5 table d'hôte and 23.0 à la carte)
Sweets and cheeses	14.5	
Teas and coffees	14.0	

You received the following memorandum today and are expected to act without delay as Mr Robin Thomas is a hard taskmaster.

Somerset Hotel, London SW1
OFFICIAL MEMORANDUM

FROM: Director of Food & Beverage
TO: Restaurant Manager – Gables
COPIES TO: Executive Chef
Assistant Food & Beverage Manager
Training Manager
Public Relations Manager
SUBJECT: IMPROVEMENTS TO THE GABLES

It is a month since our 'soft' opening of The Gables. I must say that I am not very happy about the progress we have made.

In a nutshell, during the month:

1 Our revenue has been 17.5% behind budget. In comparison to the revenue of the William's during the same month, last year a 12% drop is indicated.
2 We have lost some of our regulars as they seem to be unhappy about the new concept.
3 We have had many complaints about the service delays and other operational problems. In fact, during my three-year service at the Somerset we have not received so many complaints in a single month.
4 We have failed to get the anticipated publicity.

I intend sorting out all of the above-mentioned problems as soon as possible with the help of your dedication and hard work. Please send me a complete report with your suggestions on or before 13th of this month. Your report should cover the following:

1 Changes to the concept
2 Suitable ambience
3 An analysis of our customers and potential customers
4 Support you need from other departments
5 The standards we should maintain to face the competition in London
6 Suggestions with regard to menu presentation
7 Changes to method of service
8 A plan for 'on the job' and 'off the job training' (in consultation with the Training Manager)
9 An organisational structure for The Gables

10   A suggested job assignment sheet
11   A plan for getting better publicity (in consultation with the Public
      Relations Manager)
12   A summary of our competitor survey
13   A plan to improve the co-ordination between The Gables and the
      kitchen.
14   Comments on our pricing structure.

My secretary will type your report. If you need any clarification in this
regard please do not hestiate to contact me. At any rate, I intend
checking on your progress (with the report) during our weekly individual
meeting on the coming Friday.

Remember our aim is to make the The Gables the most successful
restaurant in London within a year!

ROBIN THOMAS

CHAPTER 10

Events

'Macbeth' Industry

'MACBETH' is a new concept we introduce in this book. 'MACBETH' covers the main segements of the business involving hotel banqueting and related areas. The 'MACBETH' Industry has seven segments, which are:

Meetings
Activities
Conventions
Banquets
Exhibitions
Theatre
Hotel events

Meetings

Meetings are assemblies for discussions. Various types of meeting are organised for different customers at hotels. Many terms such as seminar, workshop, forum, symposium, clinic, conference, summit, colloquium and lecture are given for the various types of meeting, but when compared, it appears that most types of meeting are, in fact, quite similar. More commonly used terms are:

1 **Seminar**
   A group sharing experiences in a particular field under the guidance of an expert discussion leader.

2 **Workshop**
   A general session involving participants who train each other to gain new knowledge, skills or insights into problems.

3 **Forum**
   A panel discussion by experts in a given field which provides an opportunity for audience participation; hosted by a moderator.

4 **Symposium**

A panel discussion by experts in a given field before a large audience; some audience participation but less than that of a forum.

5 **Clinic**

A workshop-type session in which the staff provide small groups with training in one particular subject.

On some occasions meetings are combined with meals (breakfast, lunch, snack or dinner).

ACTIVITIES/ENTERTAINMENT

Active special events to amuse the audience and occupy it pleasantly, such as musical shows, fashion shows, beauty pageants, sports events (e.g. boxing championship bouts held in banquet halls of Las Vegas hotels).

CONVENTIONS/CONGRESSES

Large formal assemblies (general sessions and committee meetings) of delegates belonging to a particular body or engaged in special studies; convened for a common purpose (e.g. traditional Annual General Meetings). More details are provided later in this chapter.

BANQUETS

Formal, elaborate and ceremonial public meals/feasts for selected groups. More details are provided later in this chapter.

EXHIBITIONS

Public display of works of art, industrial products, etc. More details are provided later in this chapter.

THEATRE

Dramatic performances on stage such as stage plays, café theatre (usually dinner and coffee served prior to the commencement of a play) or cinema presentation surrounded by spectators.

HOTEL EVENTS

Important happenings sponsored or organised by the hotel (e.g. Christmas lunch, New Year's Eve dinner dance, food festivals, etc.) More details are provided later in this chapter. 'MACBETH' involves transforming an area of a hotel into different forms to suit various customers and functions with a view to generating income and optimising profitability.

It is appropriate for readers to understand various terms used in the 'MACBETH' Industry. The more common terms/jargon are given at the end of this chapter.

Meeting, Convention and Exhibition Business

The growth of the convention and exhibition business has been phenomenal during the past thirty years, especially in North America. This growth has been due to several factors: meeting planners, the airline industry, the hotel industry, convention centres, convention bureaux, conference centres, meeting technology, and ground handlers. These factors are examined below.

MEETING PLANNERS

There has been an unparalleled development of the associations connected with meeting planners. These organisations grew in numbers and the list of services they offered. Other growth factors included the emergence of the independent meeting planner, formation of meeting planners' associations, an increase in the number of women planners, certification and the development of standards, and the integration of travel agents into the profession.

THE AIRLINE INDUSTRY

The development of the airline industry has made it possible for large numbers of people to travel from one point to another quickly and efficiently. This was made possible by the introduction of the jet aeroplane, an innovation that revolutionised transportation worldwide. A related factor was the deregulation of the industry. This resulted in the airlines competing more vigorously for passengers and caused a corresponding reduction in the cost of air travel.

THE HOTEL INDUSTRY

The hotel industry has recognised the financial significance of conventions and meetings and adapted accordingly. Hotels grew and became convention centres. Hoteliers learned how to adapt their services to a spectrum of different clients. Even small properties began searching for groups they were equipped to handle and learned how to work with meeting planners.

CONVENTION CENTRES

Convention centres took on new roles. They expanded in terms of exhibition space, accessibility and storage facilities. They became capable of accommodating all the activities of a convention and trade show under one roof. Traffic flow design was improved, allowing large numbers of people to move quickly from one area to another.

CONVENTION BUREAUX

Convention bureaux saw a rapid growth both in number and size of operations. They have become much more professional over the years.

CONFERENCE CENTRES

During the past twenty-five years conference centres have changed their appearance. At one time they maintained a 'business only' façade, but this has been replaced by up-to-date restaurants and recreational facilities. In addition, most contain the latest high-tech audiovisual equipment.

MEETING TECHNOLOGY

Changes in audiovisual equipment, brought about mainly by the electronics revolution, gave meeting planners a degree of flexibility and creativity never before possible. Video projectors, 360-degree projection techniques, multi-image presentations, unique sound systems and writing board photocopiers, etc., have all become common.

GROUND HANDLERS

As meetings and conventions became more complex, so did the need for effective ground arrangements. Ground arrangements can include planning tours, transportation, sightseeing and hotel reservations.

The following checklist will be useful in analysing the strengths and weaknesses of the meeting facility of a hotel.

1   Number of meeting rooms, sign boards and capacities of meeting rooms (and ceiling height);
2   Room soundproofing;
3   Rooms for staff offices, storage, and conferences;
4   Ease of access and proximity to public areas of the hotel;
5   Electrical outlets and voltage for special requirements and lighting.
6   House sound and closed-circuit television equipment;
7   Availability of risers (platforms) and special staging;
8   Distractions (e.g. columns, mirrors, wall decorations, sightlines and chandeliers);
9   Climate control, lighting, and sound controls accessible to meeting planner;
10 Visual equipment such as easels, flipcharts, boards, electric or manual pointers, overhead projectors, 35mm slide projectors, 16mm projectors, and screens.

Occasionally hotel managers are requested to help convention organisers to put their act together. Organisers without previous experience or who are not receiving external assistance (from meeting/convention planners), will certainly find guidance from the hotel banquet/convention manager and team very useful. At the same time this will help the hotel to improve the relationship with the convention organisers and increase the revenue (by charging for special services) and thus improve the profitability and marketability of the facility. The typical convention budget elements can be grouped as shown in Table 10.1.

Table 10.1 Additional convention services provided by hotels

Hotel management			
Management	Operational	Public relations	Other
1 Administrative 2 Registration 3 Printing 4 Secretarial	1 Speakers 2 Programme participants 3 Audiovisuals 4 Signs, banners, etc.	1 Food & beverage events 2 Spouse & children programmes 3 Music & entertainment 4 Press & publicity	1 Special decorations 2 Flowers 3 Stationery 4 Transportation

Table 10.2 Important factors for conventions and meetings

Importance	Factors
Most important	1 Number, size, calibre of meeting. 2 Number, size, calibre of guest rooms. 3 Quality of food service. 4 Efficiency of check-in, check-out. 5 Assignment of one staff member.
Very important	6 Availability of meeting support service. 7 Previous experience with facility staff. 8 Availability of exhibit space. 9 Number, size, calibre of suites. 10 Convenience to other transportation.
Important	11 On-site recreational facilities. 12 Proximity to shopping, restaurants, etc. 13 Proximity to airport. 14 Provision of special meeting service. 15 Newness of facility.

Table 10.2 shows the relative importance of factors influencing convention and meeting planners' choice of hotel, as shown by a recent survey.

The organisers of exhibitions consider the following factors:

1 **Exhibition area**: square footage, floor loads, ceiling height, columns, locations of restrooms, shops, etc.
2 **Accessibility**: externally and internally.
3 **Utilities**: electricity, gas, exhaust systems, steam, water, drainage and telephones.
4 **Specialist manpower**: electricians, plumbers, carpenters, cleaners, etc.
5 **Facility regulations**: liquor, fire, construction, clean-up responsibilities and licences.
6 **Insurance**: accident, damage, fire and theft.
7 **Booth decorations**: partitions, carpets, furnishings, archways, etc.
8 **Signs**: booth, aisle, directional, registration, etc.
9 **Administrative**: exhibit manager's office, transportation, storage, shipping facilities, florists, public address system, parking, press facilities, photographers, etc.
10 **Food and beverage outlets**: restaurants, fast food outlets, snacks counters, bars, etc.

Banquet Business

By and large, banqueting is the most profitable operation within the food and beverage department in most hotels. Owing to the comparatively high gross profit percentage, hotels with large banqueting facilities are often able to offset any losses incurred in other food and beverage sections (such as room service). 'Banqueting business' can also be defined as 'large numbers of guests served in a room separate from a regularly established dining room, or the restaurant in a hotel'. Banquets include breakfast, lunch, dinner, buffets, and specialities like receptions, wedding parties, and also group service for alcoholic beverages only, coffee breaks, snacks, or hors-d'oeuvres. All of these services are offered at a fixed price per person on a pre-arranged standard menu. In some cases, small party banquets are served on individual orders.

Owing to their complex nature, banqueting operations often require specialist attention and careful co-ordination. Banquets and similar hotel services may be conveniently grouped together as a distinct and separate hotel product under the heading of functions. Their users may also require sleeping accommodation and other hotel services, but several aspects distinguish functions from other parts of the food and beverage operation of the hotel. The organised nature of the customer groups, bookings made well in advance, mass production of agreed menus, and the distinctive nature of banqueting surroundings distinguish banqueting from the rest of the food and beverage operation.

In comparison to average British hotels, the London hotels (with large banqueting facilities) seem to have high banquet revenues, with an average of over 50 per cent of total food revenue and over 17 per cent of total beverage revenue. In five-star London hotels, banqueting sales represent 33 per cent of the total food and beverage sales. In most of the Park Lane hotels it is usually higher than 42 per cent.

In the United Kingdom the vast majority of business meetings held in hotels typically last for no longer than one day and are attended by 20–40 delegates only. In comparison, US and European meetings held in this way extend over two to two and a half days. The average size of sales meetings in the United Kingdom varies between fifty and one hundred people. But according to research data most of the banquets held in five-star hotels in Park Lane, London are for 400 to 1,000 people. The average number of banquet covers served in a five-star London hotel is nearly 300 per day. In London, six of the five-star hotels could accommodate over 500 guests in banquet halls (for meals) at a time. Five other hotels could provide banqueting facilities for over 200 guests at a time. Other five-star hotels have comparatively small banqueting facilities.

Banquet Management

There are two main types of banquet manager. Firstly, there is the type who specialises in banquets and outside catering operations and remains in that area throughout, without once reaching the position of banquet manager. The new trend in some hotels with significant banqueting and convention business is to promote/re-designate such professionals as 'director of catering'.

Secondly, there is the type who gains a few years experience in banquets and then moves into food and beverage management. Banqueting managers are often promoted in this way, since banqueting gives them a combination of administrative, operational and marketing experience. The banqueting manager's main functions are selling and public relations. He or she often works closely with the sales director.

In a large hotel the banquet manager is often kept at the departmental head level and is on a par with the executive chef and assistant food and beverage manager. This of course depends on the size of the hotel's banquet facilities and the seniority of the banquet manager. However, those who wish to climb the management ladder fast to reach the level of food and beverage manager should gain the valuable and essential banqueting experience, but should not over-specialise in banqueting.

The organisation structure for the banquet department of a 500-roomed hotel with a banquet capacity of 1,200 persons (for a sit-down meal) is shown in Figure 10.1. This particular hotel makes do with only two permanent waiters. The thirty casual waiters are scheduled for work on weekly rosters, according to the confirmed functions on the banquet bookings diary. The rostering is done by the maitre d' (this hotel is managed by a French company), who is fully involved in the floor-level operation, including co-ordination with the kitchen during functions. For very large functions, the food and beverage manager will arrange extra staff to be released from restaurants to banquets.

The banqueting manager is more involved in marketing and management functions. His/her main duties are:

1 Handling reservations and telephone enquiries, and maintaining the banquet reservations diary;
2 Attending to prospective banquet clients and maintaining good customer relations and periodical visits to regular clients;
3 Preparation of banqueting budget and forecast;

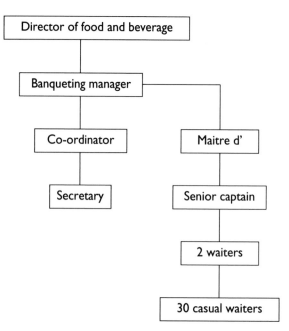

Figure 10.1 Banqueting department organisation structure

4 Comparison with the performance of competitors;
5 Checking and signing of all event orders and handling banquet correspondence;
6 Attending weekly food and beverage meetings;
7 Directing and monitoring the sales visits of the banqueting and sales co-ordinator, compiling and pricing of banquet menus;
8 Maintaining discipline in the entire banqueting department and supervising the work of the banquet co-ordinator, maitre d', banquet secretary and the other banqueting staff and co-ordinating training programmes;
9 Personal supervision of all important and large functions;
10 Personal supervision and co-ordination of all outside catering;
11 Following up outstanding payments in case of billing disputes and attending monthly credit meetings.

The banquet co-ordinator of this hotel plays a vital role as a link with different departments/persons providing supporting services. Her co-ordination work is shown in Figure 10.2. The banqueting co-ordinator's main duties are:

1 Assisting the banquet manager in
   (a) handling reservations;

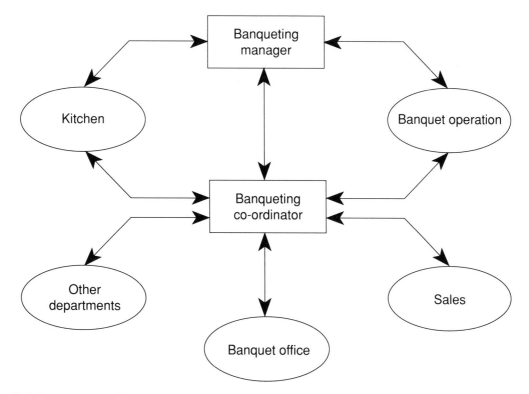

Figure 10.2 Banquet co-ordination

    (b)   attending to prospective banquet clients;
    (c)   handling telephone enquiries;
    (d)   monitoring banquet reservation diary;
    (e)   checking event orders;
    (f)   handling banquet correspondence and taking charge of duties in his/her absence.
2   Attending daily sales meetings.
3   Covering up the banquet secretary's routine duties such as typing, filing, etc., in his/her absence.
4   Following up on tentative reservations.
5   Obtaining all details and finalising event orders and assisting in the preparation of event orders.
6   Co-ordinating with all departments concerned.
7   Visiting prospective and regular banquet clients under the guidance of the banquet manager.

In hotels which have very large banqueting departments, a separate budget and a profit/loss statement is prepared. In this system the banquet kitchen costs are considered as direct banquet expenditure. Many food and beverage directors prefer one profit and loss statement (with sectional analysis) for the whole food and beverage division/ department. Most often the marketing plan and the budget are combined. Shown in Figure 10.3 is a format for the front page of the banquet budget taken from an international chain.

Hotels / Information		Our hotel	Competitor hotels			
			[A]	[B]	[C]	[D]
Lunches/dinners	Minimum					
	Maximum					
Cocktails	Minimum					
	Maximum					
Conferences	Minimum					
	Maximum					
Concerts, etc	Minimum					
	Maximum					
Space for exhibitions						
Revenue per square metre						
Number of covers						
Food & beverage check						
General reputation						
Our banquet and meeting facilities positioning						
Hotel		Strengths		Weaknesses		
Our hotel						
[A]						
[B]						
[C]						
[D]						

Figure 10.3 Banquet competitor survey

Pre-function Operation

The pre-function stage of the banquet operation is of the utmost importance. The main steps of the banquet operation at this stage are as follows.

Potential Customer Contact

Initial contact with a potential customer is made either in the hotel (banquet office, banquet hall or customer's office/residence during a sales visit).

It is essential for the person representing the hotel and banquet department (usually the banquet manager, the banquet co-ordinator, the banquet secretary or a member of the hotel sales team) to be aware of all details (such as the size of halls, capacity, menus, prices, etc.) of the banquet product. This will not be very easy in the case of a large banquet operation with many facilities, as shown in Table 10.3.

Proposal to the Potential Customer

The next step is to forward a proposal to suit the needs of the potential customer. A banquet proposal should be clear, in point form, and appealing to the customer. It is not practical to forward the whole banquet folder with several menus which may confuse some customers. Instead a more individualised approach should be used and this will be appreciated by many customers and increase the chances of your hotel getting the business/function.

Discussion and Adjustments

The next step is to discuss the proposal and obtain the views of the potential customer. It may be necessary to reduce or increase the number of dishes on a menu, change the table set-up or discount the price to suit the customer's budget. The aim here is to get the business by being more customer-oriented than the competitors, whilst making reasonable profits.

Table 10.3 Details of a large banquet facility

Meeting room	Square footage	Capacity					
		Theatre	Schoolroom	Conference	U-shaped	Reception	Banquet
Convention Level							
Marquis Ballroom	28,884	3,250	1,550	N/A	N/A	4,800	2,150
Salon I	7,552	800	400	N/A	N/A	1,250	500
Salon II	8,732	900	450	N/A	N/A	1,450	600
Salon III	6,608	800	350	N/A	N/A	1,100	420
Salon IV	5,992	750	350	N/A	N/A	1,000	420
Imperial Ballroom	16,000	1,850	700	N/A	N/A	2,650	1,200
Salon A	6,400	710	275	N/A	N/A	950	400
Salon B	9,600	990	400	N/A	N/A	1,300	600
Consulate	1,250	120	60	60	50	210	90
Summit	850	90	45	36	30	140	70
Meeting Cluster 1							
Copenhagen	836	90	45	30	25	125	60
Stockholm	1,330	130	55	40	40	210	90
Amsterdam	836	90	45	30	25	125	60
Copenhagen/Stockholm	2,166	220	100	60	60	360	150
Stockholm/Amsterdam	2,166	220	100	60	60	360	160
Copenhagen/Stockholm/Amsterdam	3,002	375	155	85	85	460	230
Trinidad	930	100	40	30	35	140	70
Madrid	682	50	30	20	20	100	50
Trinidad/Madrid	1,612	150	80	50	50	240	130
Calgary	476	50	25	25	20	60	30
Quebec	595	60	30	25	20	70	40
Meeting Cluster 2							
State	812	50	30	24	25	80	50
Cabinet	784	50	30	24	25	80	50
Sydney	1,344	110	60	45	50	200	80
Zurich	729	60	30	30	24	80	50
London	1,178	90	50	40	36	150	60
Bonn	1,680	175	75	50	50	250	100
Sydney/Zurich London/Bonn	4,931	440	215	N/A	N/A	700	330

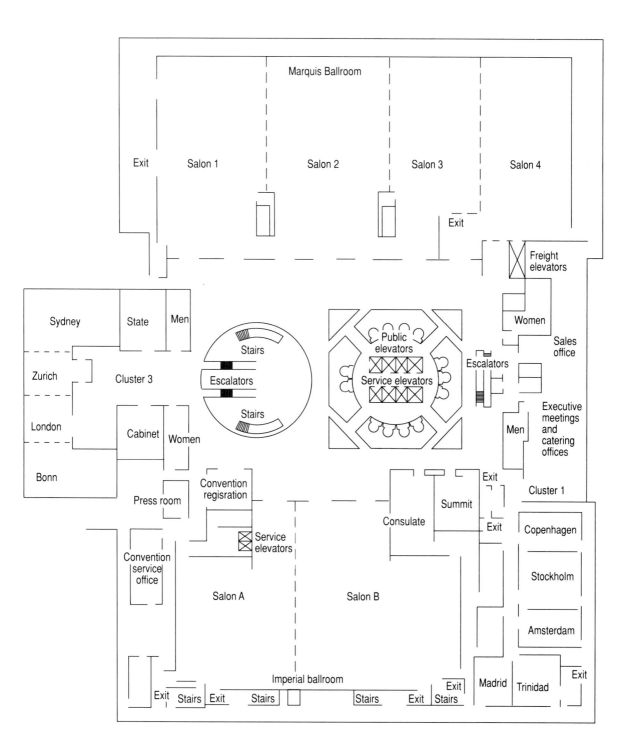

Figure 10.4 The floor plan of a large banquet facility

Signing of Contracts

It is advisable to sign a contract for even the smallest function. Usually the contracts are signed by the customer who settles the bill and the banquet manager. Many establishments will use standard contract forms drafted by the company lawyer. Of course each form will be filled in and completed by the banquet manager. The main items to be included in a contract are as follows:

- Price of menu

- Cancellation policy (most hotels will retain 50 per cent or more of the total for last-minute cancellations)

- Duration of the function

- Deposit clauses

- Insurance clauses

- Utility costs

- Hall charges

- Property damages

- Sharing with other functions (in case of a multi-room banquet operation)

- Parking facilities

- Approval for advertising and use of hotel logo (in case of entertainment events)

- Complimentary guest rooms and other facilities

- Time for rehearsals, setting up, etc.

- Corkage

- And other details mentioned in the function sheet.

Function Sheet

The function sheet is the document that gives all relevant information of a function for the purpose of informing different departments. Various other terms used in different hotels refer to the same document:

- Function prospectus

- Event order

- Banquet order.

A function sheet is a checklist used for recording the details of a function booking. This function sheet is then photocopied and distributed to the departments involved in the running of the function – food and beverage office, kitchen, engineering, housekeeping, reception, switchboard, purchasing, stores, food and beverage controls, accounts, kitchen stewarding, etc.

The main details of a function sheet are:

- Date

- Day

- Type of function

- Pax (No. of people)

- Venue (applies to establishments which have more than one function room)

- Starting time

- Finishing time

- Food requirements

- Beverage requirements

- Name, address, telephone number, etc., of the organiser

- Price

- Special requirements (which could include technical equipment such as audiovisual, computers, telephones, music bands, the colour of table linen, etc.

The layout of a function sheet will depend on the requirements of the establishment. For example the function sheet of an establishment which specialises in weddings will provide a large space for wedding requirements such as wedding cake, floral decoration, invitation cards and changing rooms. Ideally the function sheets should be distributed a week before each function. A sample function sheet is shown in Figure 10.5.

Information taken from a function sheet for a large event of an international hotel is shown in Figure 10.6. This example will show the amount of information that should be sent by a banquet manager with regard to a single event.

Type of function _____	Price _____	Date _____
_____	_____	Day _____
Venue _____ Start _____	_____	Est. No. _____
Sit-down time _____ Finish _____	Total _____	Guaranteed _____

Organiser _____

Address _____

Tel _____ Fax _____

Contact person _____ Tel _____

Beverage	Food
Special requests	Table plan
_____	
_____	
_____	
_____	
_____	
_____	
_____	
_____	
_____	
_____	

Notes
_____
_____
_____
_____
_____

Figure 10.5 A sample function sheet

Figure 10.6 Information in a function sheet

GENERAL

Ref no. 94/0977
Date: October 4
Day: Tuesday
Organisation: International Actors Association
Contact name: Miss Judy Johns, **Telephone no.:** ....
Time: 8.00 p.m. Cocktails,   9.00 p.m. dinner
Location: Ballroom/Mezzanine, **Pax:** guaranteed 900/1000
Type of function: Gala Dinner
Arrangements made by: Banquet manager, **Telephone no.:** X2210
Terms of payment: Int. Conference – Deposit Received on September 2 ($5000 Net). The Remainder to be settled prior to their departure
Billing address: 1AA, 123 Mel Road, Atlanta City
Telephone/fax:

MENU

$37 + 10% per person

Decorative seafood combination in the shape of a dragonfly, with mango and a walnut dressing

———

Light asparagus crème

———

Roast loin of veal with mixed mushrooms
William potatoes
Assorted baby vegetables, stirfried with beansprouts

———

Chocolate junk with a calamansi ice cream floating on a sea of fresh oriental fruits

———

Mocca
Petits fours

Bread rolls in baskets on table before 'sit down'
10/12 ice vases required with flowers, all white lights
Scroll menu for each guest
Cocktails (shopping arcade)
Assorted cold canapés
$10 + 10% per dozen (80 dozen)

BEVERAGES

Cocktails (shopping arcade)
One hour open bar regular brands $13 + 10% per person
Canapés/nuts/crisps

White/red house wines $19 + 10% per bottle (unlimited)
After dinner drinks
Cash basis

ROOM SET-UP

As per plans

COCKTAILS (8.00 p.m.)
Shopping arcade
Set up numerous brown casual chairs and
cocktail tables
Some palm trees, stanchions required
Waiters to circulate with drinks and canapés

DINNER
Ballroom
Pre-function
Mezzanine
Exact numbers to be advised
Tables of 12 pax
Use all white napery
All candelabras to be used
Peach candles (candles in flowers on) tables
Pls mix to give effect
Large 'band stage' for 'big band'
Two dance floors required
Trees with lights for effect
Special backdrop for banner
Casual seating – some tables to be reserved
Regal room to be used as casual sit out area
cocktail style, sofas, etc.
Bar to be set up here – confirmed
Tea/coffee with votive candles, etc.
Area to be curtained/carpeted
Programme to be confirmed after host arrival
23 September – meeting to be set up roughly
as so:

8.00 p.m.
Guests arrival by bus
Small red carpet at entrance
Ushered to cocktail area
Corsages/button holes to be pinned
Philharmonic playing on staircase

9.00 p.m.
Gong for dinner
Six pipers lead guests to dinner up stairs into
ballroom
Schoolchildren on staircase, scattering petals
Proceed to the orchid garden set-up
Ballroom – 52 tables (624 pax)
Pre-function – 19 tables (288 pax)
Mezzanine – 22 tables (264 pax)

Full capacity = 1,176 pax

10 ice vases with flowers
4 ballroom
4 Pre-function
2 Mezzanine
16 trees with small lights to lead the way –
TDC to direct
4 TV monitors cameraman
2 Pre-function
2 Mezzanine

HOUSEKEEPING

Attendants on duty
All orchids in display areas
Nice 'smell' for toilets/function areas
If raining please make allowance for coats, etc.
White napery throughout

On arrival – articles to be received at bottom
of staircase
Please put up curtain/carpet – Regal Room to
Ballroom area
Small red carpet at entrance for arrival/dept

ENGINEERING

Remove ballroom doors
Ensure sufficient air conditiong throughout
Mirror ball required for dancing
All in-house systems, please ensure we all work together for best effect – lighting ice carvings, trees – sounds of bands, etc.
No major 'cabaret' or speeches just 'dancing'
Set up a few monitors and have a camera man available
Small 'spot' at main entrance

FRONT OFFICE/SECURITY

Please ensure all shops are aware that there will be cocktails in the arcade from 8.00–9.00 p.m.
Please see that the air conditioning is turned on in this area
Bus to drop/pick up schoolchildren change room
Piper/Bus drivers – change room
All guests to arrive by buses – Donald Tours to handle
Extra doorman for arrival/departure

Concierge
Directional signs to be ready in the Lobby and at the bottom of white marble staircase by 7.00 p.m.

OTHER ARRANGEMENTS

Cashier
Six required

Allocation

European Kitchen	$36.30
Flowers	$0.50
Sundries	$0.20
Service charge	$3.70
TOTAL	$40.70

Decoration

1 Staircase $45 net
2 Table centrepiece $8 net each
3 Bracelet $3 net (500)
   Button hole $2 net (500)
4 10 ice vases $8 each
5 16 trees $16 net
6 Backdrop $33 net
7 Scroll menus $4 each

Entertainment

Please supply by band for main ballroom – 12 piece
Set up sound for pre-function area
Classical Quartet for the Mezzanine
Children (money to be given privately) $40 or put on bill
Pipes $600 net
12 piece band $2400 net
Classical Quartet $960
(includes meal allowance taken in coffee shop limit $10 net)
Monitors/Cameras $650 net (Matthew)

Issued by (banqueting manager) on 19 September 1994.

211

BANQUET SERVICE OPERATION

A detailed function sheet provides a list of duties to be carried out by different departments and co-ordinated/monitored by the banquet department. However, implementation of everything mentioned in a function sheet according to the customer's wishes and the plan depends on factors such as:

1 Team work/spirit in the whole hotel;
2 Practicality of the plan;
3 Co-ordination and tact of the banquet manager;
4 Management ability of the food and beverage director and his/her team (explained in detail in Chapter 13).

Recently, in a well-known hotel an enthusiastic director of catering wanted to revive the French classical menu. The menu planned by him and the executive chef was liked by the host of the dinner and they were requested to proceed with it. This menu is shown in Figure 10.7. On the day of the event the mistake was realised by all. It took more than three and a half hours for the service of the menu to 200 invitees. Flaming of the *Fruits à la Chef Pâtissier* was cancelled and the hotel lost one of its main banquet clients, and some of its reputation. Practicality of the plan is therefore vital. With a careful plan, attention to detail, good communication and co-ordination, one could serve long menus at banquets. As an example, Figure 10.8 shows a nine-course menu served to 500 persons at a London five-star hotel.

For this banquet a specially selected team of staff were trained. Three hours prior to the banquet the service was rehearsed until everyone knew the exact timing and their role. As a result, the waiters served and cleared together as a well-drilled team. The success of a banquet depends largely on its preliminary organisation. Each member of staff taking part must similarly organise themselves and their own section to fulfil adequately their own role in the function. It will help a waiter to know something of the arrangements which precede the banquet as well as those which apply during it. Communication of information regarding the menu and the service to the staff well in advance is vital to banqueting success.

A common feature of the banquet business worldwide is the high proportion of casual waiters. The high proportion of 95 per cent casual hands in banqueting is unique for any single hotel department. Mobility is the main feature of the hotel worker segment of casual banquet waiters. As an example, in London most of these waiters telephone the banqueting head waiters on Mondays and write down the bookings from different hotels. It is quite normal for one waiter to serve ten or twelve

Figure 10.7 The classical menu

Saumon Fumé au Caviar
Smoked Salmon with Caviar

———•———

Soupe à l'Oignon de Française
French Onion Soup

———•———

Gratin de Fruits de Mer
Gratinated Sea Food Combination

———•———

Sautées de Lapin à la Lavinia
Pan Fried Rabbit 'Lavinia Style'

———•———

Fillet Mignon
Grilled Mini Steak
Pommes de Terre à la Suisse
Swiss Potatoes
Vapeur Broccolis
Steamed Broccoli

———•———

Sorbet de Fraise
Strawberry Sorbet

———•———

Canard Rôti à l'Anglaise au Sauce d'Orange
Stuffed Roast Duck with Orange Sauce
Salade de Pommes
Apple Salad

———•———

Mousse au Carrots et Epinards
Spinach and Carrot Mousse

———•———

Glace à la Kiwi dans Tulies
Kiwi Ice Cream in a Wafer Basket

———•———

Quiche Lorraine
Open Savoury Tart

———•———

Plateau de Fromage
Assorted Cheese Platter

———•———

Fruits Flambé à la Chef Pâtissier
Fruits Flamed in Brandy Sauce

———•———

Café
Coffee

213

❧ Le Menu ❧

Terrine Covent Garden
Vegetable Terrine

Consommé de Volaille en Surprise
Chicken Consomme in a Pastry Case

Filet de Fletan en Laitue
Fillet of Halibut wrapped with Lettuce

Granité de Champagne
Champagne Water Ice

Medallion de Veau Belle Forestière
Fillet of Veal in a Wild Mushroom Sauce

Pommes de Jersey
New Jersey Potatoes

Legumes du Marché
Fresh Market Vegetables

Fromage de Chèvre et Salade
Goat Cheese Salad

Les Trois Mousses de Fruits
Three Fresh Fruit Mousses

Soufflé au Fromage
Cheese Soufflé

Café et Friandises

❧ Les Vins ❧

La Ina
Domecq

Lamberhurst Priory
Muller Thurgau
or
Chablis
Prosper Maufoux 1982

Château Meyney
St Estèphe 1977

Louis Roëderer Brut Rosé

Cognac/Liqueurs

Figure 10.8 Nine-course banquet menu

banquets at all five Park Lane hotels during the same week. Some of these waiters prefer not to be in permanent employment, as casual work provides more money and flexibility. These workers are in high demand by the five-star London hotels. Nonetheless difficulties in motivation and control of casual waiters can lower service standards. Banquet supervisors require more patience and tact in handling this worker segment.

Former Banqueting Manager (during 1940s) and later the General Manager of the Savoy, Mr Paolo Contarini wrote in his autobiography:

> I had about sixty on my permanent staff, and whenever extra help was needed I engaged the services of freelance waiters, so that the total number varied according to the number of banquets on and to their size – the usual ratio is of one waiter to every ten guests. There was certainly never any difficulty in finding staff in those days. Other banqueting staff, some of them behind the scenes, included barmen, cloakroom attendants, porters, housekeepers and maintenance men and they made an invaluable contribution to the success of the department.

Table plans are very important in banqueting service as appropriate plans can enhance the desired atmosphere and make the service less complicated. There are three main types of table plan: formal, informal and cabaret-style. Formal layouts involve lines of long tables, in some of them 'sprigs' run at right angles to a top table. Such 'sprigs' may be flush against a top table but waiters can move and work easily if space is left between them. Moreover, this facilitates draping and decorating the front of the top table. Informal layouts seat guests at separate tables. Cabaret layouts arrange smaller tables (round ten seaters are common) often leaving a centre space for dancing or entertainment. More common types of table plans are shown in Figure 10.9.

POST-FUNCTION ACTION

After a successful function it is important for the banquet manager to attend to a few important matters which can be considered as the last four stages of the banquet process. The twelve stages of the banquet process are indicated in Figure 10.10.

It is important to get feedback from the host as early as possible. Some hotels use a brief questionnaire filled out by the host soon after the function. More common practice is for the director of food and beverage to send a letter and questionnaire to the host the next day. A sample is provided in Figure 10.11.

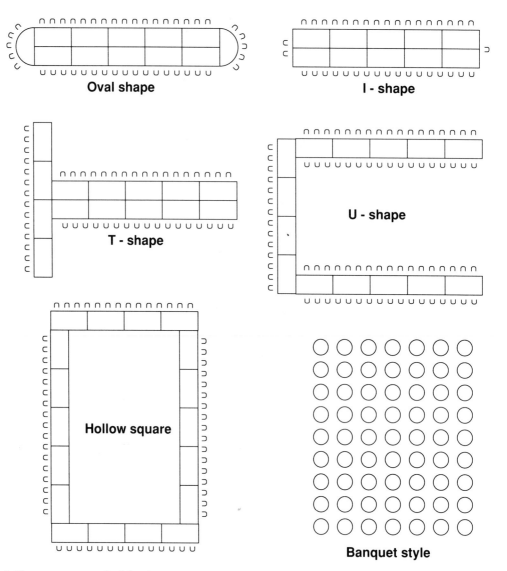

Figure 10.9 Common types of table plan

Once the feedback is received it is very important to inform the other departments with a view to improving the overall operation. Feedback is provided on a monthly basis by the banquet manager on a tabulated form. In case of important functions (e.g. royal/state banquets) feedback will be provided without delay. On some occasions special meetings are held to do a post mortem of a function which had operational problems. This type of internal communication is very relevant to ensure healthy and progressive banquet and hotel operations.

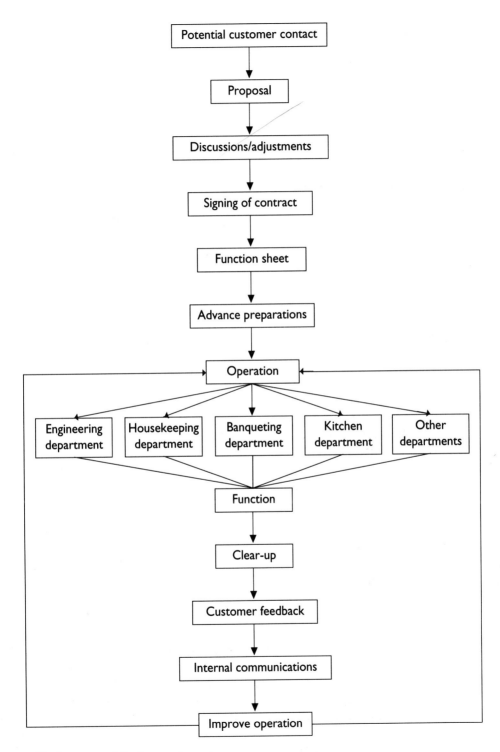

Figure 10.10 Twelve stages of the banquet process

Mr Silva
28 Combes Lane
Langport
Somerset

The Nightingale Hotel

DODINTON · LONG SUTTON · SOMERSET TA19 0ER
TELEPHONE 0245 24556

Dear Mr Silva

It was a great pleasure to be of service at your recent function held in our Hotel.

May we take this opportunity of expressing our sincere appreciation for your kind patronage.
We would welcome your comments and observations pertaining to hall arrangements, standards of our food and service, etc. We would be most grateful if you could spare a few minutes to fill in the attached form, which will be treated in confidence, and return it to us at your earliest convenience. The feed-back we receive from you will help us to upgrade our product and service for the benefit of future customers.

We look forward to having your valued patronage in the future; if you have been satisfied with us, we shall thank you to pass the word around, as there can be no better ambassador than you.

Yours sincerely,

Carlton James
Food & Beverage Director

Banquet standards

Name of client

Type of function

Number attended

Date of function

Additional comments

Please tick ✓

	😃	🙂	😐	🙁
Handling the reservation	☐	☐	☐	☐
Co-ordination	☐	☐	☐	☐
Hall arrangements	☐	☐	☐	☐
Presentation of food	☐	☐	☐	☐
Quality of food	☐	☐	☐	☐
Quantity of food	☐	☐	☐	☐
Service standard	☐	☐	☐	☐
Staff attitude	☐	☐	☐	☐
Attention of the management	☐	☐	☐	☐
Value for money	☐	☐	☐	☐

Figure 10.11 A letter and questionnaire sent to a banquet customer

Hotel Entertainment

The hotel and entertainment industries have many similarities. Both are dynamic industries aiming to ensure customer satisfaction. In most international hotels entertainment is the responsibility of the banquet manager or the food and beverage director. Entertainment is given much more attention in hotels in the Far East (e.g. Singapore) and North America (especially in cities such as Las Vegas) than in British hotels.

A variety of entertainment is vital for large resort hotels with longer average stays. Table 10.4 shows a weekly activities programme taken from a well-known resort hotel in the Far East.

Table 10.4 A weekly activities programme

Day	Animation 10 a.m.	Animation 4 p.m.	Dinner 7 p.m.	Floor show 9 p.m.
Monday	Boat trip (lake)	Hoopla (beach)	Flambé night (roof top restaurant)	Comedy act (rooftop)
Tuesday	Water polo (pool)	Aerobics (beach)	Asian buffet (terrace)	Asian dancing (terrace)
Wednesday	Volleyball (beach)	Table tennis tournament (beach hut)	Fisherman's bonfire (beach)	Fire limbo dance (beach)
Thursday	Carrom tournament (beach hut)	Boat trip (lake)	Italian buffet (garden)	Magic show (garden)
Friday	Table tennis tournament (beach hut)	Aerobics (beach)	Barbecue (poolside)	Fashion show (poolside)
Saturday	Hoopla (beach hut)	Volleyball (beach)	Chinese night (beach hut)	Staff show (beach hut)
Sunday	Elephant rides (beach)	Water polo (pool)	European buffet (ballroom)	Jazz band (ballroom)

Other daily entertainment programmes
* Terrace – live music (different bands) 7 p.m. to midnight.
* Cocktail bar – piano music 7–11 p.m.
* Oriental restaurant – calypso music 7–11 p.m.
* Dinner time – variety of music 7–9 p.m.
* Night club – DJ music 9.30 p.m.–3 a.m.

Entertainment management is a specialised job. Only some large hotels with many food and beverage outlets have entertainment managers within the food and beverage department. An organisation chart of the food and beverage department of one of the best hotels in Hong Kong is shown in Figure 10.12.

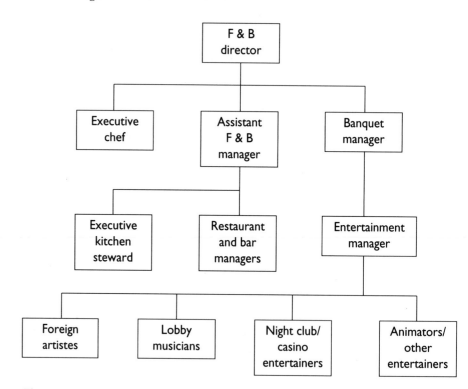

Figure 10.12 Entertainment management in a food and beverage department

Most entertainers work in hotels on a contract basis. It is important for hoteliers to pay attention to contracts with entertainers, which should cover the following basic points:

1   Names of all artistes;
2   Period;
3   Duration of each performance;
4   Fees per session/performance;
5   Taxes;
6   Providing (or not providing) musical backing, sound, equipment, etc.;
7   Meals and soft drinks on duty and the limits;
8   Laundry and valet service;
9   Changing rooms;
10   Terms for additional performances (e.g. Staff Christmas party);

11   Contract extension options;
12   Punctuality and attendance;
13   Exclusivity of performances;
14   Special performances (e.g. New Year's Eve dance);
15   Discipline and general behaviour;
16   Liabilities, etc.

However, the terms and conditions will vary depending on local laws and the role of entertainers' unions.

```
                                             Event Order Ref: 94/0977

To:  Entertainment Manager


     Please supply music for the following function:

     Name of function:         International Actors' Association
     Date of function:         Tuesday, 4 October 1994
     Time required:            8.00 p.m.
     Rehearsal/s:
     Details:                  Please supply band for main ballroom – 12 piece
                               Set up sound for pre-function area (same as
                               Australian National day).
                               Classical Quartet for the Mezzanine
     Location:                 Ballroom
     Issued by:                (Banqueting Manager)
     Issue date:               19 September 1991
     c.c. Engineering Dept
          Maître d'Hôtel, Banquet
```

Figure 10.13 Band order

Organising Hotel Events

Innovative food and beverage managers and banquet managers often create special events in order to:

1   win the support of the local community;
2   ensure guest satisfaction;
3   provide a variety of activities to generate interest among staff and thereby motivate them;
4   create a positive and active image in the minds of public/customers;
5   improve public relations;
6   gain publicity;
7   increase revenue;

8 improve profits;

9 fill the banquet halls during the low months (e.g. January in London);

10 compete with other hotels.

There is no definition of a special hotel event. There are many types and the list can become very long depending on customer needs, the creativity of the food and beverage director and the location/type of the hotel. Given below are some examples of the common types of hotel events.

- Regular events: Christmas, New Year, Easter, Mother's Day, Father's Day, Valentine's Day, Hallowe'en, Secretaries' Week, national days, cultural and religious events, festivals, etc.

- Food and beverage (theme) promotions: pool party, beach party, barbecue, oriental buffet, gourmet dinner, pastry promotion, wine promotion, cocktail promotion, lake carnival, kids' party, jungle party, river cruise party, etc.

- Special activities: music show, competition, fashion show, café theatre, beauty contest, etc.

- Food festivals with national/ethnic themes such as British, French, Chinese, Italian, Indian, German, Thai, etc.

Given in Figure 10.14 are details of special events organised by a British hotel during the Christmas season.

To organise a showbiz event or any other hotel event successfully the following are prerequisites:

- Customer orientation

- Marketing knowledge

- Management ability

- Imagination and creativity.

This is shown in Figure 10.15.

Because the Tower Hotel will be alive with the true spirit of Christmas

You can enjoy a host of seasonal events – parties, banquets, disco lunches and dinners, special menus and entertainment, carols, gospel singing, and a great New Year's Eve party with Latin and Dixieland bands, finishing with a relaxing New Year's Day brunch.

Of course we're offering very attractive room rates for revellers who really want to relax.

A five-star welcome awaits you at all our seasonal events so read on for all the details.

Christmas Parties & Banquets

There's nowhere more festive or more relaxed for your Christmas Party than the Tower Hotel.

Just give us a call and leave the rest to our expert staff. They'll tell you about the four suites, including the magnificent Triton Room: about our special Christmas lunch menu at only £24.75 per person, or our great value dinner options for small parties. And they'll tell you about your party – special menus and entertainments, not forgetting Santa if you'd like him to call.

No parking problems either with our car park under the hotel, or stay overnight with our special festive room rate offer.

So whether it's a party for eight, eighty or even one hundred and eighty, give us a call and start looking forward to a party to remember.

Winter Wonderland Disco Lunches

12th, 13th, 19th, 20th December 1994
Disco Dinner: 17th December 1994

Five-star Knightsbridge office parties await you in our Winter Wonderland. Be the Santa in your work place and join other companies in a day or evening of great food, great music and great fun – only, no dancing with elves: they're busy wrapping crackers and prizes for all!

Figure 10.14 Special events of a British hotel

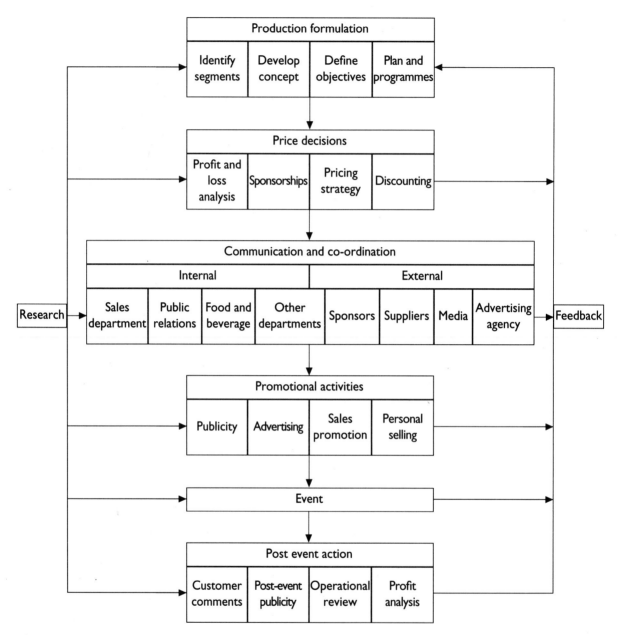

Figure 10.15 Strategic Hotel Event (SHE) model

Banquet Promotion

Target markets can be reached through many sources. The primary system of solicitation is direct mail, followed by telephone and personal solicitation, then advertising, and last, but tremendously important, internal advertising – promoting banquets by internal signs (messages on menus and drink lists; tent cards on tables, counters, and bars and handouts of sample banquet menus). In some hotels every piece of mail which goes out for any purpose (paying bills, sending out bills, etc.) has enclosures soliciting banquets. Organising the banquet promotion programme is of the utmost importance and therefore should be done systematically. A hotel should use lists of all the companies, business firms, factories, institutions (colleges, hospitals, schools), societies, clubs and all types of organisation in the area. The chamber of commerce membership list and the yellow pages are also used as the main sources. Of primary importance, above everything else, are the names of those who have held functions at the hotel in the past. Most hotels mail out banqueting solicitation letters at least once a year to former party holders and prospective clients.

In order to ensure smooth co-ordination of the banqueting operation, the salesman or woman (it could be any one person from the banqueting office) should make a note of all relevant information, such as:

- Purpose of the function
- Total budget the client has set aside for it
- Socio-economic group of the guests
- Technical knowledge of the client
- Details of timing, numbers and any other relevant facts.

Most hotels produce a list of banquets they are looking after about a week before the events take place. These lists give the number of guests to be served, the rooms to be used, the way the tables are to be set up and much other information. But such lists seldom convey any indication of the importance of the function to the clients. To most hotels the occasion normally seems just another dinner, another group of guests to be seated, fed, amused or instructed. To the clients it is a very different matter. Individual attention should be given to each function, and the size of the function should never be the criterion for judging the importance of the function.

Most banqueting brochures are very informative and it seems that a majority of hotels spend much more money on printing the banqueting brochure than the general hotel brochure.

The specimen menu is the most common and important promotional aid. Many hoteliers see the specimen menu as the most effective brochure of the banqueting product. It is also common now to sell banquets over lunch. It is felt that this provides ample time to make a full presentation in amenable surroundings, and allows the potential customer to judge the quality and standards of food and service. It was noticed that most hotels are flexible in the prices quoted for banqueting facilities. This is necessary especially to fill the spare capacity during the banqueting off-season (usually two months from Christmas Day, and June to September). Often, ten or fifteen persons are allowed free of charge, rather than offering a discount on the total bill. Large discounts (sometimes as much as 50 per cent) are given on the bedroom rates for honeymoon couples after wedding banquets.

Banqueting staff sometimes deal with the credit bills, although it is usually handled by the credit section of the accounts department. Banqueting managers seem to take much interest in the early recovery of banqueting bills. The banqueting manager of a leading hotel said, 'with £9 million annual banqueting turnover usually £1½ million is in the current debtors list. I take a personal interest in recovering the bills soon, at least within forty days of the function. I ensure that all bills are sent within 24 hours of the function and send a reminder after thirty days. It is better to deal with it early. We also have to be very tactful as almost all our clients who are given credit are very high class guests.' It was noted that credit is given only to longstanding customers and reputable individuals and organisations.

Creative banqueting seems advantageous in sales promotion as well as public relations. Many functions are held with the purpose of getting some of the guests to remember a particular point: the salespeople to remember the details of a new product, the travel agents to remember the destinations to which the airlines fly, the press to remember a company's name. It is possible to reinforce the message the client is trying to put over by introducing aspects of it into some of the areas for which the hotel is responsible – the menu for example. Other functions are held in honour of the individual or a company; when someone retires, when an association meets for its New Year Ball, when an annual staff party is held. Then the organisation would like to get the image more firmly embedded in the minds of the guests, and this too can be emphasised in the arrangements the hotel makes. The Victorians were masters of this type of creative banqueting. They named dishes after famous guests, produced a wide variety of consumable objects in sugar work and ice work, made marvellous effects with flambé cooking, and generally showed great imagination.

Terminology

Booth	The specific area assigned by the property (hotel or exhibition centre) to the exhibitor under the term of contract.
Booth area	The floor space occupied by the exhibitor.
Break-out sessions	Small groups formed from larger sessions for the purpose of discussing specific subjects.
Buffet	An assortment of foods offered on a table for self-service.
Cash bar	A separate bar set up during a function, where the guests (not the host) pay for drinks individually.
Concurrent sessions	Sessions of a meeting held at the same time in different rooms, usually allowing the participants to choose which they attend.
Consumer show	An exhibition that is open to the general public.
Corkage	A charge placed on alcoholic beverages (usually stocks of which are available in the hotel) purchased elsewhere and brought into the hotel by the host or guests.
Corner booth	An exhibit space with aisles on two sides.
Covers	The actual number of meals served at a food function.
Cut-off date	The designated date when the potential customer must release reserved (but unconfirmed) banquet/meeting room space.
Dais	A raised platform on which the head table is placed.
Exhibition manager	The manager in charge of an entire exhibition area.
Exhibitor	The company or individual sponsoring an exhibition or an exhibit booth.
Floor lectern	A full-size reading desk that rests on the floor.

Floor load	The maximum weight per square foot that the exhibit floor can safely accommodate.
Gross square feet	Total amount of space in an exhibit hall.
Guaranteed number	The minimum number of participants of a function for which the host has paid/will pay irrespective of the actual number attending. In some hotels, there is also an expected number usually being 10 per cent more than the guaranteed number. In this case, the hotel will cater for the guaranteed number but will be prepared to cater for 10 per cent more with short notice, and charge for the exact number of participants (over and above the guaranteed number).
Head count	The actual number of persons attending a function.
Hospitality suite	A room used for entertaining guests by a host.
Host (open) bar	A private room-bar set up with beverages prepaid for by the host.
Island booth	Four or more exhibition spaces with aisles on all four sides.
Letter of agreement	A document confirming all requirements, services and rates signed by the event organiser and hotel.
PDR	A small private dining room.
Peninsula booth	Two or more exhibit areas back to back with an aisle on three sides.
Perimeter booth	An exhibit area located on an outside wall.
Plenary session	A general assembly for all participants.
Podium (rostrum)	A raised platform or stage upon which the speaker stands.
Pre-con meeting	A meeting between a conference organiser and banqueting staff to discuss the details of the event.
Pre-function area	Space outside a banquet (ballroom) or PDRs for the purpose of meeting or having drinks/cocktails prior to dinner/lunch.

Proposal	The initial letter sent by the hotel outlining the menu, facilities, payments, etc., to a potential event organiser.
Reception	A stand-up social event with food and beverages being served.
Refreshment break	An interval between sessions of a meeting during which tea, coffee, soft drinks and snacks are served.
Set-up time	The time needed to arrange (or rearrange after a previous function) the facilities before a function.
Shoulder period	The period between peak season and low season.
Skirting	Cloth covers for the sides of buffet/ conference tables.
Simultaneous translation	Facility to translate a speech into several languages at the time of the speech and transmit to participants through microphone.
Table lectern	A raised reading desk that holds the speaker's papers and rests on a table.
Tabletop display	A portable display (e.g. ice carving, butter carving, flower arrangement, fruit display, etc.) that can be placed on top of a table for decorative proposes.
Tentative booking	An unconfirmed booking for a function which is not yet definite.
Theme party	An event at which food, entertainment, decorations and staff uniforms all relate to a central theme.
Trade show	An exhibition that is open only to professionals from a trade, usually by invitation.

Questions

1   What is the 'MACBETH' Industry? Explain with an emphasis on types of meeting.

2   Describe the main factors which contributed towards the phenomenal growth of the worldwide convention business and identify the important factors considered by organisers of exhibitions.

3   'High gross profit levels of banquet operations help to set off losses incurred in other food and beverage sections.' Do you agree with this statement? Discuss.

4   Draw an organisational chart for a large banquet department and explain the main duties of a banquet manager and a banquet co-ordinator.

5   Explain the five main steps during the pre-function stage of a banquet operation and analyse a function sheet collected from a hotel in your area.

6   Select a banquet menu from a British hotel and suggest a plan to serve this menu to one hundred guests.

7   Comment on different stages of the banquet process with the help of a chart and explain in detail the final four stages.

8   Suggest a weekly activities programme for a medium-sized beach resort hotel in Devon and draw up a three-month contract for a lobby pianist.

9   Plan a Hungarian food festival in your hotel with the use of the SHE model.

10 Write an essay on sales promotion in banqueting with examples from three hotels.

Case study: The Knight Hotel, Hong Kong

The Knight Hotel is a 500-roomed five-star hotel in Hong Kong (Kowloon side). It was established in 1951 with 200 rooms and two new wings were added in 1975 and in 1981. The banquet capacity (for sit-down meals) is 250 pax.

Table 10.5 Banqueting capacity of five-star Hong Kong hotels

Hotel	Capacity (meals)	Size of the main hall (m^2)
1 The Palace	1,500	1,670
2 The Milton	1,000	937
3 The Pearl Continental	800	827
4 The Royal Island	600	790
5 The Neptune	550	957
6 The Pegasus	500	661
7 The Governor's Inn	250	364
8 The Knight	250	341

Competition in banqueting seems to be more direct than the other food and beverage areas of the hotels in Hong Kong. The Palace, The Milton and The Pearl Continental could be grouped as the market leaders owing to two main factors: the location (Hong Kong side) and the size. However, any organiser of a banquet of over 1,000 people has only one obvious choice, which is going to be the Palace. The Neptune, although situated in the same location, saw their banqueting operation as being different from other Hong Kong side hotels. Its banqueting manager remarked, 'We look at different markets. In order to get out of that mass production concept, we reduced the size of our ballroom a few years ago. We now run a more successful, medium-sized banqueting operation. During the last four years our banqueting turnover has increased by 300 per cent.' Traditionally the Pegasus could be seen as being in the same competitive market as the Neptune. Considering the standards and the concept, the Knight, too, falls into the same group, despite the fact that its banqueting operation is half the size of the Neptune and the Pegasus. The Royal Island prices are much lower than those of the above-mentioned hotels and they aim at a lower spending banquet market.

The average price of a banquet meal in a Hong Kong hotel is HK $33. The approximate price of a lunch or dinner is around HK $40. A cocktail party costs approximately HK $16. The cost of sales is approximately 30 per cent.

Although comparatively small, the Knight Hotel seems to be the most prestigious and expensive banqueting operation in Hong Kong. The fact that a few of the royal functions of Her Majesty Queen Elizabeth II were held at the Knight would certainly have enriched the reputation of the Knight banquets. Attempts are made by the management of the Knight to maintain the original concept as well as high standards. The Ballroom Suite and the Mirror Room are described in their banqueting brochure:

> Designed by distinguished architect, Mr Woijgang Fernau in the early 1950s, this suite of rooms has been transformed, but nevertheless retained its original concept. Without attempting an exact replica, the colour and decoration for the entire

231

ballroom suite have to be chosen as far as possible to echo the period of the building and the initial intentions of the designer. The furniture has been retained, wherever possible, but repainted to a uniform colour. New upholstery in the form of a grey, fawn and black weave has been specially designed for the Knight and the armchairs and sofas re-covered in an American material reminiscent of the period. The light fittings are those originally supplied. In the reception room the special mirrors include techniques of glass cuttings not recently used in this country, but which are representative of the decoration of the 1950s. The combined silver mirrors and hand-cut grey mirrors give a most interesting effect. The Rotunda, which has marble architraves and skirtings, has the appearance of being entirely constructed from this material. An eighteenth-century painting technique, carried on to the present day by a few specialists, produces this very stylish result. The Arc Room retains its original panels, painted by Jane Williams and representing scenes from Shakespeare.

In the hotel the service supervisor is given an almost free hand in co-ordinating all banquet service operations, whilst the other banqueting staff spend most of their time in meeting prospective clients, public relations and office co-ordination. Most banqueting business is found in the local community. Some 30 per cent of the banqueting business comes through British citizens and British organisations in Hong Kong.

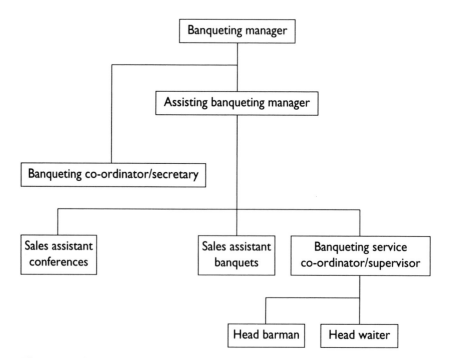

Figure 10.16 The Knight Hotel's banqueting departmental chart

The food and beverage manager of the Knight, Mr Bobby John, wishes to organise an ethnic food festival with chefs from another country once in three months. Recently he sent a letter to a friend in Sri Lanka with a view to organising a Sri Lankan food festival. This letter is reproduced below.

---

4 May 1994

010/5.4/94
Mr James Fernando
Food and Beverage Manager
Hotel Samudra
Flower Road
Colombo 3
Sri Lanka

Dear Mr Fernando

With reference to our previous correspondence, we are very happy that you will participate in the forthcoming Sri Lanka Food Promotion to be held at our hotel 8–31 August 1994 inclusive.

The details of the promotion are as follows:

Promotion theme	Sri Lanka Food Promotion.
Venue	Le Grand Café (Coffee Shop) and opening night and the closing night in the ballroom.
Date	8–31 August 1994 inclusive.
Time	Daily from 12.00 noon till 2.30 p.m. and from 7.00 p.m. till 10.00 p.m.
Concept	À la carte menu for lunch and buffet for dinner.
Specialities	Traditional dishes from Sri Lanka which are popular with the local guests.
Sponsor	Air Lanka, who will provide return flights from Colombo to Hong Kong.

We would require from you:

Menu	Proposals with recipes and a complete market list to enable us to prepare the menu and to see what is available in the local market and what has to be imported. Note: We will have free excess luggage allowance from Air Lanka.
Staff	Particulars of your participating staff including photos. As they will travel as tourists, no temporary work permits are required.

Logo	Bromides of your hotel logo are needed for the printing materials.
Handouts	Posters, leaflets, brochures of your hotel are also needed for handout to guests who are coming for a meal and display purpose.
Additional items	Your hostess should wear a traditional costume. If possible there should be some decorative items for the displays and buffet. A video cassette about Sri Lanka and some traditional music tapes would add charm to the promotion.
Giveaways	For your hotel exposure, please arrange a small giveaway for guests, perhaps not for everybody who is coming – more for the press/cocktail party and for the regular guests. Exact number to be confirmed at a later stage.

Staff entitlements are:

Rooms	We will provide rooms during the promotional period, including of course the days for the mise-en-place and for shopping after the promotion.
Duty meals	Each participant is allowed to have his/her meals including one drink at the Coffee Shop.
Laundry	We will provide laundry for uniforms and private clothes.
Bonus payment	The hotel management will offer the participants a bonus to be paid after the promotion. Amount to be confirmed.

We recommend that the participants come two days prior to the promotion so that we will be able to get everything organised, and that they remain two days after the event.

Looking forward to receiving your reply.

Yours sincerely

THE KNIGHT HOTEL HONG KONG
JOHN MARLON JACKSON
FOOD AND BEVERAGE MANAGER

c.c. Banquet Manager, The Knight

Assuming that you are the banquet manager of the Knight Hotel, prepare the following:

1   A function sheet for a press cocktail party 150 pax to be held a week before the Sri Lankan food festival;
2   An action plan (SHE model) for organising the food festival;
3   A sales promotion plan to fill the banqueting spare capacity for a year;
4   A proposal for a theme party under the theme 'Medieval England' for a 200 pax dinner to be hosted by a European company based in Hong Kong;
5   A suggested new structure for the banqueting department of the Knight Hotel;
6   A list of main duties for the banqueting supervisor.

CHAPTER 11

PRICING

Food and beverage pricing has attracted a great deal of attention in recent years. There are several reasons for this. Hotels and restaurants operate at a high level of fixed costs. What we see generally is a very high percentage of costs which are fixed and uncontrollable in the short term. At the same time variable costs are low as a percentage of total cost.

In industries where the level of variable/direct costs is high (e.g. in retailing), there is a strong and obvious link between the cost per unit and the selling price. If a loaf of bread costs £1.00 and its selling price is £1.30, the cost provides a strong base for pricing purposes. Food and beverage selling prices tend to be very high in relation to their unit costs. A portion of chicken priced at £6.00 may well have a food cost of around £0.90. In a situation like this, the unit cost provides only an approximate – indeed a very imperfect – base from which to price.

As far as profitability is concerned, the message of high fixed costs is loud and clear: high fixed costs and the resulting high profit margins enjoin that we pay particular attention to the volume of sales as, in such circumstances, net profit is very sensitive to small changes in the sales volume. Let us now discuss some of these basic considerations in more detail.

Sales Volume, Price and Profit

As the volume of sales is a critical determinant of profitability, it should be remembered that it may be increased in two different ways: (a) by increasing the level of food and beverage prices, and (b) by doing more 'physical business', i.e. selling more food and beverages. It is important to note that each of these has a very different effect on the net profit of the operation. This is explained in the following example.

EXAMPLE

In Table 11.1 we show the effect of a 10 per cent increase in sales volume and the same percentage increase in the price level on the net profit of a restaurant. As may be seen from the resulting profit figures, both increases result in a substantial change in profitability.

Table 11.1 Effect of sales volume and price on profit

	10% increase in sales vol		10% increase in price	
	£	£	£	£
F&B sales	10,000	11,000	10,000	11,000
Less F&B costs	3,000	3,300	3,000	3,000
Other variable costs	500	550	500	500
Total variable costs	3,500	3,850	3,500	3,500
Contribution	6,500	7,150	6,500	7,500
Less fixed costs	5,500	5,500	5,500	5,500
Net profit	1,000	1,650	1,000	2,000

The 10 per cent increase in the sales volume results in an increase in net profit of 65 per cent. Hence, every time we increase the sales volume by 1 per cent then – other things being equal – the net profit of this restaurant will increase by 6.5 per cent. This indicates clearly that the volume of sales has a powerful impact on the profitability of the restaurant. The 10 per cent increase in the price level has an even more dramatic effect on profit, which is in consequence increased by 100 per cent. Every time we increase food and beverage prices by 1 per cent – and manage to keep everything else constant – the net profit will increase by 10 per cent. The reason for this sharp increase in profit is simply that the price increase in the sales volume goes into net profit.

As far as food and beverage pricing is concerned, the conclusions that may be drawn from this example may be summarised as follows:

- The food and beverage price level is a most critical determinant of profitability. Indeed, its effect on net profit is greater than that of the sales volume.

- Food and beverage pricing decisions are, in consequence, of paramount importance, and should only be made by individuals who appreciate their significance and consequences.

- Food and beverage pricing should be regarded as one of the most important responsibilities of management, and should be seen as an ongoing, regular and systematic activity. Periodic, ideally monthly, price review meetings are essential to ensure the right price level and satisfactory profitability.

Range of Price Discretion

Where fixed costs are high and variable costs low, the variable cost per unit does not provide a strong enough basis for pricing purposes. Also, this particular cost structure makes cost-based pricing methods less relevant. A concept which is useful in this context is that of the 'range of price discretion', and this is illustrated in Figure 11.1.

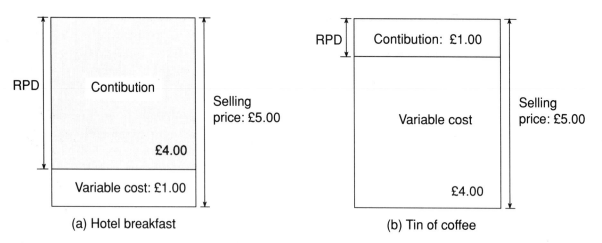

Figure 11.1 Range of price discretion

Figure 11.1 (a) shows the range of price discretion of a hotel breakfast. The selling price is £5.00 and the cost per unit £1.00. The hotel can sell the breakfast at any price between £1.00 and £5.00. The range of price discretion here is very wide. As fixed costs are fixed, any price in excess of £1.00 will result in some contribution.

Figure 11.1 (b) shows the range of price discretion in respect of a 1lb tin of coffee sold retail. The variable cost per unit is high and results in a modest contribution and a range of price discretion which is very narrow indeed.

The implications of different cost structures for food and beverage pricing may be summarised as follows:

- As the majority of food and beverage operations have a low percentage of variable costs, their range of price discretion will generally be wide – considerably wider than in many other industries.

- Low portion costs mean that practically all food and beverage items may be sold at a variety of prices. The resulting wide range of price discretion tends to make pricing decisions more difficult but, at the same time, it offers a lot of scope for food and beverage pricing which is flexible and adaptable to different situations.

- Low portion costs also suggest a particular approach to food and beverage pricing. To revert to Figure 11.1, the link between the unit cost and the selling price of the tin of coffee is strong, direct and obvious. The link between the unit cost of the hotel breakfast and its selling price is weak, indirect and rather vague. Our final conclusion is that, as portion costs do not provide a satisfactory base for pricing purposes, food and beverage prices cannot be fixed by reference to costs only. We need more and wider criteria to secure a level of prices which is, at once, acceptable to the customer and sensible in terms of our profit objectives.

Pricing: Cost and Market Orientation

We may distinguish two different approaches to food and beverage pricing: cost-oriented and market-oriented. The cost-oriented approach is prevalent in industrial and college catering, as well as in all other forms of non-commercial catering. The market-oriented approach is used extensively in hotels, restaurants, leisure centres, health clubs and similar operations. Let us now look at the two orientations in detail.

COST-ORIENTED PRICING: PRINCIPAL CHARACTERISTICS

One of the most important features of cost-oriented pricing is that unit cost (i.e. food/beverage cost per portion) constitutes the pricing base. Hence the general approach to cost-oriented pricing may be represented by the following formula:

$$Cost + Gross\ profit = Selling\ price$$

This particular approach to pricing is evident in many sectors of the hotel and catering industry, and in particular in food and beverage operations which have the characteristics outlined below.

Cost Structure

The cost-oriented sector tends to operate at a high percentage of variable costs. In many industrial canteens food cost alone tends to account for over 60 per cent of sales revenue. If we add to this the other variable costs, total variable cost will rise to at least 70 per cent of revenue. The situation is similar in college catering, local authority catering and other non-commercial types of food and beverage operation.

Profit Management

Cost-oriented food and beverage operations achieve their objectives (typically budgeted results) by manipulating costs rather than managing the revenue side of the business. In striving to secure their objectives the cost-oriented operation will place much reliance on traditional cost accounting methods and techniques (cost centres, cost control, cost analysis, cost information for management, etc.).

Stability of Demand

Cost-oriented food and beverage operations enjoy a more stable demand for their product than those which are market-oriented. In many restaurants, for example, the number of covers served at the beginning of the week is extremely low compared to business done at the end of the week. In the cost-oriented sector, on the other hand, the number of meals sold is pretty constant throughout the working week. This high degree of demand stability makes for a simple pricing structure: there is no need to shift business from peak to off-peak period through higher charges during peak periods; nor is there a need for a minimum charge, which is sometimes imposed to discourage low spenders from occupying limited space during busy periods.

Profit Margins

As cost-oriented food and beverage operations tend to have a high level of variable costs, this by definition implies a relatively low level of profit margins. The resulting narrow range of price discretion limits the scope for imaginative pricing and tends to produce a simple pricing structure.

Pricing Methods

Finally the relatively high level of variable costs tends to make a cost-based pricing method more appropriate in the cost-oriented sector. Indeed, it will be found that 'cost-plus pricing' is the most common pricing method in all types of non-commercial or welfare operation.

COST-PLUS PRICING

This, as mentioned above, is the traditional and most popular pricing method used in the cost-oriented sector of the industry. The method works as follows. We ascertain the food/beverage cost per portion and add the required percentage of gross profit to arrive at the selling price. In all pricing calculations the selling price is taken to represent 100 per cent.

EXAMPLE: GRILLED TROUT

	£	%
Food cost per portion	2.00	25
Add gross profit	6.00	75
Selling price	8.00	100

Diagramatically we may represent this method as shown in Figure 11.2.

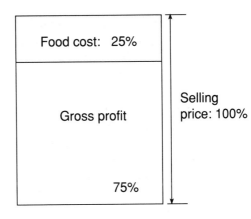

Figure 11.2 Cost-plus pricing

The cost-plus method of pricing is conceptually simple and easy to apply. It has, however, many disadvantages, as described below.

1   The method is cost-based and tends to ignore the type of customer.
2   The price is based on just one element of cost – food cost or beverage cost. In market-oriented establishments the cost of labour and the provision of the requisite comfort and atmosphere are high but these are not taken into account.
3   The method ignores the important – indeed critical – relationship between net profit and the capital invested in the establishment. It will be appreciated that, with the cost-plus method, net profit is a

function of the sales volume: the more we sell, the higher the net profit. Whatever net profit is, in fact, achieved, it may not stand in any sensible relationship to the capital invested.

4 Finally, the cost-plus method is percentage-based. We set gross profit targets in terms of percentages; we price food and beverage items through percentages; at the end of each period we compare the actual percentage gross profit with budgeted percentage gross profit. Although this is now well-established practice, it has been the subject of severe criticism in recent years. Many food and beverage managers are now of the opinion that we should see our pricing objective differently: we should strive to achieve a particular level of cash gross profit, as expenses cannot be paid out of a percentage. This is discussed in the section on 'menu engineering' later in this chapter.

MARKET-ORIENTED PRICING: PRINCIPAL CHARACTERISTICS

Market orientation is the opposite of cost orientation, and its main features may be summarised as follows.

Cost Structure

Market-oriented food and beverage establishments operate at a high percentage of fixed costs. Variable costs – which include food and beverage costs – are considerably lower than in the cost-oriented sector.

Profit Management

In endeavouring to achieve the desired profit levels, the market-oriented establishment will turn to the revenue, rather than cost, side of the business. Profit management in such circumstances means: ensuring the right level of turnover; achieving the right ASP figures for food and beverages, etc. The importance of the price level and its effect on net profit were explained earlier in this chapter. In view of the strong impact of the price level on profitability, pricing should be seen as one of the most important tools of profit management.

Stability of Demand

An important characteristic of the market-oriented sector is demand instability. The volume of business tends to follow a distinct seasonal pattern, and there is almost invariably a weekly pattern of business. Finally, a distinct daily pattern in the level of activity may also be discerned. All these sales volume fluctuations, it should be noted, occur in establishments which have a limited seating capacity. In order to accommodate all potential business, market-oriented food and beverage operations have to resort to appropriate pricing tactics. The relatively wide range of price discretion allows us to charge lower prices during the slack days of the week. Where price resistance is relatively low – as sometimes happens in banqueting operations – our prices tend to be significantly higher. A bottle of wine which is priced £12.00 lunchtime, may well fetch a somewhat higher price during the dinner service and an even higher price in the banqueting department.

Profit Margins

The profit margins of the market-oriented food and beverage sector are relatively high. This results in a wide range of price discretion and promotes the use of imaginative pricing tactics.

Pricing Methods

The relatively lower level of variable costs results in low portion costs of food and beverage items. Unit costs, though sometimes seen as a guide to pricing, are most certainly an inadequate base for pricing purposes. Cost-oriented pricing is in such circumstances inappropriate, and an alternative approach is imperative.

MARKET-ORIENTED PRICING IN PRACTICE

In market-oriented pricing our basic philosophy as well as the actual method of pricing are very different from the cost-oriented approach. In cost-oriented pricing we start with the unit cost and add a percentage of gross profit to arrive at the selling price. With market-oriented pricing we do the opposite: we fix the selling price and deduct the appropriate cost to arrive at gross profit. Hence the basic formula for market-oriented pricing is:

$$\text{Price} - \text{Cost} = \text{Profit}$$

The clear implication of the above formula is that pricing in hotels, restaurants and similar establishments is customer-oriented and that the customer profile – or type of customer – is the starting point for most major decisions. It is the type of customer that decides the kind of menus we offer, indicates the appropriate method of service, influences gross profit margins and, importantly, points to the right price level. Our customers know nothing about – and indeed are not interested in – our operating costs. What matters to them is that prices are reasonable. Thus, whatever our operating costs or desired profit margins, in the final analysis we have to ensure that our prices are acceptable to the customers.

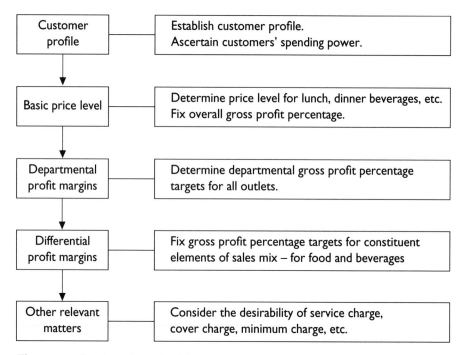

Figure 11.3 Market-oriented pricing

In market-oriented pricing, the pricing process consists of five important stages as illustrated in Figure 11.3.

Customer Profile

The first and most important step is to ascertain the customer profile. Hopefully, in an existing business we know enough about our customers: their age, sex, professional background, nationality, approximate level of income, etc. In a proposed or new business the customer profile should be investigated in adequate detail to ensure that we know who we are going to cater for. A most important point here is that, in consequence, we have a pretty good indication of our customers' spending power.

Overall Price Level

The next step is to determine the general price level of the establishment. From the description of the type of customer, as explained above, we will know his/her spending power, and this has to be translated into the key pricing decisions. We may thus decide that the appropriate charge for lunch is £12–14, and that the charge for dinner should be £16–19. It is then necessary to compile appropriate menus and ensure that whatever the customers' choices happen to be, the individual courses – starters, main dishes, desserts, etc. – when added together should fall between £12 and £14 for lunch, and £16 and £19 for dinner.

It will be appreciated that, in this context, menu planning is a critical activity. If it is badly planned and results in too high a price level, it will discourage both present and potential customers. If the resulting price level is too low, the establishment will face underachievement in terms of its sales volume. Finally, what applies to food applies equally to beverages. Selling prices for wines, spirits, beers, minerals, etc., have to be determined in relation to the customers' spending power. Also, it is necessary at this stage to make a decision on the overall percentage of gross profit at which the establishment is to operate. Most market-oriented food and beverage establishments operate at a gross profit of 60–70 per cent. Generally the higher the price level the higher the overall gross profit percentage, and vice versa.

Departmental Gross Profit Margins

In an establishment which operates a number of food and beverage outlets – for example a coffee shop, one or two restaurants, a snack bar, a banqueting department – it is essential to determine a separate gross profit percentage for each outlet. We may thus operate at gross profit margins as follows:

	%
Coffee shop	60
Restaurant	70
Banqueting department	75
Snack bar	80

The differences in the departmental gross profit levels will flow from the type of customer associated with each department. Also we would take into account any differences in operating costs – particularly the cost of labour. For instance, the cost of labour will be significantly lower in a coffee shop than in a gourmet restaurant, and this will naturally be reflected in the respective gross profit targets.

Differential Profit Margins

Step four is to fix, in respect of each element of the sales mix, a gross

245

profit percentage for pricing purposes. If, as an example, we wished to achieve an overall gross profit of 68.8 per cent, we might arrange – on the basis of past experience – differential profit margins as shown in Table 11.2.

Table 11.2 Differential profit margins: food

Sales mix	Sales	Sales mix	DPM	Gross profit
	£	%	%	£
Starters	30,000	15.0	75.0	22,000
Main dishes	90,000	45.0	60.0	54,000
Vegetables	20,000	10.0	75.0	15,000
Desserts	40,000	20.0	75.0	30,000
Teas and coffees	20,000	10.0	80.0	16,000
Total	200,000	100.0	68.8	137,500

Once we have developed a pattern of differential profit margins, pricing is a simple routine. We take the portion cost (as disclosed by our standard recipes or costing sheets), add the required percentage of gross profit, and the result is the selling price (before VAT). Differential profit margins can only be fixed in the light of experience, and they will, therefore, tend to vary somewhat from one establishment to another. What is important in all cases, however, is this. As the gross profit on some items, such as the starters and teas and coffees, is above average, we are able to accept a below-average level of gross profit on the main dishes, and thus ensure that our prices appear reasonable. Similar considerations apply to beverages. Again, on the basis of past experience and by reference to profit margins prevailing in the industry, we would develop differential profit margins, as illustrated in Table 11.3. In this example our aim is to secure an overall gross profit of 61.7 per cent.

Table 11.3 Differential profit margins: beverages

Sales mix	Sales	Sales mix	DPM	Gross profit
	£	%	%	£
Beers	60,000	20.0	45.0	27,000
Minerals	40,000	13.3	55.0	22,000
Table wines	80,000	26.7	60.0	48,000
Fortified wines	20,000	6.7	65.0	13,000
Spirits	100,000	33.3	75.0	75,000
Total	300,000	100.0	61.7	185,000

The relevant unit costs (beverage cost per tot/measure, glass, bottle, etc.) would be obtained by reference to suppliers' invoices.

Other Relevant Matters

Finally, we have to consider the desirability of charges over and above the basic charge for food and beverages. Many establishments impose a service charge. This tends to be a fixed percentage – typically 10 or $12\frac{1}{2}$ per cent – intended to make it unnecessary for the guest to tip. In some establishments, hopefully the majority, the service charge is distributed to the staff on some basis (usually a 'points system', developed for this purpose). Where the service charge is not distributed, it has a powerful impact on profitability. It increases the sales volume by at least 10 per cent, and as there is no impact on variable costs, the whole of the additional sales volume is added to the net profit.

Many customers, particularly overseas visitors unfamiliar with British customs, favour the service charge. Others pay the service charge, but insist – and rightly so – that where such a charge is imposed the standard of service should be at least satisfactory. The service charge has important implications for the sales volume, average spending power, the remuneration of staff and profitability. For this reason it deserves a great deal of attention.

A cover charge – usually a fixed amount, say £1.00 – is sometimes added to the guest's bill. This is an integral part of the sales volume, designed to cover the cost of bread, rolls, butter, etc. – i.e. items for which no specific charge is made. As some customers are unhappy about this addition to their bill, its imposition requires a great deal of thought.

Finally, a minimum charge is sometimes imposed when it is necessary to exclude low spenders during peak periods. This is not by any means a common practice. Where such a charge is imposed, due consideration should be given to its level: if the charge is too low, it will not be instrumental in excluding low spenders; if it is too high, it will exclude too many customers, create spare capacity and in this way prove counterproductive.

Market-oriented pricing, as will have been realised by now, has a number of important advantages. As food and beverage prices are determined by relevance to the customer profile, they must necessarily appear reasonable. Also, because they are based on the customers' spending power, they must presumably be affordable. In a situation like this, therefore, the price level will promote, rather than hinder, the day-to-day effort of securing an adequate volume of business. Finally, this method of pricing complements and strengthens the overall marketing policy of the business, and makes it more competitive and hence more likely to succeed in the market place.

Differential Profit Margins

Differential profit margins have already been referred to earlier in this chapter. It is time now to look at this practical aspect of pricing in more detail.

In Table 11.4 we show a comprehensive example designed to explain the role of differential profit margins in the mechanics of pricing. Readers are reminded that the selling price before VAT is always regarded as 100 per cent. All appetisers are priced at 75 per cent gross profit, entrées at 60 per cent, vegetables at 70 per cent and desserts at 75 per cent. In each case we start with the portion cost, obtained from the establishment's standard recipe or costing sheet. Thus the portion cost of fruit juice is £0.35 and the appropriate rate of gross profit here is 75 per cent. The £0.35 is therefore equivalent to 25 per cent. The VAT element – which has been assumed in this example to be 15 per cent – is then added, and so the VAT inclusive price is equivalent to 115 per cent. The calculations are shown below.

	£	%
Portion cost	0.35	25
Add gross profit	1.05	75
Selling price before VAT	1.40	100
Add VAT	0.21	15
VAT inclusive selling price	1.61	115

The selling, VAT inclusive, prices which result from the application of differential prices are sometimes odd amounts, for example the £1.61 for fruit juice or the £5.61 for the rib of beef. We would, therefore, round them off to the nearest 5p.

Table 11.4 Differential profit margins

Menu item	Portion cost	Gross profit		Selling price before VAT	VAT at 15%	Selling price
		%	Cash			
	£	%	£	£	£	£
Appetisers						
Fruit Juice	0.35	75	1.05	1.40	0.21	1.61
Grapefruit	0.45	75	1.35	1.80	0.27	2.07
Vegetable Soup	0.25	75	0.75	1.00	0.15	1.15
Chef's Pâté	0.50	75	1.50	2.00	0.30	2.30
Seafood Salad	0.55	75	1.65	2.20	0.33	2.53
Entrées						
Rib of Beef	1.95	60	2.93	4.88	0.73	5.61
Lamb Cutlets	1.45	60	2.18	3.63	0.54	4.17
Grilled Trout	1.25	60	1.88	3.13	0.47	3.60
Pork Chops	1.65	60	2.48	4.13	0.62	4.75
Spring Chicken	1.40	60	2.10	3.50	0.53	4.03
Vegetables						
New Potatoes	0.15	70	0.35	0.50	0.08	0.58
Baked Potatoes	0.20	70	0.47	0.67	0.10	0.77
French Beans	0.35	70	0.82	1.17	0.18	1.35
Cauliflower	0.25	70	0.58	0.83	0.12	0.95
Spinach	0.30	70	0.70	1.00	0.15	1.15
Desserts						
Fruit Salad	0.45	75	1.35	1.80	0.27	2.07
Crème Caramel	0.30	75	0.90	1.20	0.18	1.38
Charlotte Russe	0.35	75	1.05	1.40	0.21	1.61
Plum Pudding	0.25	75	0.75	1.00	0.15	1.15
Ice Cream	0.30	75	0.90	1.20	0.18	1.38

PRICING THROUGH CASH GROSS PROFIT

Accounting and control procedures in the hotel and catering industry have always been characterised by heavy reliance on percentages. Pricing is no exception in this respect: the two methods of pricing described above are essentially percentage-based.

The percentage approach to pricing is still in common use in most sectors of the industry. During the last ten years, however, it has been the subject of criticism, both in this country and in the USA, and an alternative, cash-based, approach is now being formulated by many hotel and catering organisations. The criticisms levelled at the percentage approach may be summarised as follows:

1 We set profit targets in terms of percentages, not cash.
2 The achievement of the targeted percentages is no guarantee that the establishment is profitable, as at the same time the cash gross profit may be quite unsatisfactory (see example below).
3 We cannot pay expenses or purchase assets with percentages.

The table below illustrates the nature of the problem: the month (February) which shows the lowest percentage of gross profit is the most profitable in terms of cash gross profit; the month (January) with the highest percentage of gross profit is the least profitable in terms of cash gross profit.

Month	Sales volume	Cost of sales	Cash GP	% GP
	£	£	£	%
Jan	50,000	17,500	32,500	65.0
Feb	60,000	24,000	36,000	60.0
Mar	55,000	20,900	34,100	62.0

Menu pricing through percentages is not safe. We will only achieve the desired results if: (a) we secure the right sales volume and (b) we maintain a constant sales mix. In practice, changes in the sales volume and the sales mix are frequent and unpredictable, which makes gross profit control an onerous task. In order to appreciate the pitfalls which may result, let us look at the example in Table 11.5, which illustrates the effect of changes in sales mix on both cash gross profit and the percentage gross profit. During both weeks we have the same menu and the same number of customers. Yet, as a result of changes in the sales mix, Week 2 shows an improvement in the percentage gross profit, but a decrease in cash gross profit. There is no doubt that the results for Week 1 are preferable to those for Week 2.

Table 11.5 Effect of sales mix on gross profit

Week 1 Menu item	Menu mix	Portion cost	Portion selling price	Portion cash GP	Total food cost	Total sales	Total cash GP
		£	£	£	£	£	£
Fish	200	1.00	3.00	2.00	200	600	400
Chicken	300	0.80	2.60	1.80	240	780	540
Grill	500	3.00	6.50	3.50	1,500	3,250	1,750
Total	1,000	—	—	—	1,940	4,630	2,690

Gross profit 58.1%
Cash gross profit/item £2.69
Total cash gross profit £2,690

Week 2 Menu item	Menu mix	Portion cost	Portion selling price	Portion cash GP	Total food cost	Total sales	Total cash GP
		£	£	£	£	£	£
Fish	500	1.00	3.00	2.00	500	1,500	1,000
Chicken	200	0.80	2.60	1.80	160	520	360
Grill	300	3.00	6.50	3.50	900	1,950	1,050
Total	1,000	—	—	—	1,560	3,970	2,410

Gross profit 60.1%
Cash gross profit/item £2.41
Total cash gross profit £2,410

Menu Engineering

The term 'menu engineering' was coined by M. L. Kasavana and
D. I. Smith, two American authors who published a book entitled *Menu
Engineering: a Practical Guide to Menu Analysis* in 1982 (Hospitality
Publications, USA). The book represents the most important
contribution to pricing through cash gross profit. Our treatment of
menu engineering is based on this American source but it places the
essential problems involved in the wider context of gross profit control
and menu profitability.

Menu engineering represents a major break with past attitudes to menu
pricing: we no longer accept the percentage approach, which has been
used for several decades. Instead we recognise that: (a) the principal aim

of menu pricing is to secure the right level of cash gross profit, and
(b) each menu item should make a sufficient contribution to overall
profitability in terms of cash gross profit. In order to achieve satisfactory
menu profitability the following are required:

1 An analysis of the popularity and profitability of each menu item. In
   this context popularity is measured by the number of items
   (portions) sold. Profitability is measured in terms of cash gross profit.
2 A continual reappraisal of the choice of menu items. Those which
   are unsatisfactory (unpopular, unprofitable or both) are examined in
   detail. If adequate improvements cannot be secured, they are
   replaced by other items which are more effective in terms of cash
   gross profit.
3 Finally, there is a continual review of menu prices, portion costs and
   sometimes menu design.

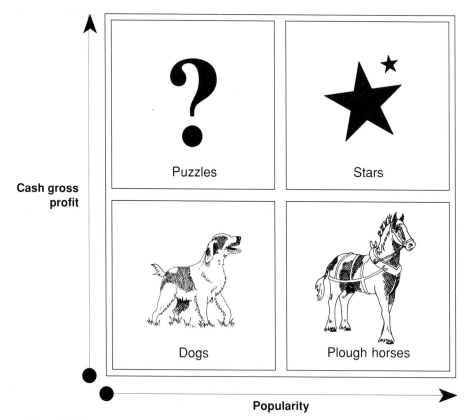

Figure 11.4 Menu item categories

Menu Engineering Terminology

We group all menu items into four separate categories:

1 A **star** is a menu item which is popular and profitable.
2 A **plough horse** is an item which is popular but does not attract a high cash gross profit per item sold.
3 A **puzzle** is an item which is profitable, but for some reason (which is a puzzle) is not popular.
4 A **dog** is a menu item which is neither popular nor profitable.

A diagrammatic representation of the four categories is shown in Figure 11.4.

Menu Engineering Worksheet

In Figure 11.5 overleaf we show the Menu Engineering Worksheet. In this example we have only the main dishes; separate worksheets would be completed in respect of the other parts of the menu, i.e. starters and desserts.

The essential aim of the Menu Engineering Worksheet is to analyse the popularity and profitability of the menu items, and to slot each item into one of the four categories already defined.

Notes on the completion of the menu Engineering Worksheet (by column)

(1) In Column 1 we show, in respect of each menu item, the total number of items sold during the period under review.

(2) Here, in Column 2, we show the percentage composition of the total of menu items sold.

(3) The food cost per portion would, of course, be obtained from the establishment's standard recipes, costing sheets, etc.

(4) The item selling price is the menu price less the VAT element.

(5) In Column 5 we show the cash gross profit per menu item. This is obtained by deducting the cost per portion in Column 3 from the item selling price shown in Column 4.

(6) Here, in Column 6, we show the total food cost of each menu item. Each figure in this column is obtained by multiplying the relevant number of menu items sold by the cost per portion shown in Column 3.

(7) Total sales in Column 7 is obtained by multiplying each number of menu items sold by the appropriate item selling price shown in Column 4.

Menu item	1 No. of items	2 Menu mix %	3 Item food cost	4 Item SP	5 Item CGP	6 Total food cost	7 Total sales	8 Total CGP Amount	8 %	8 Rank	9 CGP category	10 MM category	Notes
1 Sole Veronique	560	14.0	2.85	8.50	5.65	1,596.00	4,760.00	3,164.00	16.5	2	H	H	Star
2 Grilled Trout	500	12.5	2.65	7.95	5.30	1,325.00	3,975.00	2,650.00	13.9	3	H	H	Star
3 Chicken Kiev	630	15.7	2.55	5.95	3.40	1,606.50	3,748.50	2,142.00	11.2	5	L	H	Plough horse
4 Roast Duck	180	4.5	2.35	7.25	4.90	423.00	1,305.00	882.00	4.6	7	H	L	Puzzle
5 Calves Liver	210	5.2	2.10	4.75	2.65	441.00	997.50	556.50	2.9	9	L	L	Dog
6 Leg of Lamb	540	13.5	1.95	6.50	4.55	1,053.00	3,510.00	2,457.00	12.9	4	L	H	Plough horse
7 Lamb Chops	190	4.8	1.85	6.25	4.40	351.50	1,187.50	836.00	4.4	8	L	L	Dog
8 Irish Stew	240	6.0	1.95	4.25	2.30	468.00	1,020.00	552.00	2.9	10	L	L	Dog
9 Sirloin Steak	280	7.0	3.10	8.95	5.85	868.00	2,506.00	1,638.00	8.8	6	H	H	Star
10 Entrecote Steak	670	16.8	3.15	9.45	6.30	2,110.50	6,331.50	4,221.00	22.1	1	H	H	Star
	4,000	100.0				£10,242.50	£29,341.00	£19,098.50	100.0				

Figure 11.5 Menu engineering worksheet

(8) Under the heading 'Total cash gross profit' we enter three figures for each menu item. The amount of cash gross profit is, in each case, the difference between the relevant figures in Columns 7 and 6. Such figures may also be obtained by multiplying the appropriate amounts in Columns 1 and 5. In the next column we show the percentage composition of total cash gross profit. This is a most useful part of the Menu Engineering Worksheet in that it shows the respective contribution of each menu item to total cash gross profit. Finally, in the third column, we show the ranking of the ten menu items in terms of the contribution they make to total cash gross profit.

(9) In Column 9 we categorise all menu items in terms of their cash gross profits. This is done by reference to the weighted average cash gross profit. In this case the average cash gross profit per menu item is (£19,098.50 divided by 4,000) £4.77. Menu items with a cash gross profit loading of £4.77 or more are classified as high cash gross profit items (H); those with less than £4.77 are classified as low cash gross profit items (L).

(10) The function of Column 10 is to classify the popularity of menu items. With a menu consisting of ten items one would expect – other things being equal – each item to account for 10 per cent of the menu mix. Any item which reached at least 10 per cent of the total of menu items sold would be classified as enjoying high popularity (H); and, conversely, items which failed to reach their 'rightful share' of 10 per cent would be categorised as having low popularity (L). With this approach, half the menu items tend to be shown as being 'below average' in terms of their popularity. This in turn may call for rather frequent and fundamental revisions of the menu. It is for this reason that American food service operators use the 70 per cent formula, and regard all menu items which reach at least 70 per cent of their 'rightful share' of the menu mix as enjoying high popularity. With this approach, where a menu consists of 20 items, any item which reached (70 per cent of 5 per cent) 3.5 per cent of the menu mix would be regarded as enjoying high popularity. Whilst there is no convincing theoretical support for choosing 70 per cent rather than some other similar percentage, common sense tends to suggest that there is merit in this approach.

REMEDIAL ACTION

After an appropriate analysis of a menu, the right corrective action is required.

Stars – these are menu items which make a significant contribution to menu profitability. These items deserve a lot of attention. We must not do anything to prejudice their success. Also we must ensure that we maintain their quality through the purchase of the best possible ingredients, competent food preparation and attractive presentation.

Plough horses – these menu items do not generate a lot of cash gross profit per item sold, but they frequently contribute, in total, an amount of profit which is very reasonable indeed. Whilst it is tempting to increase their prices and convert them to stars, there may well be a significant minority of guests who favour these menu items because of their low prices. Adjustments to portion costs may be possible in certain circumstances.

Puzzles – a variety of corrective actions is possible. In some cases a lower price may increase their popularity. Some of these menu items do not sell because they do not appear attractive on the menu: a possible solution then is to rename the menu item. An important consideration here is the shelf life of the item concerned. As a general principle, the longer the shelf life the stronger the case for retaining the menu item, and vice versa.

Dogs – as a general principle, a dog should be removed and replaced by a more successful food item. Whilst their removal should not necessarily be automatic, it must be remembered that there is a dual problem here: both profitability and popularity are unsatisfactory.

SOME PROBLEMS AND LIMITATIONS

Elasticity of Demand

One of the most important practical problems in price level adjustments is that we do not know enough about elasticity of demand. However thorough the menu engineering analysis, we can never be sure of the effect on demand (number of covers) of any one change in the general level of menu prices. What applies to the menu as a whole applies equally to particular menu items. Also there is the problem of – to use economics terminology – 'cross-elasticity of demand'. This is defined as the change in the demand for one commodity (say menu item A) which would result from a given change in the price of another commodity (say menu item B). We know even less about cross-elasticity of demand for individual menu items than we do about the elasticity of demand for the menu as a whole. Therefore when we adjust the price of menu item B, any benefits arising from the adjustment may be more than offset by the change in the demand for menu item A. There is of course the knock-on effect in terms of the resulting choice of desserts, etc. It is essential to remember, therefore, that price level adjustment decisions must be underpinned by a lot of common sense, experience and knowledge of the particular circumstances of the operation concerned.

Labour Intensity

In menu engineering the most critical element is cash gross profit. Whilst no one would dispute its importance, we should not ignore the related aspect of labour intensity. The cash gross profit on a Banana Flambée may be higher than that on Poire Belle Hélène. When we take the cost of labour into account – and particularly during peak periods – it may well be that Poire Belle Hélène is the more profitable menu item to sell.

Shelf Life

Menu engineering in its crude form does not take the shelf life of menu items into account. Amongst the starters we may have on the menu (canned) Fruit Juice, showing a cash gross profit of £1.20 and a Seafood Salad with a cash gross profit of £1.40. It may well be that, especially during slack periods, the Fruit Juice is more profitable than the other starter.

Potential vs Actual Costs

Many of the figures used in menu engineering analysis are potential rather than actual figures. Thus all item food costs (and all figures of item gross profit, total food cost and total cash gross profit) are potential rather than actual figures. Whilst one should not expect undue discrepancies between potential and actual costs, it is important to realise that we are analysing intended results rather than facts. Readers will of course appreciate that any such discrepancies between potential and actual figures will depend on the size of the operation as well as the extent of the menu. Whilst in the case of a large industrial canteen the overall actual food cost may well differ by 2–3 percentage points from the potential cost, individual menu items may show more substantial discrepancies. A small up-market restaurant with an extensive menu may well find that its 'gross profit gap' (difference between potential and actual gross profit) is much higher, and that in consequence some actual portion costs may differ quite considerably from those used in its menu engineering analysis.

Operating Standards

A related problem which tends to detract from the validity of menu engineering analysis is the use of incorrect operating standards. When calculating potential portion costs we have basically two possibilities:

(a) to use 'ideal standards', when we divide the total cost of ingredients by the projected number of portions; (b) to rely on 'attainable standards', when we make an appropriate allowance for unforeseen losses during food preparation, bad portioning, leftovers, etc. The majority of American food service operators use attainable standards by adding a small percentage – frequently up to 10 per cent – in respect of 'unproductive cost'. Portion costs thus calculated are more realistic and contribute significantly to the validity of menu engineering analyses. Unfortunately most British hotel and catering companies tend to use ideal standards with the result that actual portion costs differ somewhat from potential portion costs.

Conclusion

Earlier in this chapter we said that the percentage approach is unsafe because of changes in the sales volume and sales mix. When we use the technique of menu engineering we still face these problems but, most certainly, we are more likely to succeed in achieving the right cash gross profit for the following reasons:

- We plan for and continuously monitor our cash gross profit, and this activity is not distracted by other considerations such as percentages.

- We give prominence to and control, on an ongoing basis, the determinants of menu profitability, i.e. the number of items sold and the item cash gross profit.

- We control not only total results but also the separate contribution to total results of each menu item.

- Finally, we think more analytically about menu items. This new analytical approach means that the menu offerings are not just 'menu items', but distinctly dissimilar groups which have different characteristics and require different handling in the context of gross profit control.

Pricing of Table Wines

For many decades now table wines have been priced by the percentage method. In many establishments the practice has been to use the following formula:

$$\text{Cost per bottle} \times 3 = \text{Selling price}$$

With this method we aim at a gross profit of 66.7 per cent on all table wines – irrespective of the cost per bottle and the resulting selling price, country of origin, vintage, etc. The method, though simple in application, is rigid, and it is only in recent years that we have become aware of its limitations.

With cheaper wines there is no problem. A bottle of Liebfraumilch or Soave costing £3.00 per bottle will sell at (£3.00 × 3 = £9.00, plus VAT at 17.5 per cent) £10.58 (rounded up to £10.60) – a price which is reasonable and affordable.

With better, more expensive wines, there is a real problem. A bottle of wine costing £7.00 would have to sell at (£7.00 × 3 = £21.00, plus VAT at 17.5 per cent) £24.68 – a price which can only be afforded by a relatively small minority of guests. As a result, many establishments now tend to discard the 'Cost-Times-Three' method and change over to pricing table wines through cash gross profit. The main features of the new approach are discussed below.

1   We recognise that what matters in the final analysis is the cash gross profit on each bottle sold. This may be illustrated as follows:

	Wine A		Wine B	
	£	%	£	%
Cost per bottle	3.00	33.3	12.00	60.0
Add gross profit	6.00	66.7	8.00	40.0
Selling price	9.00	100.0	20.00	100.0

From this example we see that although Wine B attracts only a modest gross profit of 40 per cent, every bottle sold produces a cash gross profit of £8.00. Wine A, even though it is priced at 66.7 per cent, is less profitable.

2   With this new approach, cash gross profit tends to increase with the cost per bottle, but not by any means in direct proportion. As a result, the percentage gross profit shows a significant decrease with each increase in the cost per bottle.

3   Establishments which have introduced this method of pricing report that it has: (a) increased their overall cash gross profits from the sale of table wines; (b) decreased their percentage of gross profit; and (c) resulted in greater guest satisfaction.

The example in Table 11.6, based on Italian wines, illustrates the impact of this method of pricing on both cash and percentage gross profits.

In conclusion, when this method is used, percentages are kept very much in the background. Our aim is to secure a satisfactory overall cash gross

Table 11.6 Pricing of table wines

Description	Bottle cost	Selling price	Gross profit	
	£	£	£	%
White wines				
Orvieto	2.85	7.75	4.90	63.2
Vermentino	3.40	8.50	5.10	60.0
Leone	3.85	9.10	5.25	57.7
Fiano	10.15	17.40	7.25	41.7
Red wines				
Valpolicella	2.80	7.60	4.80	63.2
Chianti	3.45	8.60	5.15	59.9
Montepulciano	4.80	11.00	6.20	56.4
Barbaresco	7.25	14.00	6.75	48.2

profit on table wines, and we expect each bottle to make an adequate and approximately equal contribution to overall profits. The impact on total wine sales is encouraging: from the guests' point of view this method of pricing is most attractive as wines of good quality are available at prices which are affordable.

The general manager of a well-known London residential club is a strong believer in pricing wines through cash gross profit. Irrespective of the cost per bottle, he adds £7.00 cash gross profit to arrive at the selling price. Asked about his members' reaction to this method of pricing, he said: 'They like it; for £13.00 they can have a really nice bottle of wine. I also like this pricing method: since its introduction the volume of my wine sales has increased quite appreciably.'

QUESTIONS

1 Explain what you understand by the concept of the 'range of price discretion'. What is the practical usefulness of the concept in pricing tactics?

2 Enumerate and discuss the principal characteristics of cost-oriented pricing. In which sectors of the hotel and catering industry is it prevalent?

3 What is 'cost-plus pricing'? Discuss its main advantages and disadvantages.

4 Explain what is meant by market-oriented pricing. In which sectors of the hotel and catering industry is it popular?

5   What is the role of the customer profile in market-oriented pricing?

6   Explain what you understand by 'differential profit margins'. What use is made of this concept in day-to-day pricing?

7   Explain the effect on net profit of the imposition of a cover charge?

8   What do we mean by the term 'pricing through cash gross profit'? How does it differ from pricing through percentages?

9   Give an outline of the technique of menu engineering and discuss its main advantages.

10 Define the following:

    (a) star;
    (b) plough horse;
    (c) puzzle;
    (d) dog.

    State clearly what criteria you are using for your definitions.

11 Divide the following menu items into stars, puzzles, plough horses and dogs.

	Menu Item	Portions sold	Cash GP (£)
1	Lobster	140	3.50
2	Sole	65	3.15
3	Chicken	160	1.25
4	Turkey	45	1.15
5	Kebab	55	3.20
6	Veal	135	3.35
7	Beef	40	3.60
8	Steak	70	3.05
9	Stew	125	0.95
10	Grill	165	3.45
	Total	1,000	

12 Discuss some of the practical menu engineering problems in relation to:

    (a) elasticity of demand;
    (b) labour intensity;
    (c) shelf life;
    (d) potential v. actual costs;
    (e) operating standards.

13 Give an outline of the traditional approach to the pricing of table wines and enumerate its advantages and disadvantages.

14 Explain the method of pricing table wines through cash gross profit.

15 Your managing director has been invited by the local university to speak to the hotel management students on menu engineering. He has asked you to draft some brief but comprehensive notes to ensure that the presentation is clear and logical. Prepare, in note form, an outline of the lecture, and suggest what handouts would be useful.

16 Set out below is a menu planned for the week commencing Monday 12 December 1994. Alongside each menu item is shown its portion cost as well as the relevant percentage of gross profit (i.e. differential profit margin). Assume that VAT is to be charged at $17\frac{1}{2}$ per cent and price the entire menu, rounding off the final VAT inclusive prices to the nearest 5p.

Menu item	Portion cost £	Differential profit margin %
Appetisers		
Melon	0.45	75
Fruit juice	0.30	75
Soup	0.20	75
Pâté	0.25	75
Salad	0.35	75
Entrées		
Sole	1.35	60
Chicken	0.95	60
Veal	1.30	60
Beef	2.45	60
Chops	2.15	60
Vegetables		
New potates	0.15	70
French fries	0.15	70
Cauliflower	0.20	70
French beans	0.35	70
Spinach	0.25	70
Desserts		
Fruit salad	0.45	75
Crème caramel	0.30	75
Plum pudding	0.25	75
Baked apple	0.30	75
Ice cream	0.35	75

17 Figure 11.6 shows a menu engineering worksheet which you are asked to complete. Also suggest what action is appropriate in relation to each of the desserts.

Menu item	1 No. of items	2 Menu mix %	3 Item food cost	4 Item SP	5 Item CGP	6 Total food cost	7 Total sales	8 Total CGP			9 CGP category	10 MM category	Notes
								Amount	%	Rank			
1 Fruit Salad	265		0.95	2.75									
2 Poire Belle Hélène	230		0.70	3.25									
3 Crêpes Suzettes	110		0.75	3.50									
4 Charlotte Russe	310		0.85	2.75									
5 Cherry Pie	115		0.55	1.50									
6 Baked Apple	75		0.45	1.75									
7 Fresh fruit	180		0.75	2.00									
8 Ice Creams	315		0.60	1.50									

Figure 11.6 Menu engineering worksheet
Menu period: June 1994

263

Menu item	1 No. of items	2 Menu mix %	3 Item food cost	4 Item SP	5 Item CGP	6 Total food cost	7 Total sales	8 Total CGP			9 CGP category	10 MM category	Notes
								Amount	%	Rank			
1 Grilled Trout	280		2.75	8.25									
2 Baked Haddock	250		2.55	7.75									
3 Chicken Marengo	315		2.40	5.25									
4 Grilled Duckling	90		2.30	8.50									
5 Haricot of Veal	105		2.25	5.50									
6 Kidneys Tartare	270		1.85	4.75									
7 Lamb Provencale	95		2.10	7.25									
8 Irish Stew	120		1.80	4.25									
9 Fillet of Beef	140		2.50	8.25									
10 Pork Cutlets	335		2.25	6.25									

Figure 11.7 Menu engineering worksheet
Menu period: May 1994

18 You are required to complete the menu engineering worksheet in respect of May 1994 (Figure 11.7). In the 'Notes' column, indicate whether the item is a star, puzzle, etc. State briefly what action you suggest in relation to each menu item (e.g. increase price; eliminate from menu; rename menu item, etc.).

CHAPTER 12

CONTROL

Food and beverage control is a most important part of food and beverage management for several reasons. In Chapter 5 we dealt with the major aims, policies and operating standards. It was then that we explained the need for some early and fundamental decisions. We have to decide on the major aims of the food and beverage operation and describe in detail the specific objectives that we want to achieve. We have to develop all the requisite operating standards – both for the guidance of actual operations and for control purposes. Finally we have to translate all these decisions, policies and intentions into concrete terms, which means that – as explained in Chapter 6 – we need to prepare appropriate budgets.

Food and beverage control is, very simply, the sum total of actions, procedures and devices designed to ensure that actual results are in conformity with the food and beverage policies of the establishment, and hence that they are – by the same token – in line with the budgeted results. In other words, the major aim of food and beverage control is to make sure that what is actually happening in terms of sales, costs and profit margins, etc., is what should be happening during the period under review.

Specific Aims

The specific aims of food and beverage control may be summarised as follows.

CONTROL OF CURRENT OPERATIONS

The monitoring of current operations takes place from one day/week to another. Any deviations from budgeted results may, therefore, be corrected almost as soon as they arise.

ADHERENCE TO OPERATING STANDARDS

The control of actual operations includes all the major operating standards such as yields, portion sizes and portion costs. It should therefore be regarded as an effective aid to the control of profitability and guest satisfaction.

REVENUE CONTROL

As explained in Chapter 7, in all hotels and restaurants the revenue side of the business has a powerful effect on the profitability of the establishment. Whilst the early approaches to food costing and food and beverage cost control tended to concentrate on the cost side of the business, food and beverage control is both cost- and revenue-oriented. An important task of food and beverage control is therefore to control the sales revenue of the business: total sales, sales mix, ASP, as well as sales per waiter, sales per opening hour, etc.

COST CONTROL

Readers should note that food and beverage control is concerned not only with foods and beverages, but with all the operational matters which constitute the responsibility of the food and beverage manager. Thus an important function of the food and beverage controller is to monitor not only food costs and beverage costs but all the direct/controllable costs in the food and beverage department. Payroll costs as well as control of costs in respect of laundry and dry-cleaning, contract cleaning, etc., are always seen as important ingredients of the food and beverage controller's overall responsibility.

ENSURING SATISFACTORY PROFITABILITY

The systematic checking of predetermined (budgeted) levels of ASP, portion costs and profit margins is an obvious and commonsense method of ensuring that the establishment earns a satisfactory profit from its food and beverage operations.

PREVENTION OF WASTE

Prevention of waste is not only desirable in itself; it is also indispensable if the establishment is to achieve its budgeted results in terms of unit food and beverage costs and levels of gross profit.

PREVENTION OF FRAUD

Fraud and an extensive repertoire of malpractices are, regretfully, fairly common in many hotels and restaurants. They are perpetrated by both the employees and, less frequently, the guests of the establishment. Whilst it is generally assumed that such malpractices can never be completely eliminated, the scope and opportunity for any misdeeds should be restricted through strict and systematic controls.

MANAGEMENT REPORTS

The main aim of management reports is to inform the management about the current progress of the establishment. The reporting on current food and beverage operations will need to cover appropriate periods of time (review periods). Hence we will need daily, weekly, monthly, quarterly, half-yearly and annual reports. Also it will be necessary to ensure that the reports are comprehensive and cover all the major aspects of the operation.

FOOD AND BEVERAGE RECORDS

Finally an important function of food and beverage control is to ensure that the establishment maintains adequate records. Such records relate to suitably analysed sales volumes achieved, numbers of covers served, menu and beverage prices, profit margins, payroll and other costs, etc. It should be appreciated that all such records are indispensable for future planning, and this will be clear from the budgeting examples given in Chapter 6.

The Methodology of Food and Beverage Control

The method of approach to food and beverage control and its place in food and beverage management are illustrated in Figure 12.1, where the whole field of food and beverage control is divided into three phases.

Phase 1 is the policy-making stage, where we decide what it is that we want the food and beverage operation to achieve and how we want to achieve it. All these matters are dealt with in Chapter 5. Briefly, then, it is at this stage that we decide on matters such as the required sales volume, operating expenses and the resulting profit. It is also at this stage that we determine the catering policy of the operation and the requisite

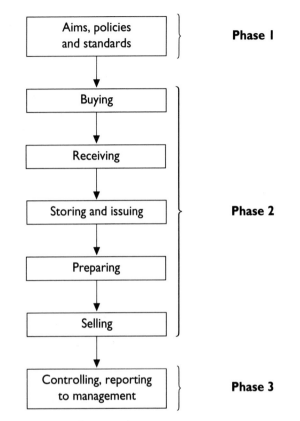

Figure 12.1 Food and beverage control

operating standards. All the matters relevant to Phase 1 are of fundamental significance to food and beverage control. It is for this reason that readers should make sure that they have read Chapter 5 before tackling the remainder of the present chapter.

Phase 2 is concerned with the five operational problems faced by all food and beverage operations – hotels, restaurants, cafés, industrial canteens, etc. – on a daily basis. They all have to purchase food and beverages, check the supplies on delivery, store the purchases and issue appropriate quantities from one day to another, cook/prepare the meals/beverages, and finally sell the food and beverages. In brief, these five operational stages are as follows:

1   Buying;
2   Receiving;
3   Storing and issuing;
4   Preparing;
5   Selling.

These five stages reflect the natural sequence of events in the catering process, and are variously described as the 'catering cycle' or the 'control cycle'. Each operational stage constitutes a highly critical aspect of the operation. Each stage, therefore, has to be controlled through effective and comprehensive checks to ensure a successful and profitable overall operation. The five stages are dealt with below.

Phase 3 is sometimes referred to as 'control after the event' or 'post-operational control'. It is mainly concerned with food and beverage reporting and the assessment of results. This phase of control is discussed in some detail in Chapter 6, and the readers' attention is particularly drawn to the practical examples in Tables 6.10, 6.11 and 6.12.

BUYING

The efficient buying of foods and beverages can make an important contribution to the profitability of the establishments. One important element here is the choice of the correct method of buying in relation to each group of commodities. The main methods of buying foods and beverages are discussed below.

Wholesale Markets

Wholesale markets for meat, fish, fruits and vegetables are an important source of supplies for hotels and restaurants, and this method of buying offers considerable advantages. As a general principle, wholesale markets provide fresh produce at competitive prices, and there is invariably a good choice available. All these factors are of great significance – particularly to high ASP establishments. Associated with this method of buying are two disadvantages: visits to wholesale markets are time-consuming and necessitate having one's own transport. However, where wholesale markets are available and situated in the vicinity of the hotel or restaurant, they are an important and attractive source of supply.

Daily Quotations

This method of buying is mainly used for fruit and vegetables, as it is in the case of these two groups of commodities that both price and quality tend to vary frequently – sometimes from one day to the next. The procedure here is as follows. The first step is to determine the quantity of the produce required for the following day. It is then necessary to ascertain what quantities are in stock; the amounts required for delivery the following morning can then be calculated. The approved suppliers would then be telephoned to obtain the necessary price quotations. The decision to place the order would not be made before securing sufficient

Old Mill Hotel Daily Quotation Sheet Date					
	Quantity required	Supplier			
	kg	1	2	3	4
Artichokes Asparagus Beans – French	20	1.40	1.45	NA	1.35
– Runner Brussels Sprouts	30	0.80	NA	0.85	0.90
Cabbage – Savoy – Spring Carrots – Large – New	40	0.90	0.95	0.80	0.95
Cauliflower Celery etc.					

Figure 12.2 Daily quotation sheet

quotations for all the food items concerned. An example of a daily quotation sheet is given in Figure 12.2.

It should be added that as a general rule the order would be placed with the supplier quoting the lowest price, especially in situations where suppliers quote on the basis of specifications and hence in respect of practically identical produce.

Cash and Carry

This method of buying is particularly suitable for smaller establishments. Its advantages are quite distinct. The location of cash and carry warehouses is usually convenient. Prices charged are generally seen as competitive. Finally, an important advantage is that it is possible to purchase foods in relatively small quantities. The main disadvantages here are the need to provide one's own transport and the supplier's insistence on cash – there are no credit facilities.

Wholesalers

Wholesale suppliers, typically quite large companies, supply a large proportion of mainly groceries and convenience foods to hotels and restaurants. As a general rule they like to supply fairly large quantities, but offer the advantage of credit facilities. Also, delivery is free, and is regular – at least once a week. Most large hotels and restaurants regard wholesale suppliers as a major source of supply.

Standing Orders

This relates to the regular, daily delivery of food items without a specific order. Standing orders are generally used for the delivery of dairy produce. Sometimes, less frequently, they are used for bakery products (bread, rolls, etc.). Standing orders may be 'fixed', when the same quantity is delivered from one day to another (10 gallons of milk daily, etc.). There are also 'flexible' standing orders in use, when the quantity delivered varies over the working week in accordance with the pattern of business.

Yield Tests

The determination of standard yields is a matter that primarily belongs to Phase 1 of food and beverage control, but it also has a bearing on Phase 2. As far as operational control is concerned, several additional points should be remembered.

Standard yields are important not only because they provide important operational standards, but also because they enable realistic costings of dishes and thus help to control the gross profit levels of the establishment. Once all the yields have been calculated, it is necessary to ensure that yields actually achieved are checked from one week to another and any major discrepancies reported on.

Yields are generally associated with yields from cuts of meat and butchering tests. They are all, however, important in relation to all foods. In addition therefore to feedback on current actual yields, it is desirable that yields should be undertaken on selected food items from one week to another. Where an operation experiences a weekly or annual pattern of business, such yield tests will normally be channelled into slack days of the week and/or slack periods of the year.

Purchase Specifications

Standard purchase specifications – or just purchase specifications – are in the same category as yield tests, in that they relate to both Phase 1 and Phase 2 (see Figure 12.1). As explained in Chapter 5, they should be written up for, at least, all the heavy-use, expensive food items. Subsequently, from the point of view of operational control, several points are important.

The writing up of purchase specifications is a time-consuming process. Therefore it is as well to ensure that the specifications are used. All the relevant suppliers should have copies of the specifications. The same applies to appropriate departments of the hotel or restaurant: the goods received department, the kitchen and of course they should be available to the food and beverage manager and food and beverage controller.

New food products continually appear on the market and, as soon as the suppliers' samples are received, such new products should be yield tested and the necessary purchase specifications written up.

PURCHASING BEVERAGES

The buying of beverages is in many ways different from the buying of foods. Three factors are responsible for such differences.

As pointed out in Chapter 1, sales instability is an important feature of practically all hotels and restaurants. This, combined with the perishability of food, means that the purchasing of food is an inherently difficult task: we have to ensure that sufficient food will be available to satisfy all the choices of our customers; we also have to make sure that we do not overbuy – as food is a highly perishable commodity.

These two factors, sales instability and perishability, do not operate to our disadvantage in the case of beverages. What wines, spirits, etc., are not sold today, will be sold tomorrow or in the weeks to come. All beverages – wines, spirits and even beers and minerals – have a sufficiently long shelf-life to ensure that we do not have to worry about their perishability.

The third factor which makes the buying of beverages different is the nature of the product. Whether it is a bottle of gin or Martini, or a can of beer, we have a standard product whose content will remain unaltered over a period of years and will not change in size from one delivery to another. Also it is a product whose price will remain stable – certainly more stable than most food prices. The nature of the beverage product is, therefore, such that we do not bother with yield tests or purchase specifications.

As far as beverages are concerned, several sources of supply are available. Wine shippers purchase wine in its country of origin for subsequent sale elsewhere. Most wine shippers tend to specialise in one particular area of a given country. Thus those importing from France would tend to concentrate on one of the following: Alsace, Bordeaux, Burgundy, the Rhône, etc. Whilst large and prestigious establishments obtain some of their supplies from wine shippers, the latter tend to deal mainly with wine and spirit wholesalers who, in turn, supply the hotel and restaurant industry. Wholesalers as a general rule offer a wide range of products and, frequently, generous credit facilities.

Large hotels and restaurants are able to purchase their spirits, beers and minerals from beverage manufacturers, who would expect the quantities involved to be quite considerable. It is for this reason that smaller establishments would tend to rely on cash-and-carry businesses as a main source of supply.

RECEIVING

Stage 2 of operational control is known as the 'receiving' stage. Hopefully, all food that has been ordered will in due course be delivered, and it is important to make sure that it is properly checked. The Goods Received Clerk will be expected to check the quantities actually delivered and the quality of the goods.

If he/she is to do the work effectively, the Goods Received Clerk will need the following.

1 Copies of all the purchase specifications – as it is on the basis of the establishment's specifications that suppliers quote prices and dispatch the foods;
2 Appropriate equipment, such as a platform scale, hanging scales, etc.;
3 Copies of the relevant purchase orders.

Whilst the checking of the quantities delivered by the suppliers is relatively easy and simple, the checking of the quality of such goods is in a different category. The majority of Goods Received Clerks do not have the technical expertise to check the quality of meat, fish, fruit and vegetables. Whenever such goods are received, the head chef or a senior member of the kitchen crew should be asked to examine them.

Expensive Food Items

In many establishments it is considered that expensive food items such as meat, smoked salmon, etc., should be subjected to additional, stricter controls. A common method of providing an additional check is to use tags. An example is shown in Figure 12.3.

Each meat tag consists of two identical parts. One part of the tag is torn off and sent to the food and beverage controller's office, the other half remains on the meat.

Tag No:	0306	Tag No:	0306
Date received:	10/7/94	Date received:	10/7/94
Weight:	16lb	Weight:	16lb
Price:	£3.75	Price:	£3.75
Cost:	£60.00	Cost:	£60.00
Supplier:	Lester Meat Co.	Supplier:	Lester Meat Co.
Date issued:	_____	Date issued:	_____

Figure 12.3 Meat tag

The tagging of food items offers several advantages:

1 All tags indicate the relevant weights and this assists in periodic stocktaking.
2 Tagging promotes a sensible rotation of stock.
3 In order to complete the tag, the storekeeper is forced to weigh the food item concerned. There is consequently stricter control over the quantities of incoming goods.
4 As tag numbers indicate what food items should be in stock, there is less scope for theft and petty pilfering.

End-of-Day Procedure

At the end of the day the Goods Received Clerk will complete a summary of all the goods received. This is done by entering all invoices and credit notes in the Goods Received Book, an example of which is given in Figure 12.4.

It should be noted that the Goods Received Book requires only the minimum of information, such as supplier's name, order number and delivery note or invoice number. Where the goods are in accordance with the purchase order, a tick is placed in the 'remarks' column. Where

GOODS RECEIVED BOOK			
Signed: J Smith		Date: 15.07.94	
Supplier's Name	Order No	Del. Note or Invoice No.	Remarks
Ealing Fish Co.	11274	0075	✓
Hanwell Cake Ltd	11891	7172	✓
Chelsea Foods Ltd	11299	0791	One case of 'Skyfroot' short
Ham Beverage Co.	11667	1348	✓
etc.			

Figure 12.4 Goods received book

there is some discrepancy, an appropriate explanatory note is made. Thus where the delivery is short, it is important to check the supplier's invoice on its arrival to ensure that the establishment is only charged for what has in fact been delivered. Where an invoice has not been adjusted for a short delivery, the Accounts Department should immediately ask the supplier for a credit note.

Receiving Beverages

The receiving of beverages is, essentially, similar to the receiving of foods. We still have to check the quantities delivered, but the quality inspection is necessarily less meticulous because we are dealing with standard products. Whilst we would expect all broken bottles and dented tins to be noted, we would tend to assume that the quality of the beverages is otherwise satisfactory. One important difference between foods and beverages is their respective values. Beverages are generally more costly and, therefore, more attention has to be paid to their security.

STORING AND ISSUING

After the delivery and inspection of foods, it becomes necessary to divide them into two categories. The dry goods will be transferred to the food store and become the responsibility of the storekeeper. The perishables – meat, poultry, fish, fresh fruit and vegetables – will be transferred to the kitchen and cold storage areas and become the responsibility of the head chef. Whilst the dry goods are stored over fairly long periods, the perishables are, typically, consumed within a day or two. The difference in the turnover of the two categories of foods necessitates different control procedures.

Perishable Foods

As the turnover of these foods is fast, it is usually considered that no useful purpose would be served by keeping detailed records for all the different joints of meat, kinds of fish, etc. By the time we made the appropriate entries, most of the foods would have been cooked and sold! Hence, in most situations it is accepted that a weekly overall record is sufficient and this is achieved by keeping an analysed Weekly Perishables Book. An example is shown in Figure 12.5.

The main function of the Weekly Perishables Book is to enable the establishment to calculate its weekly consumption of perishables. This, added to the cost of the dry goods, constitutes the weekly cost of food consumed. As may be seen from Figure 12.5, this necessitates a weekly stocktaking of perishables.

WEEKLY PERISHABLES BOOK								
Period: Week 39								
Date		Meat	Poultry	Fish	Dairy	Fruit	Veg	TOTAL
Sept 26	Opening stock	320.10	155.25	215.75	89.90	55.45	77.55	914.00
	Fresh Meat Co.	185.85						185.85
	Pericles Farm					81.25	44.37	125.62
27	Dutch Dairy Co.				96.10			96.10
	Neptune Fish Ltd			184.90				184.90
27	etc.							
27								
27								
28								
Oct 2	Total	1,235.35	605.75	806.20	355.35	204.65	301.70	3,509.00
	Closing stock	290.20	144.15	188.75	78.85	45.25	65.80	813.00
2	Consumption	945.15	461.60	617.45	276.50	159.40	235.90	2,696.00

Figure 12.5 Weekly perishables book

Dry Foods

The control of dry foods is rather more complex and time-consuming. In larger hotels and restaurants it is usual to maintain a separate record (stock card or bin card) for every food item kept in the dry store. Also, there is invariably strict control exercised over stores issues: nothing is issued from the store except against a properly authorised requisition note.

Figure 12.6 shows an example of a stock card. It should be noted that

Item: Fruit Salad			
Min. Stock: 25			
Date	In	Out	Balance
1994			
Mar 7			41
8		13	28
9		3	25
10	50		75
11		10	65

Figure 12.6 Stock card

277

stock cards (the same applies to bin cards) do not show any values – just the movements of physical stock, i.e. quantities only. Bin cards serve the same purpose as stock cards and show the same information. They are not housed in separate binders, but are usually attached to the various bins, racks and receptacles.

Figure 12.7 shows a typical stores requisition note. It should be pointed out that stores requisition notes are not normally priced when presented to the stores: at this stage they only show the quantities of foods required. They are, however, frequently priced at the end of each week to ascertain the total value of dry goods consumed. This, added to the consumption of perishable foods (see Figure 12.5), gives the weekly cost of food consumed.

Stores requisition				
Date: 10 May 1994 — **Dept:** Staff Kitchen — **No:** 0074				
PARTICULARS	Qty	Unit	£	p
Tomato ketchup	10			
Instant coffee	12kg			
Sugar – granulated	20kg			
Signed: Bill Brown				

Figure 12.7 Stores requisition note

Periodic Food Cost Calculations

All hotels and restaurants have to check their periodic gross profit performance, and this calls for the relevant food cost figures. There are two basic methods of calculating the periodic (weekly, monthly, etc.) food costs. These, briefly, are as follows:

1   Under the first method we calculate separately the cost of perishables consumed. We then price all the requisition notes presented to the food store. The combined total of these two is the periodic food cost.

2   Under the second method, we take the opening stock (of both perishable and non-perishable foods), add (the total value of) all the purchase invoices relevant to the period, and deduct the closing stock (of perishable and non-perishable foods). The resulting figure is the cost of food consumed during the period concerned.

The two methods have their respective advantages and disadvantages. It is generally considered that the first method is more convenient for shorter periods (e.g. one week), and that the second is more appropriate for monthly and quarterly food cost calculations.

Storing and Issuing of Beverages

The stock of beverages held by hotels and restaurants represents a considerable investment, frequently amounting to many thousands of pounds. Controls exercised over the beverage stock must, therefore, be strict, and in practice such controls are invariably stricter than those in respect of the stock of food. One important practice which is always very much in evidence is the restriction of access to the cellar. This, for practical purposes, means not allowing any casual access to the storage areas concerned with wines, spirits, etc. Also, even more importantly, it means limiting access to the cellar keys. Frequent changes of locks and combinations are now quite inexpensive and fairly common practice.

The high value of beverages enjoins satisfactory storage conditions. The overall storage area for beverages will therefore be divided into several distinctly separate parts. Spirits and red wines require a dry area with a temperature of 13–16°C (55–60°F). White wines and sparkling wines prefer somewhat cooler conditions and a temperature of 10°C (50°F). Bottled beers and soft drinks should be stored at a temperature of 13°C (55°F). Finally, a fairly large area is required for returnable containers, crates, kegs and empty bottles. A high proportion of these will be returned to the suppliers and, in due course, appropriate credit obtained from them.

Bin cards are quite a common feature of cellar control. An example of a typical bin card is shown in Figure 12.8.

Cellar issues are made against cellar requisitions – an example is given in Figure 12.9. It should be noticed that, in addition to the cost per unit (bottle, crate, etc.), the requisition – when finally completed by the Control Office – will show the total cost and the total value at selling price of each cellar requisition. This is necessary for control purposes. The specific controls of beverages sales through the 'sales value potential' concept are discussed later in this chapter.

Bin Card							
Item: Chateau Dillon				**Min Stock:** 12			
Bin No: 588				**Max Stock:** 48			
Date	In	Out	Bal	Date	In	Out	Bal
1994 Oct 12			37				
14		5	32				
16		10	22				
17		7	15				
18	30		45				

Figure 12.8 Bin card

Cellar Requisition						
Date: 22 May 1994		**Dept:** Main Bar	**No:** 00146			
Qty	Bin No.	Description	Unit	Cost per unit	Total cost	Sales value
5	306 ·	Gordons Gin	Bot	9.00	45.00	150.00
20	576	House Wine – White	Bot	3.00	60.00	160.00
10	588	House Wine – Red	½ Bot	1.60	16.00	50.00
		etc.				
Signed: J. B. White						

Figure 12.9 Cellar requisition

Stocktaking

Periodical stocktaking is an essential part of food and beverage operations. It is necessary for the following reasons:

1 To establish the actual physical stock at the end of each trading period. The book value of food and beverage stocks may be calculated from the stock records. This, however, is not always sufficiently accurate because of: (a) errors in issuing; (b) breakages

and other losses within the storage areas; (c) petty pilfering; and (d) inaccurate recording of receipts and issues.

2   To control food and beverage stock levels. As already mentioned, food and beverage stocks represent a considerable investment of resources, typically running into thousands of pounds. It is important to ensure that, whilst the stock is adequate in relation to the customers' needs and preferences, it is not excessive.

3   To ensure the proper rotation of stock. Even in well-managed hotels and restaurants, where adequate stock records are kept, it is not always easy to ensure the right rotation of stock – particularly during busy periods. Stocktaking is, in such circumstances, a good opportunity to rearrange the positioning of goods and make sure that they are used in accordance with the 'first-in-first-out' principle.

Unduly high stock levels inevitably lead to waste. In the case of food they result in the deterioration of highly perishable commodities. In the case of beverages any stock held over and above what is necessary is a poor investment of resources which could have been better employed elsewhere in the business.

Rate of Stock Turnover

An effective method of controlling stock levels is to calculate periodically the rate of stock turnover. This measures the speed with which the stock is turned over, i.e. repurchased or resold. A high rate of stock turnover indicates low stock levels in relation to the volume of sales; conversely a low rate of stock turnover indicates that stocks are high. The formula which is most often used to calculate the rate of stock turnover is:

$$\frac{\text{Cost of Sales}}{\text{Average Stock at Cost}} = \text{RST}$$

Average stock is normally calculated by taking the average of opening and closing stocks. Where the average stock is £2,000 and the cost of sales £80,000, the rate of stock turnover is:

$$\frac{£80,000}{£2,000} = 40 \text{ (times)}$$

The rate for stock turnover for food tends to vary between 30 and 50, which means that the typical stock of food is repurchased or resold between 30 and 50 times a year. The more extensive the menu the larger the number of food items that need to be stored, and the lower the rate of stock turnover, and vice versa. The rate of stock turnover for beverages tends to vary between 4 and 12. Again, the more extensive the choice of wines, etc., the higher the value of beverage stocks held and the lower the rate of stock turnover, and vice versa.

PREPARING

Stage 4 of the catering cycle, the preparation stage, needs careful monitoring to ensure good overall results. Two elements are of particular importance here.

First, all hotels and restaurants are subject to sales instability. The number of covers will vary from one day/week to another. Unless we introduce a system for coping with such demand instability, we will continually overproduce and underproduce food. Any over-production of food results in waste, as most cooked dishes cannot be stored and resold subsequently. When insufficient food is prepared, our customers have to be satisfied with second or third choices, and this, over a period of time, leads to loss of custom and underachievement in terms of sales volumes. The way to combat the problem of demand instability is to introduce a system of volume forecasting which is described below.

Secondly, we have the problem of portion costs. The cost per portion of any food item may fluctuate due to a variety of reasons: changes in prices paid to suppliers, erratic quality of food received, incorrect cooking methods, bad/inaccurate portioning, etc. In order to control portion costs, we need a system of pre-costing – that is, a system of determining costs in advance of the preparation of food. This is described later in this chapter.

Volume Forecasting

Volume forecasting is a method of predicting, for each day of the following week, how many customers will come and what they will choose from the menu. It is, therefore, a method of sales forecasting, in that we are trying to predict how many portions of each menu item we will sell on Sunday, Monday, Tuesday, etc. Volume forecasting is not an exact science, and no one can claim that it can be 100 per cent accurate. The point is that, with volume forecasting, our judgement with regard to the anticipated number of covers and customers' choices will be more accurate than without it. It is better to over-prepare by 10 per cent than 50 per cent! The specific objectives of volume forecasting may be summarised as follows:

1   To predict, on a daily basis, the number of covers the establishment expects to serve each week.

2 To predict customers' preferences. Thus if we expect 120 customers for dinner next Tuesday, we have to predict what they will choose from the menu: how many will have roast lamb, mixed grill, spring chicken, etc.

3 To facilitate purchasing. As we know what we are going to sell, we have no problem in placing accurate purchase orders with our suppliers. It should be noted that with a system of volume forecasting our purchasing is more rational and purpose-oriented. We buy particular quantities of meat, fish, etc., because we know we are going to sell so many of the appropriate food items. Thus if we expect to sell 40 portions of spring chicken, if one portion is half a chicken we place an order for 20 chickens. We buy on the basis of what we expect to sell not simply to maintain reasonable levels of raw materials.

4 To ensure that we have the right number of staff in all the relevant departments, i.e. kitchen, dining areas, wash-up, dispense bars, etc.

Volume forecasting must take into account a great deal of information. It is important to ascertain current levels of (guest) occupancy, advance bookings and assess the impact on the number of covers of any local events as well as the weather. However, the main and most direct indicator of what we may expect next week is the Sales History. This is a summary of the number of covers served and individual menu items sold during recent weeks. An example is given in Figure 12.10 overleaf.

Figure 12.11 shows an example of a volume forecast for a large hotel. This shows the estimated and actual number of covers for each day of the week. Comparisons of the estimated and actual figures are important because they tend to help explain any major variances and thus improve the accuracy of our forecasts. The volume forecast in Figure 12.11 is a master forecast: it only shows the projected numbers of covers for a hotel as a whole as well as the departmental figures. More detailed departmental forecasts would still be required to show the customers' choices of menu items. Figure 12.12 shows a departmental volume forecast, which is an extension of the master volume forecast in Figure 12.11. In the Restaurant of the Serendipity Hotel we expect to serve 95 covers at dinner on Tuesday 18 August. On the basis of recent sales histories we would prepare a departmental forecast such as is given in Figure 12.12 on page 286.

Cyclic Menus

Cyclic menus are an important aid to volume forecasting. A cyclic menu is one which usually covers a period of 10–28 days. When, for example,

MENU	Previous 3 Months		2 June		9 June		etc.
	Items Sold	% of Covers	Items Sold	% of Covers	Items Sold	% of Covers	
APPETISERS							
Fruit Juice	22	12.1	25	12.4			
Grapefruit	15	8.3	18	8.9			
Vegetable Soup	38	20.9	43	21.3			
Chef's Pâté	29	15.9	31	15.3			
Seafood Salad	35	19.2	42	20.8			
Total	139	76.4	159	78.7			
ENTRÉES							
Rib of Beef	29	15.9	32	15.8			
Lamb Cutlets	63	34.6	65	32.2			
Grilled Trout	27	14.9	33	16.3			
Pork Chops	25	13.7	28	13.8			
Spring Chicken	38	20.9	44	21.9			
Total	182	100.0	202	100.0			
VEGETABLES							
New Potatoes	102	56.0	115	56.9			
Baked Potatoes	75	41.2	86	42.6			
French Beans	89	48.9	95	47.0			
Cauliflower	62	34.1	67	33.2			
Spinach	30	16.5	39	19.3			
Total	358	196.7	402	199.0			
DESSERTS							
Fruit Salad	38	20.9	42	20.9			
Crème Caramel	25	13.7	29	14.3			
Charlotte Russe	18	9.9	19	9.4			
Plum Pudding	15	8.2	18	8.9			
Ice Cream	22	12.1	25	12.4			
Total	118	64.8	133	65.8			

Figure 12.10 Sales history

there is a 10-day cycle, we have ten menus. We start with the menu for day 1, then go on to menu 2, 3, etc., until we have served the tenth menu. We then revert to the menu for day 1.

Cyclic menus are particularly useful in resort hotels, where most guests stay for periods of up to fourteen days and where a fourteen-day cycle is especially convenient. The benefits of cyclic menus may be summarised as follows:

Serendipity Hotel Volume Forecast									
Week commencing: Sunday 16 August 1995									
	Sunday		Monday		Tuesday		Wednesday		etc.
	Est	Act	Est	Act	Est	Act	Est	Act	
RESTAURANT									
Breakfast	22	19	45	43	55		65		
Luncheon	55	52	120	115	140		155		
Dinner	40	38	85	82	95		110		
COFFEE SHOP									
Breakfast	105	101	120	119	140		155		
Luncheon	220	202	245	240	265		290		
Dinner	150	139	160	151	185		205		
FUNCTIONS									
Luncheons	25	25	—	—	—		75		
Dinners	125	125	—	—	65		210		
Cocktails	60	62	30	30	90		115		
FLOOR SERVICE									
Breakfast	40	35	25	23	35		45		
Luncheon	75	70	35	33	55		65		
Dinner	45	42	15	16	85		95		
Total covers	962	910	880	852	1,210		1,585		

Figure 12.11 Volume forecast

1 As there is a constant menu structure, it is easy to predict guests' choices of menu items.
2 Volume forecasting is considerably facilitated.
3 As our forecasting is more accurate, there is less waste and this leads to more satisfactory profitability.

During the last decade or so a large number of establishments introduced cyclic menus and found them not only acceptable to customers but also economical and profitable.

Pre-costing

In addition to sales instability, food and beverage operations also face the problem of fluctuations in food costs. Such fluctuations are frequently quite significant – and worrying – in the case of fresh fruit and vegetables. Other groups of commodities such as meat, fish and poultry are also subject to price instability, particularly during periods of inflation.

Serendipity Hotel Departmental Volume Forecast RESTAURANT: Tues 18 Aug 1995	
Dinner	
Menu Item	No. of Portions
Fruit Juice	10
Vegetable Soup	25
Seafood Salad	20
Chef's Pâté	15 70
Grilled Trout	25
Chicken Maryland	35
Lamb Chops	15
Mixed Grill	20 95
New Potatoes	30
French Fried	60
Spinach	25
French Beans	70 185
Crème Caramel	15
Fruit Salad	20
Summer Pudding	10
Ice Creams	10 55

Figure 12.12 Departmental volume forecast

There is no quick or simple solution to the problem of fluctuating food costs. The generally accepted view is that what is needed is a system of pre-costing. Pre-costing means determining food costs before the event – i.e. in advance of the actual preparation/cooking process. This involves building into the operation several essential operating standards, all of which have the effect of promoting food cost stability as well as steady levels of gross profit. The standards listed below have already been dealt with in Chapter 5. They are therefore discussed here only briefly in the context of operational control. Readers may find it useful to refer to Chapter 5 before tackling the remainder of the present chapter.

Standard Yields

Standard yields are an essential instrument of food cost control, in that they determine the amount or percentage of edible food available from actual cuts, etc., purchased. Whilst it is possible to calculate yields for all items of food, they are most important in the case of meat, fish and poultry, i.e. food items where inedible elements (fat and bone loss, etc.) constitute a high percentage of the total initial weight as purchased.

Standard Portion Sizes

These are especially important in the case of expensive food items such as meat, fish, poultry and game. Poor portioning and neglect of standard portion sizes tend to result in erratic portion costs and lead to inadequate profit margins.

Standard Portion Costs

The term 'standard portion cost' has little meaning unless it relates to a standard product (as determined by the standard recipe), of a standard size (as determined by the establishment's portions sizes) and is calculated by reference to the standard costs appropriate to the ingredients used.

Prices paid to suppliers will always vary to some extent, and it is important to ensure that portion costs are calculated by reference to the relevant future period. Relevance here depends on how frequently we change the menu/s. Thus where there is only one à la carte menu and this is changed four times a year, relevant portion costs are based on prices that will be paid to suppliers during the three-month period in question. Most certainly it is not right to calculate portion costs by reference to current food prices or prices 'per last invoice'.

Standard Recipes

The role and importance of standard recipes have already been discussed in considerable detail. At this stage it is necessary to note that, from the point of view of operational control, standard recipes should be seen as a critical instrument of food cost control and a major aid to pre-costing. It is for this reason that we have to ensure that we have sufficiently detailed standard recipes for all menu items. Also steps should be taken to make sure that there is adequate provision for periodic reviews of standard recipes to accommodate changes in customers' preferences as well as new products which, from time to time, appear on the market.

Preparing: Recent Progress

As far as this stage of the control cycle is concerned, a great deal of progress has been made in recent years. The vast majority of larger food and beverage operations use standard recipes; a great deal of the relevant work has been computerised and much of the control work is characterised by efficiency and professionalism. Only in one area is there still much progress to be made. Relatively few larger establishments operate a formal system of volume forecasting, and this must necessarily make the task of gross profit control more difficult.

Preparing Beverages

Fundamentally this stage of the control cycle is considerably easier in the case of beverages than the corresponding task for foods. As already mentioned, we have here essentially standard, non-perishable products. The yield (number of tots) from each bottle will remain constant from one year to another; and the same applies to the nature and essential characteristics of the product: colour, flavour, alcohol content, etc. Also, as most of the beverages are non-perishable – at least over several months – there is no need for controlling them through a system of volume forecasting. However, as the value of beverage stocks is relatively high, certain control measures are still desirable.

Standard stocks – sometimes described as par stocks – should be fixed for all sales outlets. These are necessary to ensure that each outlet has an adequate supply of beverages; also to make sure that too much capital is not invested in idle stocks. Thus, in relation to each bar, we have to decide how many bottles should be kept of each item of wines, spirits, beers, minerals, etc.

Standard drink portions are of critical importance, and therefore, the use of standard optic sizes and automatic dispensing of standard portions is now common practice. The standardisation of glassware is important from two points of view: the control of beverage sales and the presentation of beverages.

Finally, in the majority of establishments it is usual to find a number of recipes for beverages. These are recipes prepared almost exclusively for the use of the bar staff. Such recipes, therefore, tend to emphasise the quantities of ingredients and the method of preparation rather than portion costs.

SELLING

The 'selling' stage is the last stage of the control cycle. As far as the control of food is concerned, three matters stand out as particularly important.

Routine Pricing Procedures

As explained in Chapter 11, the pricing policy in relation to food and beverages will be determined before we start the actual operations. The total concept of price policy will involve, amongst other things, a decision on the overall price level, the overall percentage of gross profit, and the differential profit margins.

Once all these decisions have been made, all we have to do from one day/week to another is to make sure that we price in accordance with the pricing policy of the establishment. This routine pricing necessitates some formal mechanism for the pricing process, and most hotels and restaurants use a 'costing sheet' or a 'standard costing sheet' for this purpose. A typical example is shown in Figure 12.13 overleaf.

It should be noted that most menu items are not priced individually – on a per portion basis – but in batches. A 'standard batch' is determined for each menu item, and in this example the standard batch is 10 portions. Standard batches will depend on the size of the operation. They will normally be batches of 10, 12 or 20 portions in most restaurants, but may well be 50–100 in large-scale catering. Also, they will depend on the nature of the raw materials used: Châteaubriand will, for obvious reasons, always be priced on the basis of two portions.

The rate of VAT (which changes from time to time and is currently 17.5 per cent) has been taken as 15 per cent to simplify the calculations. The percentage of gross profit is always calculated in relation to the selling price excluding VAT, as this is in a sense the 'real' price in that the VAT element of the menu price is not the establishment's revenue, but money collected for and subsequently remitted to Customs and Excise.

Altogether six sets of columns are provided in the standard costing sheet. This is to enable a periodical re-calculation of costs and prices and is especially useful during periods of inflation.

Finally, it should be noted that our standard costing sheet is prepared in accordance with general practice in this country. As already explained in Chapter 5, most British hotels and restaurants rely on ideal, rather than attainable, standards and, in the pricing process, make no allowance for unproductive cost. Whilst this is not the best solution, our example in Figure 12.13 is intended to illustrate actual general practice, and in that sense is more realistic.

Restaurant Checking Systems

The principal aim of a restaurant checking system is to ensure that strict control is exercised over:

1   All foods and beverages requisitioned from and issued by the appropriate departments – kitchen, dispense bar, etc.;
2   The revenue generated by the food and beverage operation.

| Item | Sole Veronique | | Service | Lunch | | Ref. No. | S.R. 076 |
| No. of portions | 10 | | Menu | Table d'hôte | | VAT | 15% |

Date →			10.09.95													
Ingredients	Unit	Qty	Unit cost	Value	Unit cost	Value	Unit cost	Value	Unit cost	Value	Unit cost	Value	Unit cost	Value		
Dover sole	kg	5	3.50	17.50												
White wine	bot.	1	1.90	1.90												
Butter	kg	0.5	1.10	0.55												
Single cream	litre	0.25	0.90	0.23												
Double cream	litre	0.25	1.20	0.30												
Grapes	kg	300g	2.50	0.88												
Flour	kg	100g	0.40	0.04												
Cost per 10 portions				21.40												
Portion cost				2.14												
Selling price (incl. VAT)				6.15												
VAT				0.80												
Selling price (excl. VAT)				5.35												
Portion cost				2.14												
Gross profit £				3.21												
Gross profit %				60.0												

Figure 12.13 A standard costing sheet

There are two main types of restaurant checking system in use: the triplicate checking system and the duplicate checking system. The majority of larger hotels and restaurants use the triplicate system, whilst the duplicate system will generally be found in smaller hotels and popular catering establishments.

The triplicate system works as follows. The waiter will take the order and produce the food and beverage requisition in triplicate.

1   The top copy of each requisition will be taken to the relevant supply point. From the supply points all the top copies will be transferred, invariably in a locked box, to the control department.
2   The second copy of each requisition will be taken to the restaurant cashier, who will write up the guests' bills.
3   The third copy will be retained by the waiter as an *aide-memoire* – a means of reference during the course of the service.

With the duplicate system the waiter produces two copies of food and beverage requisitions. Again the top copy of each requisition will be taken to the appropriate supply point, whilst the second copy will be retained by the waiter for service and billing purposes. It is essential to make sure that, as in the case of the triplicate checking systems, all copies of the waiters' requisitions are in due course channelled to the control department.

In due course a copy of each food and beverage requisition as well as all the copies of the bills presented to guests will find their way to the control department. It is necessary to 'marry together' each bill with the relevant food and beverage requisitions to ensure that all requisitions have been entered on the guest's bill, and that the establishment receives full payment for all food and beverage consumed by the guest.

Readers will appreciate that this daily checking process is time-consuming and therefore costly. Whilst some establishments continue to check all the bills against the relevant requisitions, others reject 'total checking' as too costly and only check samples/batches of bills and requisitions. This is known as 'selective checking'.

Cash and Revenue Control

As each service proceeds, the restaurant cashier will be receiving copies of the food and beverage requisitions and preparing the guests' bills. Typically, a bill will be in duplicate; the top copy will be given to the guest and the second copy retained for control purposes. The cashier will, by the end of each service, have a complete report, listing all the bills and showing particulars of all cash and credit sales. A specimen example is shown in Figure 12.14 overleaf.

Selling Beverages

Beverage operations are characterised by the relatively high value of beverage stocks and the fact that a very high proportion of beverage sales

Airport Hotel								
	Grill Room			Date: 15 May '94				
Cashier: A Brown				Lunch ✔		Dinner ☐		
Bill No.	Waiter	NOC	Food	Bev.	Tobac.	Total Cash	Rm. No.	Total Credit
0274	John	2	32.10	8.15		40.25		
0275	Fred	1	16.75		3.15		116	19.90
0276	John	3	44.95	14.20	4.30	63.45		
0277	Henry etc.	2	34.10	10.20			228	44.30
		45	731.25	274.50	33.75	693.10		346.40

Figure 12.14 Cashier's Report

are cash – not credit – sales. These two characteristics demand a great deal of control over the bar staff to ensure that any malpractice is reduced to a minimum. Also, in this specific situation, an effective system of cash control is indispensable.

SOME COMMON MALPRACTICES

Bartenders, wine waiters and other staff who are involved in beverage service have many opportunities to pocket the profits of the establishment. No control system will eliminate dishonesty completely, and constant personal supervision – in addition to frequent, irregular checks – is imperative. Some of the most common malpractices are listed below.

1   Dilution of liquor – a most objectionable type of fraud, which calls for occasional checks with the aid of a hydrometer.
2   Selling by bar staff of their own liquor. A bottle of Scotch which costs £10 may have a sales value potential (see below) of, say, £35. A barman who smuggles his own bottle of Scotch into the establishment and removes £35 from the till will rob the business of £25. This kind of malpractice is difficult to check through the usual control procedures. One effective measure that may be taken is to mark, usually rubber stamp, all bottles, so that 'strange' bottles may be identified.
3   Short measures are another – regretfully quite common – malpractice. Automatic dispensing of spirits and other beverages is of considerable help here. Cocktails and other mixed drinks are particularly vulnerable in this respect.

4   Overcharging of guests (and, occasionally, undercharging of friends) is equally objectionable, and unfortunately not easy to check during busy periods.

SALES VALUE POTENTIAL

The control of beverage sales is usually linked to the value, at selling price, of the beverages sold. Hence the term, 'control by selling price'. Most beverages are sold by the measure. Thus, the standard bottle of whisky contains $26\frac{2}{3}$ liquid ounces and is expected to produce 32 measures. When an establishment charges £1.20 per measure (tot), the sales value potential of a bottle of whisky is: $32 \times £1.20 = £38.40$. If the cost per bottle is £11.00, the cash gross profit will be £27.40 and this will be equivalent to 71.4 per cent. One of the main benefits of the sales value potential concept is that it contributes to strict cash control. The example which now follows will make this clear.

EXAMPLE

The figures given below were extracted from the records of the Valley Inn at the end of Month 7.

	At cost £	At selling price £
Opening stock	3,600	8,000
Closing stock	4,200	8,900
Beverage sales	14,300	14,300
Beverages received	7,000	15,000

In order to control the percentage gross profit we have to use the 'at cost' figures, as shown below.

Beverage Sales		14,300
Less: Cost of sales:		
Opening stock	3,600	
Receipts	7,000	
	10,600	
Closing stock	4,200	6,400
Gross profit – £		7,900
Gross profit – %		55.24

The gross profit actually earned amounts to £7,900 and this is equal to 55.24 per cent of beverage sales. The actual percentage of beverage gross profit is useful: it would be compared with the budgeted percentage to assess the progress of the beverage operation.

In addition to controlling the percentage beverage profit, it is important to control the cash received from beverage operations. Cash control in this context is exercised by relying on the concept of the sales value potential, when all figures are shown at selling price.

Beverage Sales		14,300
Less: Cost of sales:		
Opening stock	8,000	
Receipts	15,000	
	23,000	
Closing stock	8,900	14,100
Bar surplus – £		200
Bar surplus – %		1.40

Cash actually received should, strictly speaking, be equal to the sales value potential. In this particular case the sales value potential is £14,100, but actual beverage sales were £14,300. There is, in consequence a 'bar surplus' of £200, equal to 1.4 per cent of beverage sales. A small percentage of bar surplus is not unusual. It is mainly due to the sale of cocktails, where the individual ingredients fetch a price higher than they would if sold as non-cocktail items.

Food and Beverage Cost Calculations

FOOD COST CALCULATIONS

The immediate aim of operational control is to ensure that, throughout the control cycle, actual results correspond as closely as possible to budgeted results. As we are in business to earn a satisfactory profit, it is clear that the ultimate aim of all control activities is to help all departments maintain satisfactory levels of profitability. This necessitates the keeping of appropriate control records and calls for certain adjustments at the end of each period. A few illustrative examples are given below.

EXAMPLE 1: MEDIUM-SIZED RESTAURANT

In smaller and medium-sized restaurants the control procedures will, of necessity, be basic and unsophisticated. In Figure 12.15 we show a food cost control sheet which gives weekly as well as cumulative results.

Food Cost Control Sheet Year commencing 1 Apr. 1995						
Week No.	Purchases		Sales		Cost %	
	This Week	To Date	This Week	To Date	This Week	To Date
	£	£	£	£	%	%
1	870	—	2,610	—	33.3	—
2	696	1,566	2,813	5,423	24.7	28.9
3	638	2,204	2,668	8,091	23.9	27.2
4	652	2,856	2,886	10,977	22.6	26.0
5	493	3,349	2,697	13,674	18.3	24.5
6	551	3,900	2,668	16,342	20.7	23.9
etc.						

Figure 12.15 **Food cost control sheet**

The column headed 'Purchases' refers, of course, to purchases (unadjusted for opening and closing stocks) and not food cost. In consequence the weekly food cost percentages tend to vary quite substantially. The 'To Date' percentages of food cost, however, are more stable, and after the initial few weeks give a good indication of the cumulative results achieved. It should be appreciated that an important advantage of this method is that it makes weekly stocktaking unnecessary.

EXAMPLE 2: LARGE FOOD AND BEVERAGE OPERATION

In larger food and beverage operations it is often considered that, in addition to ascertaining the actual food cost percentages it is desirable to monitor potential food and beverage cost savings from one month to another. A typical food and beverage potential savings sheet is given in Figure 12.16. Here the establishment operates at a standard food cost of 35 per cent and a standard beverage cost of 30 per cent.

In January, food sales amounted to £85,000, and food cost, at 35 per cent, should have been £29,750. In fact, it was £31,450 – £1,700 more than it should have been. Potential savings in food cost for January were thus £1,700. In March, beverage sales amounted to £33,820. Beverage cost, at 30 per cent, should have been – and was – £10,146. Potential savings in beverage cost for March are therefore nil.

295

	Food				Beverage			
FOOD AND BEVERAGE POTENTIAL SAVINGS Year: 1995								
Month	Sales	Cost	%	Saving	Sales	Cost	%	Saving
	£	£	%	£	£	£	%	£
Jan	85,000	31,450	37	(1,700)	32,400	10,044	31	(324)
Feb	87,410	31,464	36	(874)	33,500	10,720	32	(670)
Mar	87,800	30,730	35	—	33,820	10,146	30	—
Apr	97,410	33,116	34	974	36,210	10,500	29	362
May	114,620	37,818	33	2,292	43,210	13,396	31	(432)
etc.								

Figure 12.16 Potential food and beverage savings sheet

FOOD AND BEVERAGE TRANSFERS

At the end of each trading period, before we calculate food and beverage gross profits, it is necessary to take into account what are known as 'food and beverage transfers'. Those are amounts of food transferred to bars, amounts of beverage transferred to the kitchen, food consumed by the employees, etc. Such transfers necessitate adjustments designed to produce exact figures of net food cost and net beverage cost. A few specific examples are given below.

1 Food consumed by the employees: this should be deducted from Food Cost and added to Employee Benefits or Labour Costs.
2 Wine used in the kitchen: this should be deducted from beverage cost and added to food cost.
3 Food transferred to the bar: this should be deducted from food cost and added to beverage cost.
4 Free meals offered to travel agents: this should be deducted from food cost and added to marketing or public relations. Where the value of such meals, at selling price, is say £100, it is essential to eliminate the gross profit element (say £70) and show the adjustment in respect of the food cost involved – £30. This is because the transaction is not strictly speaking a sale – though a cost has been incurred.

EXAMPLE

The following figures were extracted from the records of the York Restaurant at 31 Dec. 1995.

	Food £	Beverage £
Purchases	520,500	185,200
Sales	1,450,000	535,000

You are required to take into account the following adjustments and calculate the restaurant's gross profit on food and beverages for 1995.

1. The cost of food used for employees' meals was £17,200.
2. Beverages transferred to the kitchen amounted to £10,700.
3. Food transferred to the bar amounted to £3,000.
4. Opening stocks at 1 January 1995 were: food £14,000, and beverages £18,200.
5. Closing stocks were: food £15,200, and beverages £22,100.

The net cost of food was:

	£
Opening stock	14,000
Add purchases	520,500
	534,500
Add beverages used in the kitchen	10,700
	545,200
Less employee meals	17,200
	528,000
Less food used in the bar	3,000
	525,000
Less closing stock	15,200
Net cost of food	509,800

The net cost of beverages was:

	£
Opening stock	18,200
Add purchases	185,200
	203,400
Add food used in the bar	3,000
	206,400
Less beverages used in the kitchen	10,700
	195,700
Less closing stock	22,100
Net cost of beverages	173,600

We are now able to calculate the gross profits.

	Food		Beverage	
	£	%	£	%
Sales	1,450,000	100.0	535,000	100.0
Less net cost of sales	509,800	35.2	173,600	32.4
Gross profit	940,200	64.8	361,400	67.6

BEVERAGE CALCULATIONS

Beverage cost figures are essential in the control of bar (percentage and cash) gross profits. Equally the concept of the potential sales value is indispensable in the control of cash received. In most situations – whether we are controlling a cocktail bar, beverages sold at a function, or room service – we will have to control three things:

1 Cash received;
2 Percentage gross profit;
3 Cash gross profit.

The numerical example which follows will illustrate the above points.

EXAMPLE: COCKTAIL BAR

A hotel cocktail bar sells a limited variety of drinks. Given in Table 12.1 are the relevant portion costs, selling prices and amounts sold in May 1995.

Table 12.1 Cocktail bar results

Drink	Portion cost	Selling price	Portions sold
	£	£	
Gin & Tonic	0.30	1.25	2,720
Bloody Mary	0.32	1.30	2,224
Scotch & Ginger	0.37	1.40	2,880
Flying Scotsman	0.35	1.35	3,622
Little Princess	0.29	1.30	1,518
Martini & Soda	0.35	1.50	5,528
Manhattan	0.40	1.50	4,230

Actual beverage cost during May was £8,050 and actual revenue (i.e. cash received) £31,990.30. You are required to prepare the necessary figures and percentages to assess the performance of the cocktail bar during the month of May.

Table 12.2 Potential cocktail bar results

Drink	Portion cost	Selling price	Portions sold	Potential beverage cost	Sales value potential	Potential gross profit
	£	£		£	£	£
Gin & Tonic	0.30	1.25	2,720	816.00	3,400.00	2,584.00
Bloody Mary	0.32	1.30	2,224	711.68	2,891.20	2,179.52
Scotch & Ginger	0.37	1.40	2,880	1,065.60	4,032.00	2,966.40
Flying Scotsman	0.35	1.35	3,622	1,267.70	4,889.70	3,622.00
Little Princess	0.29	1.30	1,518	440.22	1,973.40	1,533.18
Martini & Soda	0.35	1.50	5,528	1,934.80	8,292.00	6,357.20
Manhattan	0.40	1.50	4,230	1,692.00	6,345.00	4,653.00
				7,928.00	31,823.30	23,895.30

From the information in Table 12.2 we can see that the cocktail bar should have taken cash equal to £31,823.30. In fact, cash actually received was £31,990.30; this gives a bar surplus of £167 – i.e. 0.5 per cent. The potential cash gross profit for May was £23,895.30. The actual cash gross profit was (£31,990.30 less £8,050) £23,940.30, which is £45 more than the potential figure. Finally, to look at actual percentages, the cocktail bar should have made a gross profit of (£23,895.30 as a percentage of £31,823.30) 75.1 per cent. The actual gross profit amounted to (£23,940.30 as a percentage of £31,990.30) 74.8 per cent, giving a shortfall of 0.3 per cent.

MANAGEMENT REPORTS

The culminating point of operational control is reporting. This means the transmission to the management of daily, weekly, monthly, etc., reports on current operations. Two important points should be noted in this connection. First, as mentioned earlier in this volume, hotels and restaurants operate at a high percentage of fixed costs and, at the same time, suffer from a high degree of sales instability. This tends to create a situation in which profit levels are essentially dependent on sales volumes achieved. As far as management reports are concerned the effect of this situation is this: all reporting on current performance should give sufficient prominence to the revenue side of the business. All reports should give sufficient information on: sales volumes, sales mix, numbers of covers, average spending power, profit margins, departmental profits, etc. Secondly, all reports should give appropriate comparisons to facilitate an appreciation of current results. More often than not, current results are compared with budgeted results, and readers will find several examples of management reports at the end of Chapter 6.

Food and Beverage Records

The successful management of a food and beverage operation requires not only efficient staff, competent managers and adequate plant and equipment. Managing means, among other things, making all kinds of plans, organising the operation, making decisions on costs, prices, profit margins, etc. All these matters are difficult enough in themselves; they are, however, even more difficult in the absence of data in respect of previous trading periods.

It is of paramount importance, therefore, to ensure that at the end of each period we have a record relating to the main features of the food and beverage operation. The exact nature of the records, summaries, etc., will obviously vary from one establishment to another. Two illustrative examples are shown in Figures 12.17 and 12.18.

Blue Arrow Hotel ASP analysis: Jan–Jun 1995						
	Jan	Feb	Mar	Apr	May	Jun
Grill Room	£	£	£	£	£	£
Food	18.15	18.25	18.06	18.20	18.40	18.24
Beverage	7.22	7.20	7.31	7.35	7.12	7.31
Total	25.37	25.45	25.37	25.55	25.52	25.55
	%	%	%	%	%	%
Food	71.5	71.7	71.2	71.2	72.1	71.4
Beverage	28.5	28.3	28.8	28.8	27.9	28.6
Total	100.0	100.0	100.0	100.0	100.0	100.0
Coffee Shop	£	£	£	£	£	
Food	8.65	8.75	8.59	8.64	8.77	8.61
Beverage	2.96	2.81	3.07	3.06	2.81	3.06
Total	11.61	11.56	11.66	11.70	11.58	11.67
	%	%	%	%	%	%
Food	74.5	75.7	73.7	73.8	75.7	73.8
Beverage	25.5	24.3	26.3	26.2	24.3	26.2
Total	100.0	100.0	100.0	100.0	100.0	100.0

Figure 12.17 ASP analysis

Blue Arrow Hotel						
NOC analysis: Jan–Jun 1995						
	Jan	Feb	Mar	Apr	May	Jun
Covers						
Grill Room	1,716	1,824	2,147	2,215	2,195	2,206
Coffee Shop	2,667	2,771	2,984	3,388	3,476	3,912
Chinese Room	1,296	1,336	1,451	1,393	1,557	1,691
Total	5,679	5,931	6,582	6,996	7,228	7,809
NOC mix	%	%	%	%	%	%
Grill Room	30.2	30.8	32.6	31.7	30.4	28.2
Coffee Shop	47.0	46.7	45.3	48.4	48.1	50.1
Chinese Room	22.8	22.5	22.1	19.9	21.5	21.7
Total	100.0	100.0	100.0	100.0	100.0	100.0
Functions	2,914	3,067	2,895	3,316	2,292	1,204

Figure 12.18 NOC analysis

QUESTIONS

1   What do you understand by 'food and beverage control'? What are its specific aims?

2   List the main control procedures and methods relevant to each of the following stages of the control cycle:

(a) buying;
(b) receiving;
(c) storing and issuing;
(d) preparing;
(e) selling.

3   Give an outline of the main methods of buying suitable for a medium-sized provincial hotel.

4   Explain what you understand by a 'sales history'. What are the functions of sales histories?

5   What is a 'volume forecast'? How is it compiled and what purpose does it serve?

6   Explain what is meant by 'pre-costing' and indicate its aims and advantages.

7 It is often suggested that the control of beverages is considerably easier than the control of food. State, giving reasons, whether or not you agree with this view.

8 The information given below was extracted from the records of the Bridge Restaurant at 31 December 1995. You are required to prepare the restaurant's profit and loss account for the year to the above date and comment on its profitability.

	£000
Food sales	2,920
Beverage sales	1,090
Food purchases	1,050
Beverage purchases	375
Payroll	995
Employee benefits	90
Direct operating expenses	205
Music and entertainment	195
Advertising and sales promotion	115
Gas and electricity	55
Administrative and general	175
Repairs and maintenance	45
Rent	180
Depreciation	55

You are required to take the following notes into account:

(a) Opening stocks: Food £25,000
Beverages £35,000
(b) Closing stocks: Food £30,000
Beverages £40,000
(c) The cost of employees' meals amounted to £35,000.
(d) Beverages transferred to the kitchen during the year amounted to £25,000.
(e) Food transferred to the bar during the year amounted to £9,500.
(f) Food and beverages used for the annual staff party amounted to £2,000 and £3,000 respectively.

9 Examine critically the role of the following at the preparation stage of the control cycle:

(a) standard recipes;
(b) volume forecasts;
(c) sales histories.

10 The balances shown below were extracted from the records of the Buffalo Restaurant at 31 December 1994.

	£000
Food sales	920,000
Beverage sales	380,000
Food purchases	345,000
Beverage purchases	95,000
Employee benefits	50,000
Direct operating expenses	72,000
Music and entertainment	76,000
Advertising and sales promotion	41,000
Gas and electricity	22,000
Administrative and general	49,000
Repairs and maintenance	14,000
Payroll	355,000
Rent	47,000
Depreciation	16,000

You are informed that:

(a) Opening stocks were: Food   £15,000
                             Beverages £14,000
(b) Closing stocks were: Food   £17,000
                             Beverages £16,000
(c) The cost of employees' meals included in the above figure of purchases was £21,000.
(d) Food transferred to the bar during the year amounted to £6,000.
(e) Wines used in the kitchen cost a total of £4,000.
(f) The number of covers served during the year was 59,000.
(g) Food sales consisted of:

Soups and appetisers	£138,000
Meat and fish	414,000
Vegetables	90,000
Sweets	142,000
Teas and coffees	136,000

(h) Beverage sales consisted of:

Beers	£26,000
Minerals	71,000
Table wines	102,000
Fortified wines	53,000
Spirits	128,000

You are required to:

(i) Prepare the restaurant's profit and loss account in respect of the year ended 31 December 1994.

(ii) Calculate the average spending power.

(iii) Calculate the sales mix – separately for food and beverages.

(iv) Comment on the results achieved by the restaurant.

11 Explain what you understand by the term 'potential sales value'. What is the importance of this concept in:

(a) cash control;

(b) gross profit control?

12 Set out in Table 12.3 are the actual figures relating to the food and beverage operation of the Newcastle Hotel. The standard food cost is 35 per cent and the standard beverage cost 30 per cent.

Table 12.3 Newcastle Hotel's F&B figures

	Food sales	Food cost	Beverage sales	Beverage cost
	£	£	£	£
Jan	42,500	15,725	16,200	5,022
Feb	43,705	15,732	16,750	5,360
Mar	43,900	15,365	16,910	5,073
Apr	48,705	16,558	18,105	5,250
May	57,310	18,909	21,605	6,698
Jun	72,100	25,235	26,450	7,671
Jul	88,705	30,158	32,970	10,221
Aug	88,400	33,592	32,745	10,478
Sep	69,305	24,948	26,115	7,835
Oct	47,500	17,575	17,520	5,431
Nov	45,105	15,785	17,130	5,482
Dec	43,800	14,454	16,475	4,778

You are required to design a suitable 'Potential Food and Beverage Cost Savings' sheet, enter the above figures and show the monthly and annual savings for food and beverages. Comment on your results.

13 The banqueting beverage control sheet given in Figure 12.19 shows all the beverages sold at a wedding reception.

You are required to complete the sheet and calculate the potential:

(a) beverage cost;

(b) cash gross profit;

(c) sales value;

(d) gross profit percentage.

	Opening stock	Closing stock	Consumed	Cost/ bottle	Selling price per tot	Potential beverage cost	Potential gross profit	Potential sales value
				£	£	£	£	£
Teachers	4 bot	1 16/32	2 16/32	10.88	1.20			
J. Walker	3 bot	1 6/32	1 26/32	10.88	1.20			
Gordon's	2 bot	0 16/32	1 16/32	9.28	1.10			
Smirnoff	3 bot	1 10/32		8.96	1.10			
Martell	2 bot	0 25/35		15.75	1.60			
Tia Maria	2 bot	0 16/31		11.78	1.00			
Drambuie	1 bot	0 4/28		12.88	1.30			
Sandeman's	4 bot	1 6/13		5.59	1.20			
Double Century	3 bot	0 5/13		3.90	0.80			
Martini	2 bot	0 10/30		6.60	0.80			

OLD MILL HOTEL
BANQUETING BEVERAGE CONTROL
Function: Mr and Mrs Hill Wedding: 13 Jan 1995

Figure 12.19 A banqueting beverage control sheet

14 From the information given below, calculate the food and beverage gross profit (cash and percentage) in respect of May 1995.

	Food £	Beverage £
Opening Stocks	2,505	8,405
Closing Stocks	2,455	7,895
Purchases	7,250	2,690
Sales	21,945	8,385

Transfers and Adjustments:	£
Beverages for Cooking	130
Cooks' Beer	255
Food used in Bars	190
Food for Employees' Meals	615
Beverages for Staff Party	145
Food for Staff Party	290

305

CHAPTER 13

MANAGEMENT

Management means using the available resources to achieve organisational objectives. The main resources involved are:

1 Men
2 Money
3 Machinery
4 Materials
5 Methods
6 Minutes.

These resources are identified as the six Ms. Using the six Ms effectively to increase the productivity of the organisation is the main responsibility of the management. All managers manage the six Ms by using their knowledge, experience and skills in:

1 Planning (planning and scheduling);
2 Organising (communicating, delegating, directing, motivating and co-ordinating);
3 Controlling (reporting, evaluating, controlling, analysing and reviewing).

Management Functions

The above-mentioned three key activities of management may be subdivided into twelve management functions as shown below.

PLANNING

Planning
This means defining organisational objectives by deciding who is to do what, where, when and how. Planning is pre-thinking to implement the organisational policies and to achieve objectives. Planners may get expert advice, depending on the project, or get the whole team involved (e.g. brain-storming sessions, quality circles and planning committees). The managers should consider the following:

(a) Where are we? SWOT Analysis (strengths, weaknesses, opportunities and threats). Other factors to be analysed at this stage are corporate policy, company culture as well as political, economic, social and technological (PEST) factors affecting the macro environment.

(b) Where do we go from here? Long-term, short-term goals and objectives.

(c) How do we get there? Strategies (long-term) and tactics (short-term) (e.g. planning of a New Year's Eve dinner party to achieve a given level of profit).

Answers to the last question usually form the basic plan to achieve the objectives and targets identified.

Scheduling

This necessitates a detailed plan with timetables, programmes of activities, tasks and persons responsible (e.g. deciding on tasks such as the menu, table plan, decorations, music, etc.).

ORGANISING

Communicating

These are objectives and tasks translated into words to inform those concerned through memoranda, meetings, minutes, manuals, etc. (e.g. informing the food and beverage management team of a proposed party and the relevant plans) through horizontal and vertical channels.

Delegating

This means entrusting different duties to specific departments, teams or individuals and giving them authority to take appropriate decisions within the relevant framework (e.g. allowing the executive chef and banqueting manager to decide on the menu and price).

Directing

This means guiding individuals towards achieving tasks and secondary objectives (e.g. advising the executive chef to keep the cost of the menu at an agreed food cost percentage).

Motivating

This means creating a desire amongst the employees to achieve the goals set by understanding individual needs, appreciating good performances and encouraging effort (e.g. commending the bar manager for obtaining a special sponsorship for a function from a wine supplier, or thanking the executive chef, in public, for a well-balanced menu planned for some occasion).

Co-ordinating

This means synchronising the activities that have been delegated for better results. This involves checking progress and harmonising the work of different individuals by avoiding conflicts, duplication, overlapping, delays and waste (e.g. the executive chef checking the purchasing of items for a menu and monitoring the progress of advance preparations in different sections of the kitchen.

CONTROLLING

Reporting

This means ensuring a system of timely reports sent up through vertical channels of communication (e.g. daily food cost report from the food and beverage controller or a profit and loss projection from the food and beverage manager to the general manager regarding the proposed function).

Evaluating

This involves checking the actual performance against the plan (e.g. checking the progress of a New Year's Eve party ticket sales against predetermined targets, or checking the cost of decorations against projected budget levels).

Controlling

This means developing standards and establishing the rules. The six Ms should be controlled according to the policy of the organisation. Also it means taking any action of a disciplinary nature (e.g. disciplinary action in respect of an employee found to have deliberately undercharged a customer).

Analysing

This involves the examination of all the separate elements of an operation, with a view to tracing the reasons for success or failure (e.g. trying to ascertain the reasons why the actual food cost of a function was 5 per cent more than budgeted).

Reviewing

This consists of a periodical review of an operation, normally with the aim of improving future performance (e.g. discussing the results of a

New Year's party early in January and ensuring that the food and beverage manager has full feedback from all concerned).

Managing the Six Ms (M6M Theory)

No manager has all the resources he or she needs for a perfect operation. The good manager determines the best way to utilise the available resources to attain the objectives. All three key management activities should be used in managing the six Ms.

A good manager puts the basic management principles into practice. Also, using experience and, importantly, common sense, he/she will ensure that all management functions are interlinked. Management is the art of getting things done through others. The six Ms are the tools available and the twelve management functions provide the techniques for performing this art.

The traditional viewpoint that a hotel general manager's 'all round' experience in all departments is an essential prerequisite is no longer accepted. Most present-day general managers have climbed the management ladder from the food and beverage side of the operation. There are some with a strong rooms division background and a few from a marketing and finance background. Food and beverage management is, however, seen as the real springboard to general management.

It seems that a thorough knowledge of the food and beverage operation is often the key reason for the success of general managers. This may be due to the fact that the food and beverage department is the most complex, most technical and the most versatile department in any hotel. A former general manager of the London Dorchester expressed the opinion that 'in Europe, hotel management education and training mainly involves food and beverage operations, but in the USA priority is given to finance, marketing, computer technology and management. I think the best background for a general manager as well as a food and beverage manager is a blend of these two concepts of education and training.' This is absolutely correct. A food and beverage manager must have a good knowledge of the following four main areas, as shown in Figure 13.1.

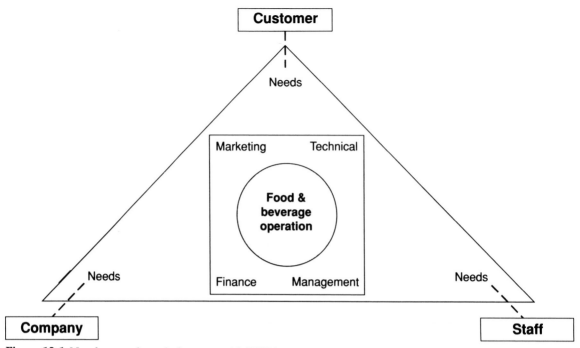

Figure 13.1 Need versus knowledge pyramid (NKP)

TECHNICAL

Kitchens, bars, banqueting, coffee shops, restaurants, and the stewarding department.

MARKETING

- Product formulation (menus, wine lists, food festivals, special theme weeks, etc.);

- Pricing (menus, wine lists, banquets, special events, etc.);

- Promotion (new restaurants, new menus, banquet sales, events, in-house advertising, etc.);

- Place (distribution – in the case of outside catering).

FINANCE

Budgeting (profit and loss statements, statistical reports), feasibility studies for new food and beverage outlets, etc.

MANAGEMENT

Management of all the six resources are as follows.

Men

In a large hotel the food and beverage manager is usually in charge of around half of all employees. They will be responsible for manpower planning, recruiting, training, developing, rostering and control of all their staff.

Money

In most hotels the food and beverage department generates 30–50 per cent of total revenue (depending on the size of the banqueting operation). Many hotels expect the food and beverage department to achieve a departmental profit of about 20 per cent. This is not normally easy as all food and beverage operations entail a high labour cost – in addition, of course, to food and beverage costs and other departmental expenses such as laundry, cleaning and printing. In such circumstances a good knowledge of planning and (cost and revenue) control techniques is absolutely vital for success in food and beverage management.

Machinery

Apart from the engineering department and the computer section of an average hotel, the food and beverage department has the most valuable equipment (kitchen plant, cold rooms, etc.) and a great deal of small operating equipment (silverware, glassware, china, etc.). Food and beverage managers have an important role in deciding on the relevant operating standards, planning and training in the proper use of such equipment.

Materials

Food stores and wine cellars usually stock most of the expensive materials in hotels. Food and beverage managers are responsible for co-ordinating market surveys, yield tests, standard purchase specifications and standard recipes, as well as the storage and handling of food and beverage.

Methods

Owing to the complexity of the food and beverage operation, a great deal of space in hotel operations manuals is devoted to systems and procedures for the food and beverage department. The implementation, analysis and improvement of such methods are all responsibilities of the food and beverage manager.

Minutes

Most food and beverage managers frequently work long hours. This is because of the complex role of administrator, businessman and host all rolled into one. Effective time-management is therefore vital.

The Role of the Food and Beverage Manager

As explained above and shown in Figure 13.1, for a successful and profitable food and beverage operation the most essential element is the technical, marketing, finance and management knowledge of the food and beverage manager. However, managers with a sound knowledge and experience in these key areas sometimes fail to achieve profits, fail to maintain standards and, even worse, fail to analyse the reasons for such failures.

It is essential in this context to satisfy the needs and expectations of the three main interested parties (segments):

1 Customers;
2 Company;
3 Staff.

Food and beverage managers should operate with a good understanding of the different needs of these three segments. One can only be successful if the main needs of the above segments are satisfied by the proper use of the four main knowledge/skill areas. Needs and expectations are different and vary from hotel to hotel, from company to company and from one country to another. The understanding, therefore, of different hotel cultures, company cultures and national cultures is the key to success for any food and beverage manager. The next step is to adjust the skills mix to satisfy the needs of the three segments; essentially to operate in a flexible manner in the context of the following varied expectations.

CUSTOMERS

- Good food

- Friendly service

- Value for money

- Pleasant environment

- Attentive management

- Good choice of food and beverage

- Accessibility

- Good reputation

- Good hygienic conditions

COMPANY

- Optimisation of long-term profits

- Control of short-term profits

- Minimisation of expenses

- Controlling of costs in line with the budget

- Securing repeat business

- Good reputation/image

- Positive publicity

- Absence of customer complaints

- Growth of business

- High productivity

- Good employee relations

- Team work and co-operation

STAFF

- Job security

- Job satisfaction

- Good working conditions

- Fair pay

- Promotion prospects

- Friendly and understanding management

- Facilities for training

The role of the food and beverage operation cannot be assessed purely in terms of the profits it makes. It helps in establishing the right image of a hotel's quality. The reputation of the food and beverage operation should be considered as the backbone of the hotel. An interesting example from the USA may be quoted to illustrate this. The Plaza Hotel had one of the leading food and beverage operations in New York. It enjoyed good food and beverage business as well as a high room rate and an impressive occupancy level. The hotel is considered as one of the finest and most profitable hotels in the world. Twenty years after the opening of the Plaza a much more modern and in many ways better hotel, named Savoy Plaza, was opened close to the existing Plaza Hotel. Unfortunately for the new competitor, which had limited catering facilities, it could not ensure a good name for its food and beverage operation and, as a result, the Savoy Plaza was demolished and an office building erected in its place.

Some Relevant Changes

Through most of the first half of the twentieth century, food and beverage occupied a minor position of importance in the minds of hotel operators. In some cases it was treated as a necessary evil – a service to be made available just in case the guest should desire it. From an economic standpoint it was important to attempt to break even, if possible, or to lose as little as possible. At the same time there was an emphasis on the rooms, because this was where the money was made. As long as one could fill the guest rooms, the profit figures on food and beverage were relatively unimportant.

The outlook changed gradually towards the 1960s. Hoteliers started wondering whether there were profits to be made in food and beverage. The answer appeared to be affirmative: after all, individual restaurants, whose only source of income was food and beverage sales, had made profits for many years. Even in London and Paris, where eating out had been fashionable and popular for many decades, hotel restaurants were often considered too expensive. Most of London hotel guests used to go out to restaurants instead of patronising the hotel food and beverage outlets. Improving profits and standards, cutting costs and marketing the food and beverage outlets in international five-star city hotels seemed to be extremely difficult. In fact it is still a difficult task. However, the limited managerial ability of the traditional catering manager, head cook and the restaurant head waiter who came up from the ranks appeared to be insufficient to face the new trends and demands of the food and beverage operation which indicated high complexity in all the aspects. The American concept of the 'Food and Beverage Manager', combining the management skills with technical know-how, proved to be a satisfactory alternative.

In the 1960s this new concept was accepted by some of the leading hotel companies. As a result the food and beverage manager who co-ordinates all operations relevant to the food and beverage activities from purchasing to the billing stage has become an accepted feature of the majority of large hotels. This position requires a fully experienced food service or business-educated person who co-ordinates and encourages open communication with managerial assistance, the kitchen and serving staff. However, the ideal food and beverage manager will be an energetic administrator with a clear perception of quality and profitability and a full understanding of technical aspects of the operation.

The food and beverage operation involves a high degree of technical knowledge and skill – perhaps more than any other managerial position in the hotel industry. Almost all the leading hotel groups consider experience in food and beverage management a prerequisite for promotion to general management. In large hotel chains, executives with proven ability in the rooms division and other areas of the operation who have shown the potential for developing their careers in general management are often transferred to the food and beverage department prior to being promoted. This is done with a view to providing the essential food and beverage experience and know-how needed by a general manager. In the 1980s the designation of food and beverage director became popular, especially in large hotels. Today both designations are being used and there is no difference in the main duties. In some large hotels the assistant to the General Manager handles the department and the designation of Executive Assistant Manager (Food and Beverage) is used.

Some Relevant Opinions

A recent hotel survey asked the question 'How important is the food and beverage operation in the context of the whole business?' Of those interviewed, 95 per cent answered without hesitation, 'Vital.' It seems the obvious answer. A number of similar relevant opinions noted during this survey are quoted below. A senior consultant to the hotel industry commented: 'One cannot do without it; it is obviously an essential element of the total product that is being offered and one which cannot be separated. But profit centres should be carefully analysed by the management to increase the productivity of the operations.' The general manager of a large hotel commented: 'Food and beverage reflects the image of the hotel more than any other department. Rooms are quite standardised in international hotels and it is the food and beverage operation which makes each of the hotels different from all others.' The food and beverage manager of a five-star London hotel stated that 'Food and beverage makes or breaks the reputation of hotels. The image of the hotel is based on what the guest sees, and the most noticeable aspect for residents as well as the non-residents is the standard of the food and beverage operations.'

The Vice-President for Food and Beverage Operations of an American hotel corporation expressed a similar view and added, 'Earlier on the rooms received the first priority and food and beverage operations was a supplement.' The situation has changed completely and food and beverages is now the image-builder. If a hotel is strong in food and beverage operations, the question of building more rooms is considered. This is a common view of most leading hotels of the world. The food and beverage manager of a leading hotel in Switzerland (who had been a rooms division/front office manager during most of his career) said, 'The food and beverage operation is more complex and important than any other service provided in the hotel in the context of obtaining publicity and creating an overall image. People want to stay in hotels providing good food.'

In most hotels it has been the food more than anything else that has created hotel and hoteliers' reputations. The names of Cesar Ritz and Escoffier are but two of the many who made their hotels, and in particular the London Savoy Hotel and the Ritz, internationally famous, mainly because of the standards in their magnificent restaurants. 'We cannot charge £200 for a room unless we provide an excellent food and beverage product,' stated the new food and beverage manager of an international hotel in Knightsbridge, London. He continued, 'Guests are concerned with the food and beverage facilities even though many do not use them; frankly, only very few hotels in London make a considerable profit in food and beverage departments. However, food and beverage must attempt to stand on its own feet.' The director of a London-based consulting group stated that, 'Financially very few hotels make a profit from food and beverage operations after charging all the relevant expenses, but it is an important service that has to be provided.' In this situation hotels may attempt to cut down on food and beverage facilities whilst maintaining high standards. But the experience of another food and beverage manager has proved that this could not be the solution. The manager of one Japanese-owned 500-bedroomed hotel trimmed the food and beverage operation, after a lot of thought and careful planning. The move failed totally and they reverted to the original method of operation.

Duties of the Food and Beverage Manager

In order to understand the duties and responsibilities of the food and beverage manager, one should initially analyse the food and beverage division of a large hotel. Hoteliers who do not have experience in large international hotels frequently underestimate the wide range of duties of food and beverage directors/managers. As shown in Table 13.1, a large food and beverage division may be divided into approximately twenty sections.

Table 13.1 Facets of a large food and beverage operation

Front of house		Back of house	
Section	**In charge**	**Section**	**In charge**
Outside catering	Banqueting manager	Cashiering*	Food & beverage controller/accountant
Conventions	Banqueting manager	Bars (dispense)	Bar manager
Banqueting	Banqueting manager	Stewarding	Executive kitchen steward
Pastry shop	Coffee shop manager	Kitchens	Executive chef
Night club	Night club manager	Staff cafeteria	Executive kitchen steward/ executive chef
Bars (public/residents)	Bar manager	Kitchen stores	Executive chef
Coffee shop	Coffee shop manager	Food and beverage controls*	Food and beverage controller
Entertainment	Entertainment manager	Room service	Room-service manager
		Stores*	Stores manager
		Receiving*	Receiving officer
		Purchasing*	Purchasing officer
		Administration	Assistant food and beverage manager

*Indirect responsibility of the food and beverage director.

In a large operation the food and beverage director has to co-ordinate with many specialists such as the executive chef, entertainment manager, and banquet manager. Obviously the food and beverage director cannot be an expert in all areas coming under their purview. In a large operation they become more of a generalist with a fair amount of knowledge, sufficient to understand each specialist's function. In this context this management, marketing and finance knowledge may play a more important role than the actual technical knowledge. The manner in which the knowledge mix may change according to the size of the operation is shown in Figure 13.2.

Figure 13.2 Knowledge mix in different food and beverage operations

In a small food and beverage operation the required knowledge of the food and beverage manager can be listed (in order of importance) as follows:

1   Technical;
2   Management;
3   Finance;
4   Marketing.

On the other hand, in a very large food and beverage operation the importance of the required knowledge of the food and beverage director will be completely different as shown below:

1 Marketing;
2 Finance;
3 Management;
4 Technical.

Therefore, a very successful food and beverage director in charge of a large operation may fail in a smaller operation, and vice versa, if this shift of emphasis is not understood.

Technical knowledge is undoubtedly essential for one to climb the ladder to become a food and beverage director of a large operation. However, having reached that position the food and beverage manager will not use this knowledge as often as his or her knowledge in marketing and finance. Managers should be prepared for this change and adjust quickly to improve their business service to be effective in larger operations.

Knowledge usage and time spent (in percentages) in different areas by food and beverage managers/directors is shown in Table 13.2.

Table 13.2 Knowledge usage in different food and beverage operations (%)

Knowledge / Size of operation	Marketing	Finance	Management	Technical
Very large	35	30	25	10
Large	25	25	25	25
Medium	15	20	25	40
Small	10	10	25	55

Organisation Structure

An organisation chart is essential in indicating the basic framework within which the whole organisation and its departments function. It also indicates the following:

- Span of control – simply the number of subordinates that an individual supervises.

- Levels of management – different tiers through which management operates.

- Channels of communication – vertical and horizontal lines of communication.

- Delegation of authority – entrusting duties by a manager/supervisor to subordinates. What is delegated is authority to carry out instructions, but not the responsibility (which will remain with the superior).

- Division of work – grouping of work and departmentation.

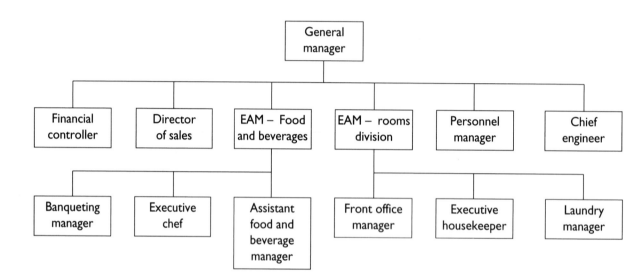

Figure 13.3 Typical organisation chart of a large international hotel

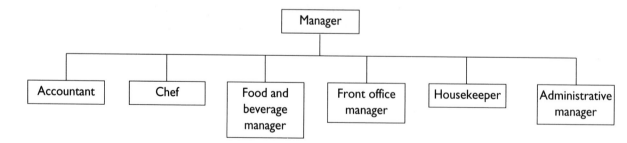

Figure 13.4 The top tiers of a typical organisation chart of a medium-sized hotel

In the 1990s most hotels are in the process of simplifying their organisation structure. Despite attempts to reduce the tiers in hotels, the following levels are still common in most hotel organisation structures:

1 General manager
2 Resident manager/executive assistant manager (EAM)
3 Divisional heads (e.g. in larger hotels food and beverage director)
4 Departmental heads (e.g. executive chef)
5 Assistant departmental heads (e.g. assistant front office manager)
6 Junior managers/executives (e.g. restaurant manager)
7 Supervisors (e.g. housekeeping floor supervisor)
8 Skilled level employees (e.g. barmen)
9 Semi-skilled employees (e.g. kitchen steward)
10 Trainees, etc. (e.g. trainee waiter)

Personnel Management

Although large hotels and small hotels attached to hotel groups have specialist personnel managers, food and beverage managers should be involved in personnel administrative functions such as:

1 *Human resource planning* – deciding on required numbers, job descriptions and man specifications.
2 *Recruitment* – assisting personnel managers to screen applications, interview and select suitable employees.
3 *Training* – planning, organising and co-ordinating 'on the job training' of food and beverage staff to ensure the required levels of skills.
4 *Development* – identifying potential for long-term career development of suitable employees and planning, implementing and reviewing of such programmes in consultation with personnel manager/training manager.
5 *Appraisals* – carrying out periodical appraisal of executives and supervisors in the department and planning the appraisals of other staff to be done by executives/supervisors.
6 *Promotion and increments* – making suitable recommendations.
7 *Worker participation* – implementing concepts such as 'Quality Circles' and other concepts to improve productivity by motivating worker participation in problem-solving. Also staff welfare matters.
8 *Disciplinary action* -- when required, conducting departmental investigations and making recommendations to the personnel manager.

9 *Termination of employment* – making recommendations to the personnel manager with regard to dismissals, redundancies and retirement.

10 *Manpower reviewing* – carrying out periodical reviewing of above-mentioned human resources management functions and ensuring improvements in consultation with the personnel manager and the general manager.

Staffing Levels

Staffing levels vary from country to country, hotel to hotel, restaurant to restaurant and bar to bar depending on:

1 Grade of hotel/restaurant;
2 Labour costs;
3 Productivity of staff;
4 Skill/training level;
5 Layout of the hotel;
6 Quality of equipment;
7 Operational standards maintained;
8 Influence of the unions;
9 Labour laws;
10 Company policies;
11 Attitude of staff;
12 Labour turnover rate.

In most hotels, payroll costs are around 30 per cent of revenue. In some Asian countries this will be as low as 15 per cent and this means more attentive service provided without much affecting profitability levels. In the United Kingdom, obviously the five-star London hotels seem to have higher staffing levels. After a survey carried out in five-star London hotels we arrived at the following averages:

- Number of covers per waiter in a gourmet restaurant – 10:1.

- Number of covers per waiter in all restaurants – 15:1.

- % of food and beverage staff of the total hotel staff – 48%.

- % of food production staff (kitchen) of the total food and beverage staff – 26%.

A sectional breakdown of food and beverage employees is given in Table 13.3.

Table 13.3 Staff of London five-star hotels

Section	% of total food & beverage staff	% of total staff
Kitchen	26	12
Restaurant (average 3 outlets)	23	11
Stewarding	17	8
Room service	16	8
Bar/lounge (average 2 outlets)	8	4
Banqueting	6	3
Other	4	2
Total	100	48

Once a decision is taken on the productivity level (number of covers per waiter or per cook), calculating the total number of employees per section of the food and beverage department becomes an easy task if the following formula is used.

$$\frac{\text{Average covers per day}}{\text{Productivity level}} \times \frac{\text{Number of operative days}}{\text{Number of working days}} = \text{Required total staff}$$

Let us take a London restaurant as an example and assume the following:

Average covers	100 per day
Productivity level per waiter	16 covers a day
Restaurant is open on all 365 days of the year	
Non-working days per waiter	104 days off
	21 days holiday
	7 days official holidays
	5 days no pay (average)

Total = 137 days a year

Number of working days per waiter	= 365 minus 137 days
	= 228 days

Now, by using our simple formula we arrive at the required number of waiters:

$$\frac{100}{16} \times \frac{365}{228} = 10$$

Once this calculation is done, it should be ensured that rostering balances off days and holidays to match peak periods and low days.

Food and Beverage Communication

Communication is one of the most important management functions of the food and beverage manager. They have to be a good communicator as they deal with many departments and sections within the overall food and beverage operations. In addition to the internal communications they also have to communicate with many others externally.

Figure 13.5 Food and beverage manager as a communicator

Meetings and minutes are used as the main mode of communication by food and beverage managers. The usual meetings attended by the food and beverage manager are shown in Table 13.4.

Table 13.4 Meeting schedule of a large hotel

Frequency	Meeting	Chaired by
Daily	Morning briefing	General Manager
	Food & beverage briefing	Food & Beverage Manager/ Outlet Managers
Weekly	Induction	Training Manager
	Individual meeting (with General Manager)	General Manager
	Departmental heads meeting	General Manager
	Food & beverage meeting	Food & Beverage Manager
Monthly	All executive meeting	General Manager
	Credit meeting	Financial Controller
	Controls meeting	Financial Controller
	Sales meeting	Director of Sales
	Advertising meeting	General Manager
	Purchasing committee meeting	Financial Controller
	Entertainment meeting	Food & Beverage Manager
Other	Budget meeting	General Manager
	Marketing meeting	General Manager
	Development meeting	General Manager
	Christmas and New Year meeting	Food & Beverage Manager
	Special events co-ordination meetings	Food & Beverage Manager

In order to ensure effective co-ordination in the department, the food and beverage manager should prepare for all meetings. The following routine is suggested for food and beverage meetings.

1 Observations/notes by food and beverage manager (during the week).
2 Information from executives/departmental heads meetings, etc.
3 Food and beverage departmental meeting
   • Breaking the ice
   • Thanks/special announcements
   • Performance analysis/statistics

- Matters arising from last meeting
- General matters
- Specific matters per section (kitchen, banqueting, etc.)
- Next meeting: date, time, venue, etc.

4   Minutes – draft (soon after the meeting).
5   Minutes distributed (on the same day as the meeting, preferably within four hours after the meeting).
6   Sectional meetings (e.g. coffee shop staff chaired by coffee shop manager on the same day).
7   Feedback – daily (during the week).
8   Follow-up (during the week).
9   Advice to members of the team if needed.
10 Observations/notes (for the next week's meeting).

We have seen many hotels in different regions of the world ensuring effective communication and quick action with the implementation of similar meeting routines. It is important to schedule all meetings objectively and logically in order to improve internal communication. An example to illustrate the speed of communication between the general manager and coffee shop waiting staff (using the proper communication channels) is given in Figure 13.6.

Decision by General Manager (at weekly departmental heads meeting 4 p.m. Tuesday)

↓

Announcement by food and beverage manager (at weekly food and beverage meeting 10 a.m. Wednesday)

↓

Announcement/Notice by Coffee Shop Manager (at daily briefing 3 p.m. Wednesday)

↓

Action by waiting staff (4 p.m. Wednesday)

Figure 13.6 Speed of communication

Prerequisites for Success

The job of food and beverage manager is one of the most challenging in the hotel industry. It is evident from comments already made earlier in the chapter that an average executive working eight hours a day cannot cope with its demands.

To be successful as a food and beverage manager of an international hotel one should preferably have the following attributes.

1 Qualifications (minimum a diploma), skills and knowledge (technical, management, finance and marketing);
2 Experience (minimum 10 years), efficiency, dedication and creativity;
3 Management ability (M6M), leadership qualities and ambition;
4 Adaptability, ability to learn from 'CSCSO' (Customers, Supervisors, Colleagues, Subordinates and Others);
5 Sociability, ability to establish useful contacts and mobility (free to move from one country to another at short notice without delays).

Food and beverage management is, by and large, the most demanding, dynamic, complex and indeed the most interesting area of hotel management.

QUESTIONS

1 Discuss the twelve key management functions with examples from a food and beverage operation.

2 Explain the 'M6M' theory with emphasis on the 'Needs v. Knowledge' pyramid in food and beverage operations.

3 'For a successful and profitable food and beverage operation the most essential element is the technical, marketing, finance and management knowledge of the food and beverage manager.' Discuss this statement.

4 Analyse and compare the needs of customers, company and staff of a small hotel and a large hotel.

5 'The food and beverage manager is a key divisional head in most hotels nowadays, although it was a new concept thirty years ago.' Discuss this statement, highlighting the main reasons for creating this post.

6 'How important is the food and beverage operation in the context of the whole hospitality business?' Carry out a survey and compare the views of five hotel general managers.

7 Assume that you are the food and beverage manager of a 100-roomed three-star Manchester hotel with two restaurants and two bars. In the absence of a personnel manager, you are required to organise the personnel function of your department. Suggest a plan.

8   Analyse the food and beverage department of a large hotel and identify the executives in charge of each section.

9   'The ideal food and beverage director of a large hotel should be a generalist with a good understanding of the functions of specialists in his/her division'. Discuss this statement comparing the type of knowledge needed by a food and beverage manager of a small hotel.

10   'A food and beverage manager without good communication skills will fail to be successful.' Discuss this statement, explaining the complexity of communication in the food and beverage division of a large international hotel, and suggest a routine for food and beverage meetings.

CASE STUDY: 'SKYWAY HOTEL'

Skyway Hotel is a four-star 200-roomed hotel situated near Birmingham Airport. The hotel was opened fifteen years ago and was managed by the owning company: Birmingham Foods Ltd, a catering company which also owns two supermarkets in Birmingham. Four months ago the board of directors decided to hand over the hotel on a management contract for five years to a lesser-known London-based international hotel corporation: Hospitality International. The management was taken over on the first of last month and Hospitality International took over the control of the property in a very 'businesslike' fashion. This is their first management contract in Birmingham. Three better-reputed hotel companies were interested in the contract, but the board of directors decided in favour of Hospitality International, mainly owing to considerably lower management fees and the reputation of Mr Brian Johnson, the new general manager representing the management company. Hospitality International has to improve the image of the hotel, occupancy levels and profits within the first year of the new partnership as this will be vital for the growth of the company in the Birmingham area.

Skyway Hotel has a popular coffee shop, a grill room (dinner only) and a Mexican restaurant (running at a loss). The 24-hour room service is also running at a loss. Two bars are located on the ground floor (next to the banquet rooms with a seating capacity of 400). The banqueting manager Mr Jim Williams is the most senior person in the food and beverage team, having started at the very inception of the hotel as an assistant banquet head waiter. Executive chef Mr Jean-Paul Ducray is a Swiss-born chef who joined the hotel seven years ago. His wife is from Birmingham. Mr Ducray had a total free hand before the takeover, and is unhappy about many of the instructions he has received since last month. With the takeover both food and beverage manager and his assistant left. Mr Harry Taylor, an MHCIMA with thirteen years of hotel experience in the Hospitality International chain, was appointed as the food and beverage manager. He is searching for a good assistant food and beverage manager who, if he/she proves him/herself, will be promoted as the food and beverage manager after six months. Mr Taylor is tipped to be promoted as the assistant general manager by then. At present the new sales director and the new financial controller (both from the chain) pay special attention to food and beverage revenue and profits. The organisation chart is given in Figure 13.7.

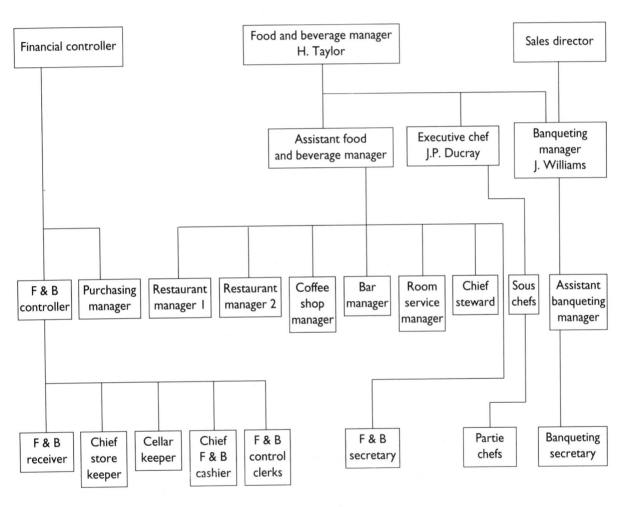

Figure 13.7 Skyway Hotel's food and beverage organisation chart

The job description for the assistant food and beverage manager is as follows:

Job Position
Assistant Food & Beverage Manager.

Category
Executive/Sub-departmental Head.

Responsible to
Food & Beverage Manager and through him/her the General Manager and Vice-President (Food & Beverage).

Job Definition
To assist the F&B Manager in total operations with special emphasis on innovations. Will be directly responsible for certain activities assigned and will also look after F&B Manager's job during his/her absence.

Duties and Responsibilities
Administrative
1   To look after food and beverage operations in association with the F&B manager.
2   To liaise with the training manager to organise programmes for staff in the department.
3   To help the F&B manager, in co-ordination with the Personnel Division, in keeping the payroll down.
4   To attend the following meetings along with the F&B manager.

    (a)   General manager's meeting for departmental heads;
    (b)   Energy conservation meeting;
    (c)   Tasting committee meeting;
    (d)   As deputy for the F&B manager in other committee meetings as required;
    (e)   Departmental meetings.

Production
1   To study the kitchen operations and suggest to the F&B manager and the executive chef methods for reducing wastage and saving costs.
2   To help the F&B manager plan various menus for the outlets and ensure the change of menus at regular intervals.
3   To check the storage of various foodstuffs at the optimum temperature and also to ensure that the stacking is proper and the items are of the required standard.

4 To assist the F&B manager in grading new products in the market and checking procured items from time to time so as to ensure that these items are of the prescribed standards.
5 To assist the executive kitchen steward in maintaining the quality of food served in the cafeteria.

Service
1 To take rounds of various F&B outlets and ensure that the service standards and specifications are maintained in every way.
2 To co-ordinate with the outlet managers and suggest and implement methods of improving service, as well as the image of the hotel.
3 To attend staff briefing of various outlets and suggest improvements in service.
4 To help in uniform inspection of various outlets and co-ordinate with the housekeeper for improvements if any.

Controls
1 To analyse the operations and suggest improvements.
2 To work out the par stock of specific foodstuffs and recommend to the F&B manager to implement the same.
3 To help the F&B manager in co-ordination with controls for setting and implementing procedures of yield tests/market surveys/ inventories/shortages/bar control/menu sales summary, etc.
4 To keep the inventory record of the various furniture items and ensure that the department does not run short at any time.
5 To make random checks and ensure that the quantities of various items indicated in the cardex are the same as in the physical inventory.
6 To implement the advice of the F&B controller regarding food portions, quality and pricing.

Other
1 To co-ordinate with kitchen stewarding to obtain maximum efficiency of various equipment being used and ensure optimum usefulness.
2 To analyse guest comments and ensure that any negative factors in food quality and service are removed without causing further damage.
3 To assist the F&B manager in organising local entertainment.
4 To ensure that pest control in various areas is undertaken at regular intervals and regular schedules are maintained for same.

Supervise
Operationally and administratively all food and beverage service personnel.

Area of Operation

All food and beverage areas of the hotel.

Hours of Operation

Hired for job completion and not for hours of work put in.

Authority

Supervise all restaurant managers in the department. Recommend increments, transfers and promotions as well as disciplinary action.

Interdepartmental Co-ordination

With the front office for daily forecast of arrival of groups and convention arrivals to aid in increasing revenue from food and beverage sales.

With the Housekeeping Department for maintaining a smooth flow of linen and uniform requirements and the maintenance of cleanliness in all food and beverage areas (public).

With the Engineering Department for the maintenance of all food and beverage production and service, equipment and fittings in these areas and also air conditioning and refrigeration.

With the Accounts Department to analyse all financial statements and accounts reports pertaining to the Food and Beverage Department.

With the Personnel Department for ensuring the maintenance of employees' discipline as per the house rules.

With the Training Department for ensuring that all F&B personnel are well versed in the latest systems and methods pertaining to service and guest handling.

With the Unit Sales Director and the Vice-President (Sales and Marketing) regarding food and beverage sales and its further development.

With the Purchasing Department for setting of standards and specifications of food and beverage items. Testing, grading and approving of new products in the market (as per committee).

Other

In addition to the above-mentioned duties and job functions, any other assignments given occasionally or on a daily basis by the immediate supervisor or the management.

The Vice-President Food and Beverage after his first visit to Skyway Hotel last week, suggested the following:

1 Appropriate recruitment policy to blend the old and new employees, hard core and transient employees, trained and untrained employees.
2 Proper training and career development programmes and to motivate staff by promoting suitable individuals.
3 A tactful approach in staff management.
4 Keeping the staff informed regarding the relevant departmental and hotel activities.
5 Improving the team spirit.
6 Encouraging healthy interdepartmental and inter-sectional competitions in standards and sales targets.
7 Better control of cost of sales.
8 Create an image for the hotel for creative food and beverage promotions/ events.
9 Calculating appropriate staffing levels for the following outlets.

Outlet	Covers per waiter	Operative days for the year	Total covers for the year
Coffee Shop	20	365	70,000
Grill Room	10	313	12,000
Mexican Restaurant	15	260	8,000
Room Service	12	365	14,000
Banquet	15	—	48,000
Total	—	—	152,000

You have been selected as the assistant food and beverage manager with effect from the first of next month. If your work is satisfactory you will be promoted as the food and beverage manager in six months' time. Mr Harry Taylor is too involved in general administration, in the absence of an assistant general manager, and he expects you virtually to take over the department after a two-week orientation programme at London Head Office and in all the departments of Skyway Hotel. Suggest a plan of action for the next six months with a view to getting the promotion.

INDEX